AF477532

Stabilization and Growth in Latin America

Stabilization and Growth in Latin America

A Critique and Reconstruction from Post-Keynesian and Structuralist Perspectives

Leonardo Vera

palgrave

First published 2000 by
PALGRAVE
175 Fifth Avenue, New York, N.Y. 10010 and
Houndmills, Basingstoke, Hampshire RG21 6XS
Companies and representatives throughout the world

PALGRAVE is the new global publishing imprint of
St. Martin's Press LLC Scholarly and Reference Division and
Palgrave Publishers Ltd (formerly Macmillan Press Ltd).

ISBN 0-312-23269-1 hardback

A catalogue record for this book is available
from the British Library.

Library of Congress Cataloging-in-Publication Data
Vera, Leonardo.
    Stabilization and Growth in Latin America: A Critique and
    Reconstruction from Post-Keynesian and
    Structuralist Perspectives / Leonardo Vera.
        p. cm.
    Includes bibliographical references and index.
    ISBN 0-312-23269-1 (cloth)

    1. Latin America—Economic Policy. 2. Latin America—
Economic conditions—1982- 3. International Monetary Fund—
Latin America. 4. World Bank—Latin America.

HC125 .V463 2000
338.98—dc21   00-040464

First edition: June, 2001
10 9 8 7 6 5 4 3 2 1

Design by Newgen Imaging Systems (P) Ltd, Chennai, India

Printed in the United States of America

Contents

Acknowledgements

One cannot achieve anything without the help and support of others, and naturally I have many debts. Some of my debts go back a long way, to my student days at the Central University of Venezuela. There, Enzo del Bufalo and some others taught me macro-economics in a way that allowed me to see more than neoclassical economics. The process was fostered in very different ways by my post-graduate studies at Roosevelt University. A number of people gave me inspiration and invaluable guidance at Roosevelt. Sam Rosenberg, Fred Lee, and Gary Langer deserve special mention. The work has taken shape finally in recent years at University of East London. I am conscious of my intellectual debt to Philip Arestis (East London) and Howard Stein (Roosevelt), and I should like to take this opportunity to thank them for their kindness and encouragement. Howard gave generously of his time and offered me his expertise and criticism. At every stage I have been helped immeasurably by Philip, who made many effective comments on substance and presentation.

Finally, I express my love and appreciation to my wife and my family for sacrificing time and convenience to see this effort bear fruit.

Acronyms

AID   Agency for International Development
BOP   balance-of-payment
EDI   Economic Development Institute
EFF   Extended Fund Facility
ESAF   Enhanced Structural Adjustment Facility
FAO   Food and Agriculture Organization
GDP   Gross Domestic Product
IBRD   International Bank of Reconstruction and Development
ICOR   incremental capital output relationship
IDA   International Development Association
IMF   International Monetary Fund
LDC   less-developed country
NIC   new industrialized country
NIBP   non-inflationary basics price
PPP   purchasing power parity
SAF   Structural Adjustment Facility
SAL   structural adjustment lending
SAP   Special Action Program
SECAL   Sectoral Adjustment Loan
WB   World Bank

Introduction

Even though economic reforms were initiated in Latin America as early as 1973 in Chile and Uruguay, in the other Latin American countries it was the debt crisis of 1982 that triggered a series of reforms that to some degree have become the foundation of the overall economic strategy all over the region. The move towards reforms started when the large external borrowing of the 1970s and early 1980s proved to be unsustainable after the interest rate and terms of trade shocks of the early 1980s. The abrupt limitations on access to international capital markets submerged Latin America into a deep recession. The severity of the crisis was such that simple solutions were not available. With no international agency specifically charged with managing the staggering debt and growing international conflicts, Latin American countries initiated during the 1980s a reorientation of economic policies, in particular in the form of stabilization and structural adjustment policies in whose formulation and implementation the International Monetary Fund (IMF) and the World Bank (WB) have played a key role. Thus, when other alternatives have proved ineffective, very often a Latin American country with balance of payments problems ends up requesting a line of credit or some kind of external loan from the IMF and/or the WB. The Bretton Woods institutions have by now gained an unprecedented and pervasive influence over policy-making in Latin America. In exchange for the loan, the borrowing country pledges to reform its economic policies to meet the requirements of these institutions. For many Latin American countries there is nothing new in this, as conditionality and "orthodox" therapies have been standard since the 1950s in cases where countries had to borrow from the IMF. But since the 1980s one country after another embarked on general orthodox stabilization and adjustment programs.

The orthodox programs, whose internal logic has remained surprisingly unchanged over the years, have not achieved the expected results. After almost two decades of harsh stabilization and adjustment programs in

Latin America, stabilization has not been completely achieved, and the prospects for economic growth and development are far from promising.

Two questions arise at this junction: first, why have orthodox programs remained so unsuccessful? and second, is there an available alternative? Regarding the first, we think that if we want to explain the relative failure of orthodox policies, then the discussion has to explore theoretical questions and examine practical consequences or observable events. At the theoretical level, it is important to identify the reasoning and the theoretical models that underlie the policy packages employed by the Bretton Woods institutions. It is also important to illustrate the possible shortcomings of the theory by examining country experiences and the evidence offered by the existing literature.

Our hypothesis here is that in dealing with each of the major aspects of stabilization and adjustment in less-developed countries (LDCs), the orthodox approach falls short of providing a convincing explanation and viable solutions. In some cases, we will argue, it is because the assumptions underlying the orthodox models are completely at variance with what is known about the realities of Latin American economies. In other cases, it is because the models fail to account for certain types of historically observed phenomena. In a few cases, it is because the logic of the models themselves is questionable.

The answer to the second question is perhaps the core of our study. We believe that the current economic problems of Latin American economies can be better studied on the basis of an alternative, and more coherent, body of contemporary thought. The framework I propose is rooted in both the post-Keynesian approach and the Latin American structuralist tradition. The post-Keynesian tradition, unlike mainstream economic thinking, adopts an approach to economic reality based on a money-production–distribution-class relationship. In this perspective economic analysis is based upon "stylized facts" or empirical generalizations elaborated hierarchically at the macro, sectoral, and micro levels. The post-Keynesian alternative benefits from some complementary frames of reference provided by the structuralist tradition. The structuralist emphasis on sectoral distinctions, production and foreign exchange bottlenecks, and the leading role that a constrained public sector plays in any development strategy is critical to any serious analysis of Latin American economies. Thus, our synthesis will provide us with an instrument for a better theoretical understanding of the economic realities of the region, and for the development of some innovative economic policies that could be more useful and relevant than those provided by the orthodox analysis.

Chapter 1 describes briefly the particular economic situation in the Latin American region and analyzes the macroeconomic issues at stake. We examine the statistical evidence and demonstrate that no significant economic improvement was observed in the region during the 1980s and early 1990s. While the poor performance is not simply the result of IMF/WB management, it is nevertheless fairly clear that under the generalized control by these multilateral agencies, the region seems to have behaved in ways not previously observed. A brief discussion on the origin, nature, and evolution of IMF/WB conditionality in Latin America follows. We illustrate how the number of programs in Latin America have fluctuated over time, but we also show how the 1980s and 1990s have witnessed a dramatic increase in the number of agreements and conditionality strictness. It is important to note that no attempt is made here to evaluate and discuss the nature and extent of IMF surveillance, a topic that has received a lot of attention very recently. Rather, it is financing and the accompanying exercise of "conditionality" that concern us here. The aim of chapter 1 is to serve as a starting point for the subsequent discussion.

In chapter 2 we present a systematic and comprehensive review of orthodox approaches to stabilization and structural adjustment, and demonstrate how these views relate to the models that are used in the design of IMF/WB programs. The importance we attach to this detailed reconstruction is due to the scarcity of serious discussion about the premises underlying the IMF/WB policy approach. Despite the widespread interest in this subject, very little material has been written that describes and analyzes the macromodels that inspire policy-based lending. In general, the existing literature is incomplete and not very well integrated. Our exposition in this part is extensive in the sense that we cover the assumptions and essential elements of the macroeconomic policy-oriented models that have inspired for almost four decades the prescriptions of the Bretton Woods institutions. We also show how policy prescriptions are rooted in the analytic premises of these models.

The argument developed in chapter 2 enables us to understand the shortcomings and limitations of the orthodox approach. It is on this basis that the third chapter proceeds with a critical evaluation of the orthodox stabilization and adjustment packages. We argue in this chapter that the weaknesses of the orthodox approach have three basic sources. First, there are theoretical weaknesses that are intrinsic to the models. Second, there are weaknesses that are the result of mistaken premises and assumptions. And finally, there are weaknesses that can be observed at the empirical level when the theory is subjected to the historical evidence.

In chapter 4 we present what we consider an alternative framework for dealing with stabilization and growth issues in Latin American countries. We proceed in two stages here. We first offer an introduction to the methodology employed by the post-Keynesian school and the structuralist tradition. We then discuss the basic principles of reasoning from which each of these paradigms construct their theories. Our purpose is not to provide a comprehensive account of these schools; rather, it is to give the reader an opportunity to understand the reasons for our preference for the proposed synthesis, to become familiar with certain fundamental ideas and concepts, and above all, to analyze the capitalist economies of the Latin American region, which are to be found in the model that we present in the following stage. In a second stage, we outline a macroeconomic framework for the analysis of alternative policies in LDCs that could eventually lead to growth with equity, while trying to avoid inflationary pressures and imbalances in the internal, external, and fiscal sectors. The basic model we propose differs from the conventional macro-models for stabilization and adjustment in many respects. It is post-Keynesian in the sense that it takes as its central focus an approach to economic reality based on a money-production–distribution-class relationship. Oligopolistic product markets, collective bargaining in labor markets, and differentiated marginal propensities to save help us to determine output, employment, prices, and real profit and wage shares. We make some minimal, but essential sectoral distinctions so as to reflect the principal internal characteristics of LDCs. As an important distinctive feature, the model is not set up in real terms but includes prices and income flows in nominal (or money) terms, and also important asymmetries among productive sectors. A primary (food or necessities) and industrial sector are clearly distinguished, where production, pricing, and demand formation are set according to specific structural features. As an innovation the model includes not only primary- and secondary-sector supply-and-demand constraints, respectively, but also a foreign exchange and a government-budget constraint (introducing additional transmission mechanisms for policy variables). By covering production, demand, income distribution, market clearing conditions, external finance and fiscal balance, role of credit, and inflation dynamics, the model allows us to derive a short-run equilibrium representation and to examine the macroeconomic stabilization conditions in order to deal effectively with employment, inflation, and the external imbalances. Moreover, the model can be extended to study the long-run interactions between investments, production capacities, and income distribution in a growth context.

We turn in chapter 5 to policy-oriented issues, a topic that remains unexplored in the literature. The need to rethink the direction and overall form of economic policy is implied in our model. Without denying that specific aspects of policy reform may have been successful, Latin American countries' poor performance (after demand restraint policies, exchange rate adjustment, and overall liberalization) suggests that stabilization and adjustment policies as a whole must be judged unsuccessful. We suggest, however, that there is a potential mix of measures capable of reconciling a high level of activity, low inflation, and an adequate level of international reserves. Of course, this implies that the underlying policy framework in Latin America needs to change.

Among our main arguments we may state the following: First, in terms of demand management, an increase in public sector savings, as we have described it, improves the fiscal balance and the level of economic activity. But we will also show that without incentives to manage manufacturing exports and supply-side policies (capital-augmenting investment), it is only a matter of time before the external sector constraint and the supply-side bottleneck provoke a severe drainage of reserves along with inflation.

Second, besides the short-run stabilization issues, the type of model we employ can address factors that affect prospects for economic growth and equitable distribution. In our model, growth can be financed in various ways. In particular, we explore the impact generated by those changes in government and foreign saving and external shocks.

At the level of economic policymaking, it is hoped that the present study, by helping advance the process of integrating the key tenets of structuralism into a more general open economy and fiscally constrained post-Keynesian framework, makes a contribution by creating an improved basis for policy-oriented analysis in economies afflicted by chronic inflation, external constraints, and low income and growth rates.

CHAPTER 1

On the Origin and Extent of Orthodox IMF/World Bank Programs in Latin America

1.1 The Latin American Impasse

In the early 1980s and especially between 1982 and 1984, almost all indebted countries of the third world as well as of the Eastern European bloc were forced to declare some form of moratorium on debt servicing, and to start negotiations with the International Monetary Fund (IMF), the World Bank, and/or the private banks for the rescheduling of their debts. An abrupt slowdown in international lending (after more than a decade of very rapid expansion) started before the Mexican suspension of payments in the summer of 1982. The banks had already perceived the difficulties into which debt relations were falling. This unprecedented situation contrasted with the dramatic increase in the international supply of funds, and the more fluid and sophisticated local financial markets that the world economy had experienced since 1950. Excess liquidity and the uncontrollable nature of international capital markets (in particular the eurocurrency market) had allowed many less-developed countries (LCDs) to finance current account deficits by borrowing abroad. This was especially so in the late 1970s and early 1980s, when investment opportunities in the industrialized countries were limited and Latin American countries in particular, began to absorb an important proportion of surpluses in the capital markets. In the meantime, deflationary policies in the industrialized countries, and especially the U.S. macropolicy shift aimed at containing inflation through tight monetary policy, pushed interest rates up to record levels. High interest rates made it difficult for most indebted countries to service their debt, as they already were struggling with low prices for their exports and a fall in export volumes.[1] The rise in interest rates had a far bigger effect on Latin American countries than on those in Asia and Africa, since a larger proportion of the Latin American debt was of the floating rate variety (Singh 1995).

The onset of the debt crisis in the early 1980s compelled Latin American countries to adopt stabilization and adjustment programs supported by the IMF and the World Bank. The change in market sentiment led to a violent reversal of capital inflows, causing several episodes of balance-of-payments crisis. Without official financing, the crisis would have forced on the authorities disruptive adjustment, with potentially high costs in terms of output and employment losses. In addition, it is taken for granted that for countries whose economic fundamentals justify access to private capital, access might be available only at high costs. However, after the eruption of the debt crisis, capital was not available at all for Latin American countries.

Despite the fact that the Bretton Woods institutions were not designed to cope with financial crises, by the early 1980s both the IMF and the World Bank had been involved in credit concessions to borrowing countries.[2] But IMF/World Bank lending activities, like other activities, are guided by specific purposes. Sometimes the purposes or objectives have been described as ensuring that borrowing countries do indeed pursue prompt and orderly stabilization and structural adjustment (Guitian 1981). Sometimes, it is argued, the IMF and World Bank lend to borrowing countries in order to ensure a sufficient supply of money from debtors to the private banking system (Roddick 1988). Recently, some have argued that these multilateral agencies certify the quality of government policies and place a seal of approval on a country, providing information to investors at large (Rodrik 1995). The fact of the matter is that these institutions will not lend money today to a country merely because the country wants to borrow. Both institutions must be convinced that extending credit promotes their purposes. Thus, conditionality, the right to demand policy changes from governments that ask for loans from multilateral agencies, plays a crucial role here. Without doubt, conditionality is the hallmark of multilateral institutions today.

From this scenario, the IMF and the World Bank emerged as two immensely powerful institutions with the power to interfere in domestic policy decisions by providing emergency rescue packages under strict conditionality. At the center of the scene Latin American countries have been among the major victims of the debt "financial scandal," and the IMF/World

Bank duet has become a sort of global capitalist authority. During the 1980s, Latin American countries suffered a deep depression, which was worse than that of the 1930s in terms of its duration, and more significantly, in terms of the damage done to long-term development prospects. As we will show, most macroeconomic and social indicators deteriorated sharply during this period. It was towards the beginning of the 1990s that Latin American economies started a slow recovery and a gradual disinflation process. The revival of international capital inflows is perhaps the most visible economic change in the region during the last decade. However, growth prospects are low; unemployment remains high; and the region seems to experience a historical reconstruction of current account deficits, increased financial instability and worsened exchange rate crises, high unemployment, falling average wages, and a widening income distribution. We believe that even restricting the discussion to the difficulties of Latin American countries (which is our modest purpose), it is easy to understand parallel events in other regions of the third world.

A simple logic here would blame much of the relatively poor performance in Latin America on multilateral misguided policies, and, in fact, the historical evidence does suggest that countries that apply the orthodox recipes experience considerable problems. It is difficult, however, to blame the poor performance of the region since the debt crisis entirely on IMF/World Bank management. There have been a variety of factors that these institutions can argue have been beyond their control: domestic mismanagement, slow reforms, and external conditions have played major roles. However, the inability to alter the current economic crisis has been part of the problem, because despite the clear importance of factors beyond the control of multilateral agencies, the IMF and the World Bank still stress individual and purely orthodox domestic adjustment. Moreover, it is fairly clear that under the generalized control by these institutions, the region seems to have behaved in ways not previously observed, and economic and social conditions have not improved. We are not attempting to test the relative importance of multilateral management and external factors in causing the poor performance of the region. We will just argue (in later steps) that the framework, which has given rise to current conditionality practices, suffers from severe theoretical and empirical shortcomings. However, before fully describing and evaluating the theoretical framework and the analytical tools and models that underlie conditionality, we want to indicate how the Latin American region has behaved since the debt crisis (a period in which domestic-policy intervention by multilateral institutions has been decisive) and show how conditionality has evolved over time.

Between 1982 and 1984 most Latin American countries entering into open debt rescheduling negotiations were first obliged to sign agreements with the IMF (see table 1.1). On only a few occasions, as in the case of Venezuela's debt rescheduling, was the IMF left completely out of the negotiations.[3] In 1980 (just before the capital supply shock) the outstanding external debt in Latin American countries accounted for about $216,194 million. Since then, debt restructuring has been a part of most countries' effort to come to grips with their economic difficulties. This has involved spreading out repayment of maturing principal over a number of years into the future, and has also entailed rolling over short-term debt; but a variety of schemes—debt buy-backs, securitization, debt-equity swaps—have emerged in recent years in an effort to find a way out of the debt problem through voluntary actions on the part of creditors and under the support of the IMF. Despite the popularity of these market-based solutions to the debt problem, there has been surprisingly little sensible alleviation of the problem. Table 1.1 shows how by 1999 the total debt outstanding had risen to over $729 billion in the same selected group of Latin American countries.

The capital supply shocks to which Latin American countries were subjected after 1982 emanated from "contagion effect" whereby, following the Mexican debt crisis, voluntary private capital flows to most of these countries were greatly reduced if not stopped altogether. Besides capital supply shocks, Latin American countries have faced highly unstable terms of trade shocks at various times over the past two decades. We should remark here that the importance for many of these countries of primary-commodity exports with exogenously determined prices accounts for a significant source of macroeconomic instability. Prices of primary commodities tend to fluctuate sharply with a downward trend, as illustrated for a selected group of such commodities in figure 1.1. In spite of the important increase in the share of manufactured goods in LDCs' exports over the past decades, most Latin American country exports still consist largely of primary commodities. The share of primary commodities in the exports of a selected group of countries within the region is given in table 1.2.

It may be appreciated that deterioration in the external position of any of these countries has extremely serious consequences for all spheres of the economy, real as well as financial. The external constraint can become so binding that the country has to curtail imports required for maintaining the existing level of production. In fact, imported intermediate and capital goods still play an important role in the aggregate production function(s) in Latin American countries. Figure 1.2 clearly shows that the composition of real imports in Latin America as a whole has not changed in the last decades.

Table 1.1   Request for IMF Rescue Intervention or Debt Rescheduling and Total External Debt in Selected Latin American Countries

| | 1982–84 | | Total External Debt ($ Millions) | |
	IMF	Debt Rescheduling	1980	1995
Argentina	Yes	Yes	27,157	89,679
Bolivia	No	Yes	2,340	4,528
Brazil	Yes	Yes	64,000	164,836
Chile	Yes	Yes	11,207	21,825
Colombia	No	No	6,805	23,431
Costa Rica	Yes	Yes	2,209	3,794
Ecuador	Yes	Yes	4,167	13,934
El Salvador	Yes	Yes	1,176	2,243
Guatemala	Yes	No	1,053	2,107
Honduras	Yes	Yes	1,388	4,372
Mexico	Yes	Yes	50,700	161,100
Nicaragua	No	Yes	1,825	10,240
Panama	Yes	Yes	2,271	3,710
Peru	Yes	No	9,515	27,487
Dominicana	Yes	Yes	2,173	4,001
Uruguay	Yes	Yes	1,165	4,852
Venezuela	No	Yes	26,963	35,200
Total Selected Countries			216,194	577,341

Sources: P.C. Padoan (1986) and ECLAC (1996).

The adverse external conditions and the stabilization and adjustment policies carried out after the debt crisis were not without cost. Overall, the 1980s was a lost decade for the region. Even though Latin America was rapidly able to transform a trade deficit of $3.5 billion in 1981 into a trade surplus of over $37.8 billion in 1984 (Pastor 1990, p. 156), that was not a reason for optimism since the improvement in the trade balance was accomplished largely through import restraint.[4] Because of the structure of industry in most Latin American economies, a fall in imports on this scale was largely the result of contractionary policies. Gross Domestic Product (GDP), per-capita GDP, and its evolution are shown in table 1.3. Per-capita GDP fell more than ten percentage points between 1981 and 1990, and the average annual rate between 1981 and 1990 was −1.19 percent. Inflation remained high and was accelerating by the end of the decade, reaching an average rate of

Figure 1.1 World Prices of Some Important Commodities for Latin America

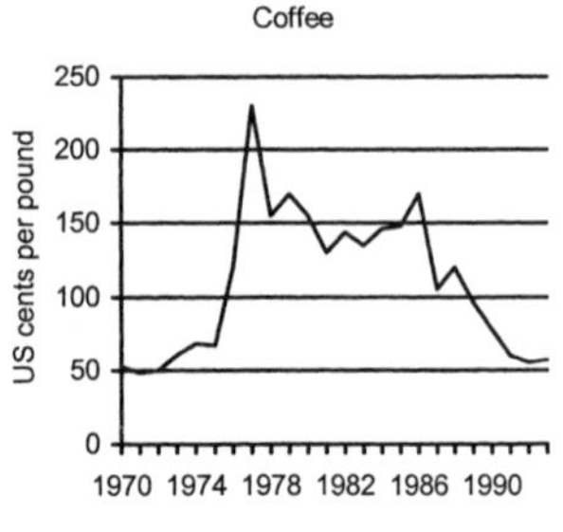

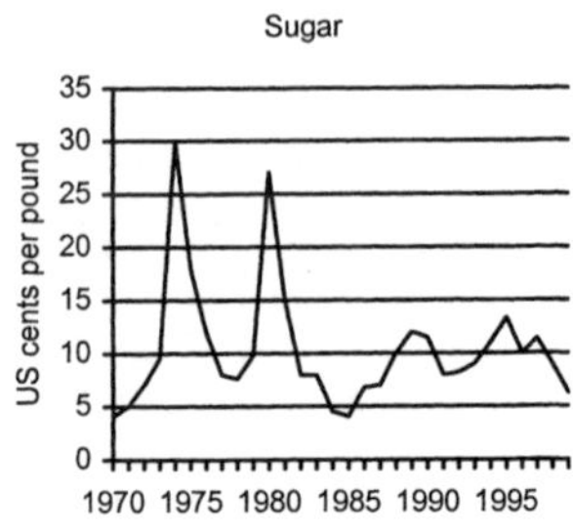

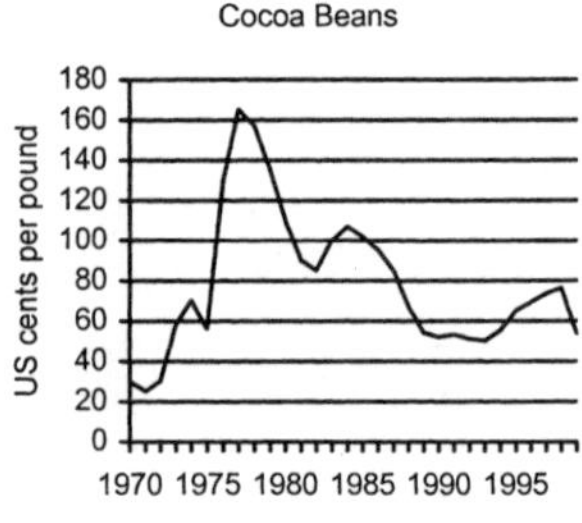

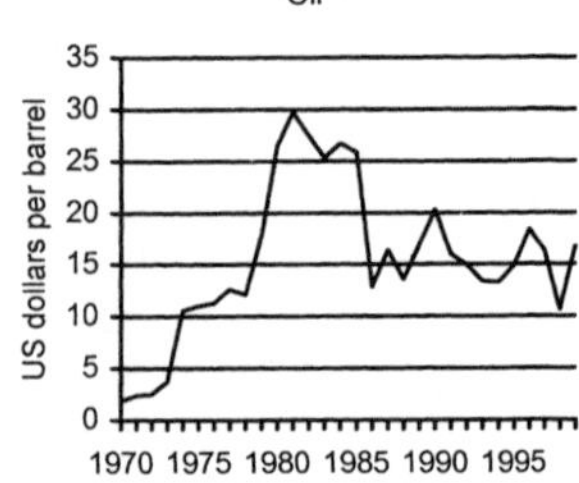

Source: ECLAC and Reuters.

Table 1.2 Export Share of Primary Commodities (1991)

Selected Latin American Countries	*Export Share (%)*
Bolivia	95
Brazil	44
Chile	85
Colombia	67
Costa Rica	74
Ecuador	98
Haiti	58
Jamaica	44
Mexico	55
Venezuela	88

Sources: Agenor and Montiel (1996).

Figure 1.2   Composition of Real Imports in Latin America

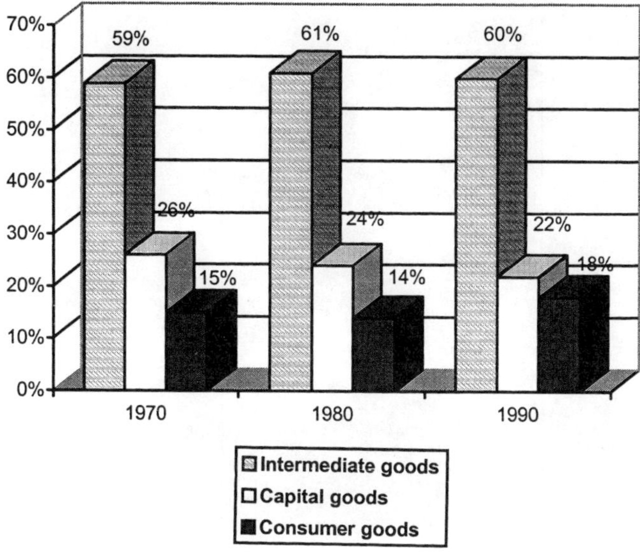

Source: Inter-American Development Bank.

413 percent between 1981 and 1990. Human capital has been undermined, and between 1981 and 1990 physical capital formation was reduced drastically (Roddick 1988 and table 1.3). Education spending as a part of the central government's total spending decreased in 14 out of 17 Latin American countries reported (Cardoso and Helwege 1992). The coefficient of savings remained static while the average Latin American per-capita consumption in 1988 was approximately 7 percent less than in 1980 (Eyzaguirre 1989). An increase in unemployment (Van der Hoeven 1987) was accompanied by falling real urban minimum wages, whose average variation between 1981 and 1989 was −2.79 percent per year (own calculations from Cardoso and Helwege data, 1992). In most cases the combined effect of these two of course increased urban poverty. According to the World Bank Development Report (1990), by 1985, 31 percent of the population in Latin America were considered "poor" or "extremely poor." Estimates by Altimir (1996) put at 35 percent the households living in poverty in 1980, increasing to 37 percent in 1986 and reaching 39 percent in 1990. By 1990 the region as a whole was still carrying an annual external debt service of 34.4 percent of its export earnings

Table 1.3   Latin American Leading Economic Indicators, 1981–90

	1981	1982	1983	1984	1985	1986	1987	1988	1989	1990
GDP (Billions of $ in 1988)[1]	769	761	741	769	795	821	842	843	848	840
GDP Per Capita ($)[1]	2,161	2,092	1,991	2,020	2,044	2,066	2,074	2,034	2,003	1,946
Growth of GDP Per Capita	−1.9	−3.2	−4.8	1.5	1.2	1.1	0.4	−1.9	−1.5	−2.8
Gross Investment/GDP[2]	24.2	21.7	17.4	16.8	17.7	17.7	20.4	20.9	19.5	19.0
CPI Inflation Rate (%)[3,4,5]	58	85	131	185	275	65	199	233	340	438
Net Foreign Resource[3]										
Transfer (Billions of $)	11.3	−18.7	−31.6	26.9	−32.3	−22.7	−16.0	−28.8	−28.3	−16.0
External Debt Service[1]										
(Billions of U.S. $)	55.5	59.1	50.4	51.8	47.9	47.7	46.2	54.9	45.5	43.6

[1]IDB, *Progreso Económico y Social en América Latina*: Informe 1991.
[2]G. Rosenthal (1992).
[3]World Bank (1991), World Tables.
[4] ECLAC (1990).
[5]IMF, *World Economic Outlook*, May 1996.

(IMF 1996). The net transfer of capital from 1982 to 1990 was negative and reached a staggering $221 billion (table 1.3).

It was towards the beginning of the 1990s that the Latin American economies started a modest recovery, which came from a slow increase in the output growth rate and from a gradual disinflation process. However, during the 1990s the average growth rate was low by comparison, with average growth rate registered between the mid sixties and the high seventies, and the rate of inflation has been higher than the average one registered during the 1960s (see figure 1.3).

Reduction of the share of the budget deficit was the single most important policy goal of the 1990s. The rise of the fiscal deficit-to-GDP ratio to 6.8 percent in 1983 was unprecedented in Latin America. This was in the depths of the recession, and coincided with the adverse external conditions. The fiscal deficit was reduced only to 5.3 percent in 1984 and remained above 5 percent for the rest of the decade. But as illustrated in figure 1.4, from 1987 public expenditure became restrictive and started to fall dramatically. By 1993 public expenditure had fallen to 23 percent of GDP from a peak of 32 percent registered in 1987.

The recent evolution of sectoral balances also throws some interesting light. As we can see from table 1.4, in industrial countries as a whole, the

Figure 1.3   Inflation and Growth in Latin America, 1966–98

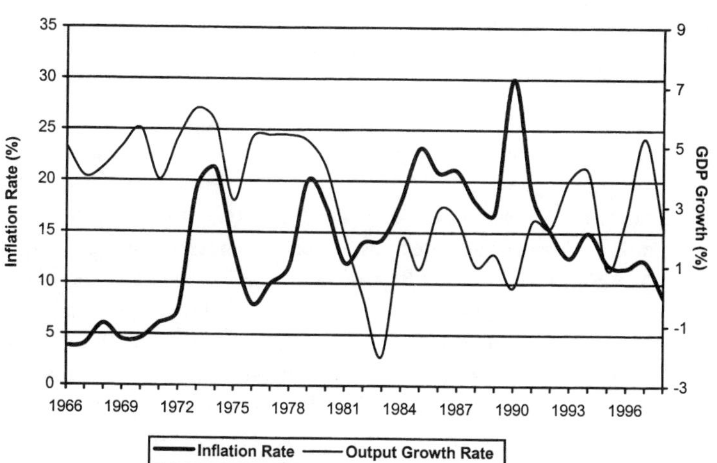

Source: IDB (1997), *Progreso Económico y Social en América Latina* and IDB Statistics and Quantitative Analysis Unit.

Figure 1.4 Evolution of the Fiscal Accounts in Latin America, 1983–96

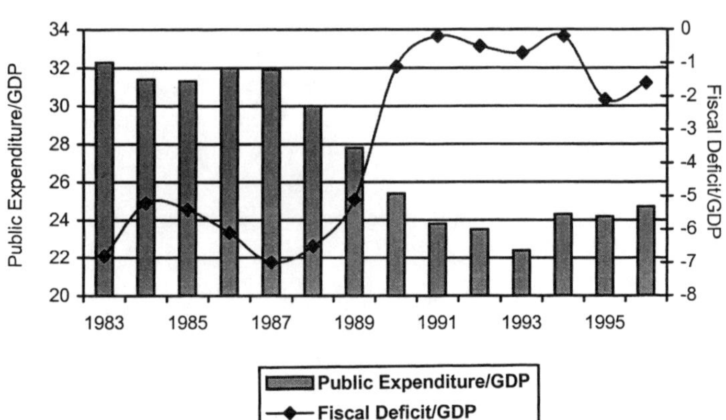

Source: IDB (1997), *Progreso Económico y Social en América Latina.*

Table 1.4 Public and Private Balances in Industrial and Latin American Countries (in Percent of GDP)

	1988			*1994*		
	Public	*Private*	*External*	*Public*	*Private*	*External*
Industrial Countries	−2.0	1.6	−0.4	−3.6	3.5	−0.2
Latin America	−5.3	4.0	−1.3	−0.6	2.5	−3.1

Sources: Fitzgerald (1996).

deterioration of the public net balance has been accompanied by an improvement in the private balance. In Latin America, between 1988 and 1994, there is a dramatic improvement in the public sector balance, and as we will remark in a moment, the same happened with respect to the autonomous inflow of capital; but unfortunately the effect of increased liquidity has deteriorated the external balance. In this regard, it can be observed that after a significant improvement in the current account balance of the mid-1980s, during the 1990s the current account has deteriorated (see figure 1.5). Certainly, this recent widening current account deficit has been more than financed by capital flows. But, in spite of this, there is a lot of uncertainty regarding the extent to which the current external situation is sustainable or not.

Between 1990 and 1994 the turnaround in private capital inflows to the region was impressive (see figure 1.6). By 1991 the region received

Figure 1.5   Current Account Balance in Latin America, 1987–97 (Billions of $U.S.)

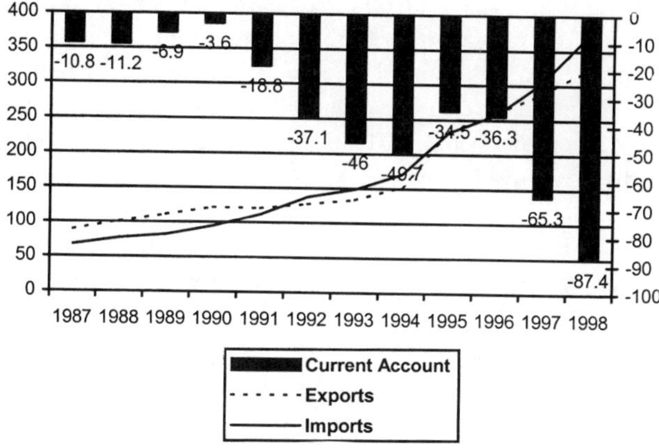

Source: ECLAC, *Preliminary Overview of the Latin American and Caribbean Economy,* several years.

Figure 1.6   Annual Private Capital Net Flows in Latin America, 1979–98 (Percentage of GDP)

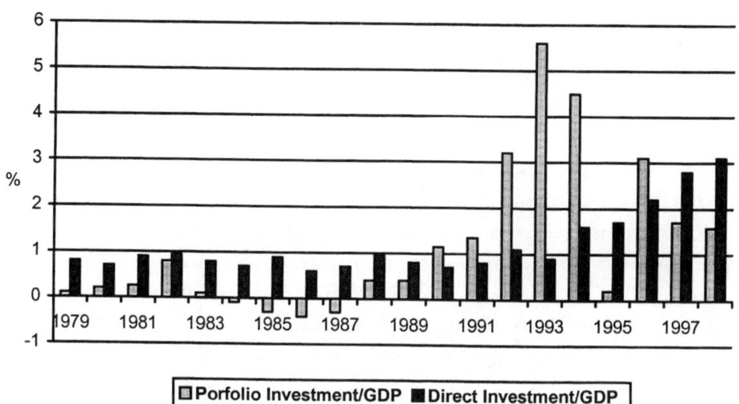

Source: IDB Statistics and Quantitative Analysis Unit.

$40.000 million, a substantially higher amount than the $13.400 attracted in 1990 (Sagasti and Arvelo 1992). Annual long-term private capital net flows also increased. An air of triumph dominated public discourse and was echoed by multilateral institutions. However, three aspects of these capital movements must be evaluated. First, these resources were concentrated in a few countries (Mexico received 40 percent, Brazil 24 percent, Argentina and Venezuela 12 percent each, and Chile 4 percent). Second, recent econometric studies have investigated the causes of portfolio capital investments in major Latin American countries, and all conclude that external factors were a major cause of these inflows, so a reversal of these conditions may lead to a future capital outflow (see Calvo *et al.* 1993, Fernandez-Arias and Montiel 1996, and Frankel and Okongwu 1996).[5] Third, the volatile nature of these capitals are cause for concern since an important proportion of them have taken the form of equity instruments, both direct and portfolio (syndicated bank loans are relatively unimportant).[6]

The sudden and deep crisis of the Mexican peso in late 1994 revealed the false premises of the speculation-led economic growth model in which huge current account deficits are financed by short-term capital inflows. During the Salinas administration and under the support of the IMF, Mexico liberalized completely its financial markets.[7] In addition, a trade liberalization program was financed with $1 billion in loans from the World Bank. Within the financial liberalization program, important events included the development of the money market, the freeing of interest rates on bank assets and liabilities, the elimination of priority lending quotas, the phaseout of both reserve requirements and liquidity coefficients, and, ultimately, the privatization of 18 banks in 14 months—June 1991 through July 1992. Relatively high real interest rates in Mexico and low rates in the United States precipitated large inflows of foreign capital. This short-term foreign investment flowing into Mexico was being used to finance a $28 billion deficit in the current account created by an increasing appetite for cheap imports. In 1994 alone, the trade deficit on current account reached record proportions of 8 percent of GDP. The deficit convinced financial markets that the peso will decline, and that, along with rising U.S. interest rates, triggered movement out of the peso. Other forces contributed to the loss of confidence by foreign investors: political unrest and a history of post-elections devaluations.[8] Between February 1994 and November 1994 foreign currency reserves fell from $29.3 billion to $12.8 billion. On December 20, the finance secretary announced the devaluation of the peso.

It can be argued that stabilization and adjustment can only be judged successful if they bring about a rate of growth of output that allows for a steady improvement in employment and living standards. Even though the results of massive and successive stabilization and structural adjustment programs in Latin America have been modest so far, these have been accomplished while preserving very low real wages, and increasing unemployment, inequality, and poverty. Figure 1.7 charts the annual average real wage and the average rate of unemployment in Latin America from 1982 to 1996. Unemployment increased dramatically as the economy plunged precipitously in the recession of the early 1980s. Unemployment declined from 13 percent in 1985 to 9 percent in 1993, but since then it has increased steadily. The average real wage declined with no interruptions after 1982 and has remained stagnant during the 1990s. This resulted in widening income inequality and higher poverty measures. Figure 1.8 provides the Gini index and a poverty line measure for the period 1980 to 1995. As the graph shows, both measures increased over the years.

One can never be too sure about prospects of the Latin American region. The experience of the 1990s confounded both optimists and pessimists, and the scene is uncertain. Although capital inflows were large in the early 1990s (until the Mexican crisis in 1994) compared with those in the 1982–89 period; they have been somewhat smaller than in the preceding period,

Figure 1.7   Real Wages and Unemployment in Latin America 1980–96

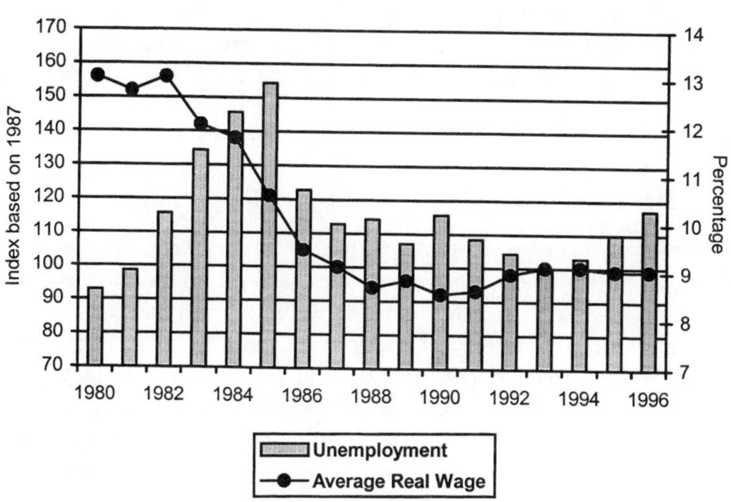

Source: IDB (1997) *Progreso Económico y Social en América Latina.*

Figure 1.8 Poverty and Inequality in Latin America, 1980–95

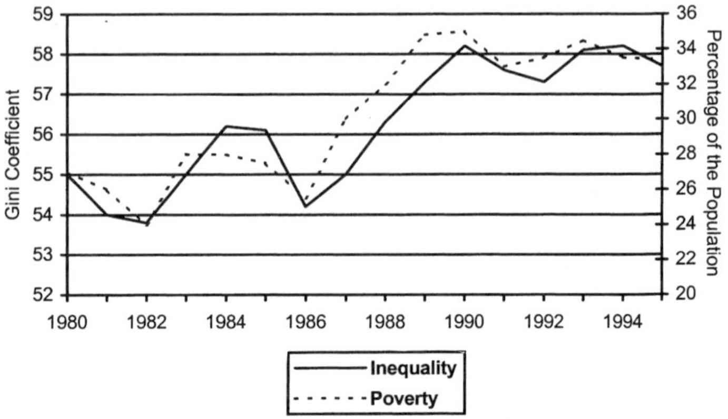

Source: IDB (1997) *Progreso Económico y Social en América Latina.*

1978–81 (Dooley *et al.* 1996). Gross domestic product growth showed a modest increase in 1993 and 1994 but it was adversely affected in 1998 and 1999 after the financial debacle of East Asian countries. Even though GDP expanded at the average annual rate of 4 percent in 2000, now there are prospects of recession in Argentina, Ecuador, Colombia, and Peru. Table 1.5 shows that annual inflation decreased in 1997 to 8.7 percent (a low level by Latin American standards), but it averaged 138 percent during the period 1990 to 1998. Moreover, trade flows have been far from satisfactory, and the region has accumulated a current account deficit of $379 billion during the last seven years (from 1991 to 1998). Furthermore, external debt service has remained high and continued to grow during the 1990s.

1.2 IMF Conditionality: Origin, Nature, and Evolution

Despite the fact that over the years the use of IMF resources has come to be viewed as desirable only when other alternatives have been exhausted, very often an LDC with balance-of-payment (BOP) problems ends up requesting a line of credit, or some kind of external loan, from the IMF. The reason is that under the present arrangements in the global economic system, the IMF is the final source of cash (the lender of last resort) for economies to which commercial banks, capital markets, and/or donors no longer care to lend.[9]

In exchange for the loan, the borrowing country pledges to reform its economic policies to meet the requirements of the IMF. Since countries cannot present collateral, conditionality substitutes for this to provide the

Table 1.5   Leading Economic Indicators for Latin America, 1989–98

	1978–88	1989	1990	1991	1992	1993	1994	1995	1996	1997	1998	1990–98
GDP (Real Growth in %)	3.2	0.7	0.0	3.7	3.2	3.9	5.2	0.9	3.9	5.3	2.3	3.1
GDP Per Capita												
(Real Growth in %)	0.7	−0.8	−0.9	1.3	0.9	1.2	2.9	−0.8	2.2	3.6	0.7	1.2
CPI (Growth Rate in %)	98.1	340.0	438.6	128.8	151.5	209.5	233.7	37.9	21.7	12.2	8.7	138.0
Terms of Trade												
(Percentage Change)	−2.5	1.7	−1	0.1	−5.5	−2.1	2.8	6.2	1.7	−1.6	−5.5	−0.5
Current Account												
(Billions of U.S. $)		−7.8	−1.2	−17.6	−33.8	−45.5	−50.9	−37.1	−38.5	−65.6	−90.5	−42.3
External Debt												
(Billions of U.S. $)		408.2	419.2	432.0	451.7	500.4	544.6	602.3	630.2	664.0	—	
External Debt Service												
(Billions of U.S. $)		52.7	44.8	46.1	52.6	62.4	67.2	84.6	114.3	132.5	—	

Sources: IMF, *World Economic Outlook*, several years; IDB Statistics and Quantitative Analysis Unit.

assurance that policy changes will be undertaken to generate the resources for repayment. From this perspective conditionality is perfectly legitimate. But as Steward and FitzGerald (1998) point out, there are many alternative policy packages that would offer the promise of generating enough foreign exchange to guarantee repayment. The IMF, however, insists on just one possibility—its own policy package.

Since conditionality was put in practice, its purpose has been to maintain the revolving nature of IMF resources by ensuring that members' drawings are purely temporary. Buira (1983) and Loxley (1986) have correctly pointed out that conditionality was a practice not envisaged in Keynes's original proposal for an international monetary institution. Conditionality was also bitterly opposed by European nations, the main debtors at that time, which believed that the IMF should not interfere in this way with national autonomy. Diaz Alejandro (1984) brilliantly summarized the implications of conditionality: "the key justification for conditionality is that if you ask for a gift, you must listen to your patron" (p. 359). In the end the Executive Board formally accepted conditionality as a principle in February 1952 (under the pressure of the United States), although it was not written into articles of the IMF until 1969.

Latin America was the first visible target when the IMF invented the concept of conditionality. The practice of attaching economic policy conditions and performance criteria to IMF loans was gradually developed in the 1950s, mainly using Latin American economies as testing grounds for such techniques. In 1954, conditionality of the type we currently see first appeared when Peru signed the first stand-by agreement.[10]

While there was no mention of stand-by arrangements in the original Articles of Agreement signed at Bretton Woods; the instrument evolved in practice throughout the late 1950s and 1960s and has been by far the major form of interaction between the IMF and its Latin American members. The country can draw on the credit as long as the promised policy changes are instituted, and macroeconomic indicators behave according to the pre-specified performance criteria. In fact, the policy revisions and the criteria together amount to conditionality. An agreement includes a number of performance criteria that are written into a letter of intent from the member, and continuing access to credit is conditional upon adequate progress in fulfilling the criteria. Usually, IMF officials devise the basic framework of the programs with little contribution from local officials. The IMF's targets for the main macroeconomic variables have to be revised due to lack of target fulfillment. IMF teams arrive in a country periodically and stay for two or three weeks evaluating the progress in fulfilling the criteria. A negative evaluation can interrupt the flow of external funds until conversations with each country's policymakers are reinitiated. The conversations take months, and during this time governments can do nothing but wait.[11] Most programs contain a near-identical set of polices, and local officials may make some contribution when magnitudes and sequencing have to be established. Indeed, IMF's officials have recognized that the impression that economic stabilization is too rigid and dogmatic to accommodate the differing and changing circumstances of member countries is not entirely without foundation (see Mussa and Savastano 1999). A degree of conservatism is imparted by a highly disciplined bureaucracy that has long tenure in the IMF; and that operates in accord with established, and only gradually evolving, policies and procedures, and within a legal framework that imposes constraints on what is acceptable in IMF arrangements.

Under a stand-by agreement a member's access to IMF resources is expressed in terms of tranches, equal to 25 percent of its quota to the IMF. The first of these tranches (the reserve tranche) is available automatically on request and without conditions, and the next (the first credit tranche) is subject to minimal conditions. However, for borrowing in the so-called upper credit tranches, finance is available if the member government guarantees that the credit is in support of an "adequate" program of domestic policies. The objectives of the program, especially in the first three decades of conditional loans, were perceived as essentially short-term, comprising the resolution of an immediate balance-of-payments problem and a reduction of the rate of inflation to tolerable levels (which were problems assumed to be short term in nature). Consequently, the economic models from which policy actions and recommendations were drawn were short-run, demand-oriented models, and the policy prescriptions derived from these models were accordingly aimed at demand management. Traditionally, demand management policies to solve BOP problems and inflation have been known as "stabilization," even though what seems to define the term is more the policy targets than the policy instruments.

In an IMF stabilization program, the source of disequilibrium is normally identified as excess aggregate demand. This imbalance is supposed to be reflected in the prevalence of inflation and BOP deficits. This view logically leads to a concentration on demand management techniques of fiscal and monetary policy combined with exchange rate adjustments. Perhaps the only change that this traditional view has experienced in recent years is the fact that stabilization programs have come to be viewed with a longer-term horizon that includes changes in the supply side. However, the short-term demand side aspect of stabilization still remains an essential element of current programs, and it is for this reason that the IMF's stabilization policies look remarkably similar over space and time.

The packages endorsed by the IMF in Latin America in the 1950s incorporated policies that would remain central to the IMF's perception of how to establish BOP equilibrium and stabilize the price level. Well-known models of balance-of-payments adjustments took shape thanks to experience with stabilization program in Latin America (as in the case of the absorption approach and Polak's model, for example). Particularly important was the IMF's work with Latin American central banks, many of which were sympathetic to the IMF's policy packages. Kahler (1990) illustrates how domestic economic policy in Mexico in the late 1940s and early 1950s served as a basis for the construction of IMF theory with respect to the need to devalue the domestic currency.[12] By the 1950s, reduction in the fiscal deficit, control of domestic credit expansion (particularly of credit extended to the public sector), and establishment of a "realistic" exchange rate were all key ingredients in IMF programs. Felix (1954) has also reported income policies (an aspect often neglected in the literature). In Chile, for instance, during the so-called Klein-Saks period,[13] and in the subsequent 1959 IMF stabilization effort, the rise in money wages was held down by restricting wage increases to an annual fraction of the previous year's rise in the cost of living. In Argentina, in their first stand-by arrangement signed with the IMF (in December 1958), the principal device used seems to have been a tougher policy toward unions on part of the government. The earlier stabilization programs of the 1950s and 1960s did not encourage a dramatic change of commercial policy or financial control (Diaz Alejandro 1981). By the late 1960s and early 1970s, however, a renewed interest in trade regimes and liberalization,[14] and the works of McKinnon (1973) and Shaw (1973) on "financial repression," produced a new consensus highly critical of the import substitution model and of financial controls in LDCs. This consensus, which was to become a firm part of the so-called new orthodoxy,[15] held that outward-oriented trade, realistic exchange rates, and financial liberalization were likely to ensure more successful adjustments to external imbalances and higher rates of economic growth in LDCs. Moreover, the structuralist-monetarist debate in the 1960s in Latin America increased the interest of orthodox and neoclassical economists in economic growth, so that some structuralist claims (such as the need for growth-oriented programs) were picked up by the old orthodoxy (Kahler 1990). Thus, the concept of structural adjustment was accepted by the IMF and gave rise in 1974 to the Extended Fund Facility (EFF), allowing countries to prolong their adjustment programs up to three years. Therefore, contrary to the common belief, structural adjustment is not something new and experimental, but dates back to the mid-1970s and has been widely practiced. Stabilization programs in the so-called Southern Cone countries, notably Chile (from 1975), Argentina (from 1976), and Uruguay (1974), emphasized the need to supplement traditional demand-management policies by commercial and financial reforms that aimed to extend the role of the price mechanism as the allocative instrument.

The EFF reflects greater emphasis on supply-side elements in the conditionality of the programs. The types of measures that were included reflected the new orthodoxy: trade liberalization, public sector reforms, removal of price subsidies, and policies affecting interest rates. By the end of 1983 Angel Buira, a former executive director of the IMF, stated: "In practice this facility has not been sufficiently developed to make it fully meaningful and, as a result, most of the so-called structural adjustment programmes undertaken remain essentially a chain of conventional demand management programmes built around the usual ceilings on credit expansion, fiscal deficit, etc . . . , to which ad-hoc measures of trade liberalization and production incentives have been added to stimulate a supply side response" (Buira 1983, p. 131).

Today, a typical program in Latin America—whether stand-by or EFF—embodies a variety of policies that reflect the broadening of orthodoxy criteria: devaluation of the national currency (which is viewed as a precondition); monetary restraint; reduction in budget deficits (specifically by removing state subsidies to food, fuel, and transport, and reducing social expenditure); the reduction of tariff and elimination of some import controls; liberalization of interest rates to their "natural" market level; and sometimes (as in the southern cone stabilization programs of the 1950s and 1970s) some form of administrative ceilings on money wages.

1.3 Phases of IMF Conditionality in Latin America

Lichtensztenj (1983) has identified three phases of IMF conditionality in Latin America, which are to our understanding still valid. In the first phase, the IMF intervenes actively (from the mid-1950s to the late 1960s), pursuing a change in certain aspects of foreign trade regimes, the international mobility of capital, and domestic performance through conventional stabilization policies. In the second phase (on the threshold of the 1970s), there was an evident decline in IMF intervention. In the third phase (still running), the IMF has created strong links with the international banking system, and in coordination with the World Bank has strengthened its conditionality.

During the early phase, the amounts and terms of the IMF's financial assistance, and the nature and desirability of the conditions attached to its credits, was the subject of intense debate. The stand-by arrangements (the main and almost unique facility used by the IMF) were in effect for a maximum of one year,[16] and conditionality was very demanding. Credit tightening and fiscal reform were the main instrument policy in all programs, but devaluation was also present. Lichtensztejn (1983) and Felix (1964) mention as some major examples in the 1950s the participation of the IMF in Chile in 1955 (the Klein-Saks mission), the Adair mission sent to Bolivia in 1956, the IMF reform program in Paraguay in 1957, the stabilization program in collaboration with the Eximbank in Colombia in 1958 (a pioneer program that resembles the contemporary IMF/World Bank approach), the monetary and exchange rate reform in Uruguay in 1959, and others. Between 1954 and 1970, Latin American countries signed a total of 164 stand-by agreements,[17] and were overwhelmingly the main users of IMF facilities. These figures confirm that the IMF's intervention in Latin American countries is by no means new; on the contrary, it has been repeated since the creation of the Bretton Woods's financial structure.

It is interesting to note that IMF intervention in national economies seems to be greater when there are few alternative sources of finance available. This was the case in the 1950s and '60s when both private and other multilateral official credit flows were at very low levels. Taylor (1987, p. 33) has correctly pointed out that "conditionality strictness fluctuates over time... due at least in part to shifts in the resources of the IMF relative to the demand placed upon them." The fact is that by the early 1970s, the number of stand-by arrangements requested by Latin American countries and globally by LDCs had declined (Kahler 1990). This reflected the second phase of IMF conditionality. The phenomenon reflected the fact that countries were reluctant to draw on the upper credit tranches of the IMF except as a last resort. This reluctance, in turn, was naturally fueled by the new successes of Latin America in contracting loans from capital-laden western banks.

The pressure of global economic changes forced the IMF to adapt its facilities in other directions (Loxley 1986, Pastor 1987), and to reduce conditionality. In 1974 it introduced the Extended Financing Facility, which was supposed to provide members with longer-term funding for supply-oriented programs designed to confront balance-of-payments problems.[18] However, the EFF and many other facilities of primary or exclusive relevance to LDCs—the Compensatory Financing Facility, the Buffer Stock Financing Facility, the Trust Fund, and the Subsidy Accounts—were of limited importance since the maximum sums that could be drawn on were clearly insufficient and many countries refused to use them fully (Sutton 1984, Williamson 1987). Feinberg (1987) also claims that the IMF was disappointed with the early EFF multi-year programs due to the difficulties in the design, so that the EFF finally fell into disuse. Nevertheless, the EFF was revitalized in Latin America in the mid-1980s when applications came from Chile (1985), Venezuela (1989), Mexico (1989), and later from Argentina (1992) and Peru (1993). The conditions included in these more recent arrangements placed considerable emphasis on structural adjustment.

It is important to note that third phase of IMF conditionality in Latin America develops in a different economic environment from the one that inspired Bretton Woods. In the Bretton Woods conception, private capital flows were not expected to be a major factor, and capital account convertibility was not expected to be the rule. However, the development of open financial markets and the exposure to private capital flows volatility has radically change the rationale for IMF financing. For countries whose economic fundamentals justify access to private capital, access might not be available at all, and this excludes countries from the efficient allocation of capital. Moreover, for other countries a change in market sentiment can lead to violent reversal of the capital inflows, causing a balance-of-payments crisis. In fact, as Mussa (1997) has emphasized, today the general rationale for the IMF's role needs to be grounded in the existence of market imperfections or in the inadequate provision of public goods, both of which IMF surveillance and its lending activities can help to alleviate.[19]

The first boom of capital flows into Latin America during the period that followed the 1973 oil shock came to an abrupt end with deep financial and

Figure 1.9   IMF Intervention in Latin American Countries under an SBA, EFF, SAF or ESAF (1954–97)

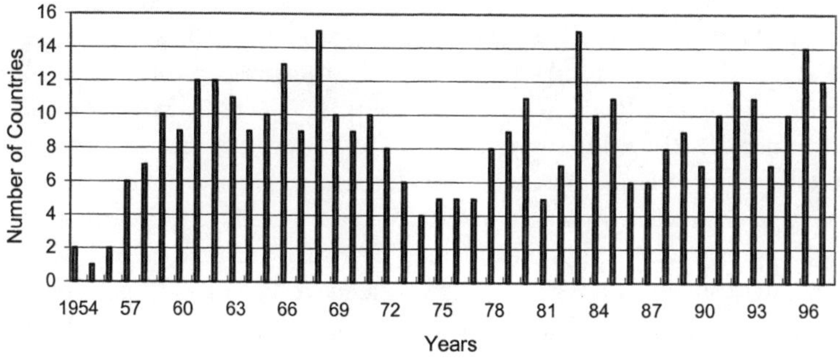

Source: Korner *et al.* (1986), and IMF, *Annual Reports*, 1985–98.

external crisis. Thus, the 1980s witnessed a dramatic increase in the IMF's power and influence compared with the levels of the 1970s. In the mid-1970s, for instance, less than one-third of all Latin American countries were operating under IMF programs. By late 1983, however, more than three-quarters of the same set were operating under IMF programs, and all of these were upper credit arrangements (Pastor 1987). Figure 1.9 presents a graphic picture of this reality. It shows how the influence of the IMF has evolved over time, by simply registering the number of Latin American countries under stand-by, EFF, SAF, or ESAF arrangements. After a fall in 1981, a clear and sharp increase in the number of countries under the supervision of the IMF occurred. What is worse, a hardening in conditionality was reported by Sutton (1984) and Buira (1983). In fact, the Reagan administration, in particular the Treasury, pressed for stricter monetary and fiscal policies from the borrowing countries and expressed the wish to resist any weakening of conditionality. In this context Buira (1983) reports: "U.S. spokesmen expressed the view that the IMF should not become a financial intermediary but, rather, that it should promote a stricter conditionality in order to preserve its resources and accelerate the adjustment process" (p. 113). Thus the relative increase in the resources that countries could borrow, which was one of the achievements of the policy of enlarged access,[20] was undermined by the strict conditionality attached to the programs. Loxley (1986) reports that virtually 100 percent of IMF finance in 1981/83 was highly conditional, compared with 24 percent in 1979/80 and 6.6 percent in 1975/76. He comes to this conclusion after considering the Compensatory Facility to be highly conditional and deducting drawings on the reserve tranche. We may presume that policy conditionality of the IMF has grown in influence over recent years (after the "tequila effect") as the number of countries involved has risen (typically under 8 in 1994; up to 10 in 1995; rising to 14 in 1996 and 12 in 1997).

In March 1986 the IMF established the Structural Adjustment Facility (SAF), and two years later the Enhanced Structural Adjustment Facility (ESAF). Major differences in conditionality exist between SAF and more traditional IMF credit arrangements. The former are disbursed in one installment per year, so the IMF has no leverage until the next year's letter of intent is negotiated. Apart from this difference in enforcement power, the IMF applies weaker conditionality under SAF than under other facilities; the structural content of a SAF arrangement tends to be less well specified and less action oriented, with greater acceptance of studies (Polak 1991). By and large, only African countries are given access to SAF. Since 1987 only two countries in Latin America, Haiti and Bolivia, have had access to a SAF program, and four to an ESAF (in contrast with about 30 countries in Africa). In fact, between 1990 and 1997, 19 out 21 Latin American countries that were under an agreement with the IMF were using either a stand-by or an EFF facility.

1.4 The World Bank: From Development Projects to Policy-based Lending

The World Bank, which consists of two institutions, the International Bank of Reconstruction and Development (IBRD) and its soft loan affiliate, the International Development Association (IDA), has traditionally had a mandate to finance long-term reconstruction and development. With respect to LDCs, the Bank always put emphasis on loans devoted to agriculture, rural development, infrastructure, education, training, etc. Big development projects like dams and irrigation systems, highways, and agricultural and forest programs were also funded by the Bank. In the 1980s, however, it introduced new forms of lending, which had much more in common with the IMF facilities than with conventional forms of Bank assistance. Little by little, the Bank moved away from its original emphasis on discrete development projects to macroeconomic adjustment.

A few years after it was created, the World Bank oriented its efforts and organization to help LDCs handle the multitude of different problems that arise during the course of development. In this sense the Bank was a pragmatic institution, with an outstanding capacity to learn from experience. In the late 1950s, for example, after a mission to Tunisia, the Bank recognized that the process of development demanded a much more complex response than simply providing resources for physical capital, so it started to finance education in order to improve entrepreneurship, to train workers, and to secure all other unquantifiable benefits that education could bring to the transformation of an economy (Kamarck 1984). The Bank's involvement with training government officials arose from a similar concern. As a result, in 1955 it established the Economic Development Institute to help train senior government officials. Moreover, close relationships with the Food and Agricultural Organization (FAO) were established in the 1950s, including the recruitment of special FAO staff to work with the Bank. Up to the end of the 1970s, the Bank frequently required as a condition for the issue of loans the definition of investment priorities (Görgens 1998). To identify these investment steering priorities, Chenery (then vice president of the World Bank) wanted to use "normal structures" to reflect the typical proportions of value creation in the domestic product by different industries in the development process. Under McNamara's leadership in the 1970s, the Bank adopted a well-publicized antipoverty policy, and a growing interest in channeling funds to assure adequate "basic needs" formed part of the agenda in the late 1970s (after the International Labor Office World Employment Conference). Loxley (1986), for instance, provides data showing an important shift of emphasis in lending away from infrastructure toward rural development, water supply, education, urbanization, and other basic needs. How successful this effort was in alleviating poverty in LDCs remains controversial.

The emergence of the debt crisis significantly changed the relationship between the Bank and LDCs. By providing multilateral finance, the Bank assisted indebted countries in restructuring their debt and gradually changed its interest from the antipoverty approach to the promotion of macroeconomic adjustment. Precise dating of the change in paradigm is difficult because no official statement of a change of course was ever made. In personal terms, Görgens (1998) suggests, it can be linked with the entry of Krueger as the vice president of the World Bank in 1982 and Lal's entry into the research department.

But well before that, in 1979, the Bank introduced a new lending facility called Structural Adjustment Lending (SAL). This new lending program represents a clear example of the gradual change experienced by the Bank. With SALs, the improvement of the BOP was for the first time an explicit objective of the Bank's lending programs. Medium-term BOP support was offered "in order that the current account deficits of many LDCs do not become so large as to jeopardize seriously the implementation of current investment programs and foreign exchange-producing activities" (World Bank Annual Report 1980, pp. 67–68). Thus, SAL programs came to reflect the new orthodoxy by emphasizing policy-based lending on an unprecedented scale.

At the Bank-Fund Annual Meetings in Seoul in 1985, U.S. Treasury Secretary James Baker made a series of proposals to address the problem of "debt fatigue." The Baker initiative called for action by the major debtor countries to undertake structural adjustment programs, and called for help from the commercial banks and the Bretton Woods institutions to finance these efforts and help countries design and implement the necessary adjustments. With respect to SAL programs, Baker stated at the meeting: "[SALs] have been effective and we believe it should be retained and even prudently expanded, as long as there is a serious need and desire for more SALs linked to appropriate policy reforms" (quoted in Bacha and Feinberg 1986, p. 186).

Following the adverse developments in the international economy in the early 1980s, adjustment lending intensified and its scope widened with the introduction of sectoral adjustment loans (SECALs). The aim of SECALs was to support programs of policy necessary to modify the structure of an economy so that it can maintain both its growth and the viability of its balance of payments. Moreover, in 1983, the Bank developed the Special Action Program (SAP) to expand support for adjustment in LDCs. Under SAPs, the Bank was supposed to increase substantially the speed of its disbursements, while expanding its policy dialogue to facilitate structural reforms among its members (Bock and Michalopoulos 1986). Close co-operation between the Bank and the IMF enhanced financial assistance to member countries.

From a modest start the share of SALs and SECALs in World Bank lending steadily increased beginning in the early 1980s, and, by the end of the decade, structural adjustment lending was accounting for a third of total lending (Noorbakhash and Paloni 1997). Conditionality under SALs, SECALs, and SAPs implies the need to take action to increase resource mobilization with the objective of encouraging externally oriented growth. Policies designed to improve resource mobilization have included the adjustment of exchange rates, trade liberalization, the movement toward positive real interest rates, the introduction of tax reforms, greater reliance on price incentives, and an expanded role for the private sector at the expense of the public sector.

It is interesting to note that the Bank sees overvalued exchange rates, inadequate price incentives to producers, and incompetence in credit markets as the major causes of poor export performances in many countries (Loxley 1986). It also holds state intervention and import substitution industrialization responsible for such "distortions," which, in turn impede the mobilization and efficient allocation of resources (Stein 1991). These views of the causes of poor performances in LDCs are to be found in several Bank publications specifically in relation to sub-Saharan Africa.[21]

Even though the conditionality of SALs, SECALs, and SAPs seems to focus on what we have termed supply-side stimulation, the Bank believes that demand restraint and exchange rate policy is often a necessary prerequisite to successful adjustment efforts. The Bank, for example, assumes that its own programs "will usually follow closely on the heels of the successful negotiation of an IMF Extended Facility" (Loxley 1986, p. 131), and, therefore, envisages its own assistance and conditionality as closely complementing those of the IMF. David Bock and Constantine Michalopoulos, at the time both staff directors at the Bank, in their description of Bank's adjustment programs for growth, stated: "The first key objective is to achieve and maintain a stable macroeconomic environment. This entails a strong and sustained commitment to several basic actions: bringing the fiscal deficit under control . . . maintaining monetary discipline, and establishing a realistic exchange rate regime" (Bock and Michalopoulos 1986, p. 24).

In an evaluation of structural adjustment lending over the years 1980–92 in 42 countries, the World Bank (1995) reports that 24 of the 42 countries reduced their fiscal deficit, 35 of the countries experienced real devaluations during the adjustment period, and 37 increased their interest rate differential.

Much of the Bank's attention in recent years has been directed toward assisting low-income African countries, particularly the countries of sub-Saharan Africa, and the transition economies of Eastern Europe. In fact the concentration of World Bank lending programs in sub-Saharan Africa and Asia during the 1990s was quite evident. With respect to Latin America, Feinberg (1990) has pointed out the decline in Bank attention to the region since the 1970s. By April 1984, for example, the bank had approved over $4 billion in SALs to 16 countries, out of which only four were Latin American countries (Bolivia, Guyana, Colombia, and Panama).[22] With the exemption of Colombia all of these countries had received first an IMF facility. It is very interesting to note that in its review of the effectiveness of 15 years of Bank support in the Caribbean region, a Bank report recommends that "given the poor past experience, reliance on SAL-type operations should remain limited" (p. 8).

In recent years, with the idea of funneling quick-disbursing credits to Latin America, the Bank instead of negotiating SALs has used Special Action Programs (Feinberg 1990). But it must be admitted that the expectations aroused by SAPs, at least with respect to the acceleration of economic growth, have not been fulfilled. According to Görgens (1998) the deficiencies lie mainly in the underestimation of the problems of political–economic implementation. But Mosley, Harrigan, and Toye (1990) reproach that the World Bank have used a "standard model" for its SAPs that takes too little account of specific features.

To overcome these defects, the World Bank for sectoral investment programs has presented new proposals. So far, only the contours of this concept are discernible. Moreover, in the welcoming address to the Annual World Bank Conference on Development Economics in 1998, James Wolfenson, current president of the World Bank, noted his belief that a new consensus on development policies should go beyond the so-called Washington Consensus.[23] Joseph Stiglitz, former senior vice president and chief economist of the Bank, has gone further by claiming the need of "providing the foundations of an alternative paradigm, especially one relevant to the least developing country" (1998, pp. 1–2). It is by no means certain, however, that we will see something new under the sun and that we will see some changes in emphasis and views.

1.5 Rationalizing the IMF and World Bank Cooperation

As late as the 1970s, the division of labor between the World Bank and the IMF seemed straightforward, with the IMF concentrating on balance-of-payments equilibrium and control of inflationary pressures through demand management, and the Bank taking a longer-term perspective, analyzing the composition and appropriateness of development programs in infrastructure and sectoral projects. There is no doubt that the distinctions gradually blurred over time. The movement of the World Bank into the area of general balance of payments, at the very time that the IMF was introducing longer-term, supply-oriented programs, leads us to conclude that their roles were converging. The creation of the Extended Fund Facility (EFF) and the Structural Adjustment Facility (SAF) by the IMF, and the Structural Adjustment Lending (SAL) and Special Action Program (SAP) by the Bank were a clear demonstration of the existence of this trend.

As we mentioned before, the introduction of SAL programs moved the Bank away from a nearly exclusive emphasis on discrete projects, to the granting of non-project balance-of-payments loans aimed at broader economic reforms. In the meantime, by introducing the EFF the IMF has been paying more attention to the promotion of adjustment through growth. As a consequence, supply-side transformation of the economy is now also required by the IMF (completing the isolated demand management). In fact, authoritative IMF staff has firmly stated: "Structural reforms are now part and parcel of adjustment programmes, and the basic concern of the Fund is how such reforms can help in achieving the objectives of medium-term external and internal balance . . . Thus, policies which influence aggregate demand and structural policies are to be view as complements" (Frenkel and Khan 1992, p. 6).

With the establishment of the EFF and the SAL, the IMF and the Bank were both providing BOP loans, over a period of one to three years, with medium-term amortization periods. Both types of program supported the new forms of conditionality, as well as the conditions previously imposed by the traditional IMF's short-run packages.

We mentioned in the previous section that the Bank policy prescriptions seemed to be concentrated on the supply side but with the proviso that the member country first pursues a consistent stabilization package to correct imbalances. In fact, Bank staffers believe that without stabilization a structural adjustment program will fail. In practice, SALs and sometimes project loans have been held up by a borrower's accord with the IMF. This is shown in table 1.6 in which it is clear that structural and sector adjustment loans in Latin America have followed a previous IMF facility. As a consequence, Bank policy-based programs are unique in the sense that they are accompanied by an unprecedented degree of conditionality; first, because in practice they

Table 1.6 Policy Based Loans from the World Bank to Latin American Countries, 1979–88

	World Bank Structural and Sector Adjustment Loans		*Stand-bys and EFF from the IMF*	
Argentina	Agriculture	4/86	SBA	1/83
	Trade Sector	5/87	SBA	12/84
	Banking Sector	3/88	SBA	7/87
	Trade Policy	10/88		
Bolivia	SAL		SBA	2/80
Brazil	Agriculture and Exports	10/83	EEF	3/83
	Exports Development	10/83		
	Agriculture	6/86		
Chile	SAL I	10/85		
	SAL II	11/86	SBA	1/83
	SAL III	12/87	EFF	8/85
Colombia	Trade Sector	5/85		
	Trade and Agriculture	4/86		
	Power Sector	12/87		
Costa Rica	Exports Development	5/83	SBA	12/82
	SAL I	4/85	SBA	3/85
	SAL II	12/88	SBA	10/87
Guyana	SAL	2/81	EFF	7/80
Mexico	Export Development	10/83	EFF	1/83
	Trade Policy	7/86	SBA	11/86
	Trade Sector	11/87		
	Agriculture	3/88		
	Fertilizer	3/88		
Panama	SAL	11/83	SBA	6/83

Sources: IMF, *Annual Reports*, 1900–1988; World Bank, *Annual Reports*, 1980–1988; and World Bank, *Structural Adjustment Lending Progress Report*, 1984.

assume IMF conditionality as a precondition, and second, because they then impose a variety of exacting, detailed conditions on top of that.

Similarly, as noted by Feinberg (1990), Fund-supported programs started to stress variables of particular interest to the Bank. For example, Feinberg found that between 1980 and 1984, energy prices were addressed in 46 percent of Fund-supported programs, the mobilization of domestic savings in 54 percent, and the transfer of public enterprises to the private sector in 29 percent.

All the elements just mentioned, the convergence of the functions of the two institutions, the enhanced policy approach, the attachment of Bank programs to previous IMF intervention, and the consideration of the same policy variables, suggest the existence of what the late Sidney Dell has called "cross conditionality."[24]

Cross conditionality and the essential harmony of viewpoint that the IMF/World Bank duet share on the causes of instability, and their appropriate remedies, found its ultimate expression in the Fund's establishment Fund of the Structural Adjustment Facility (SAF) in March 1986. The SAF programs marked a significant new phase in the IMF/Bank collaboration since the policy framework of this facility is developed jointly by the staff of the two institutions. In fact, a description of the general outlines of a three-year program and a delineation of the expected path of macroeconomic policies should be contained in a paper developed by IMF/Bank staff as a prerequisite for access to a credit line.

1.6 Concluding Remarks

There is no single conclusion that can be reached in a description of this sort, but perhaps precisely for that reason, concluding remarks are necessary to draw the discussion to a logical end. Certainly, the performance of Latin American countries after the debt crisis has been influenced by a heavy debt burden, by declining or volatile commodity prices, by financial instability, and eventually by domestic mismanagement. However, the debt crisis of 1982 gave the IMF and the World Bank unprecedented powers and heavily involved them with policy design in Latin American countries. Though IMF/World Bank inherence is unlikely to be the unique or even the principal factor determining success or failure, there is no reason for failing to see the unsuitability of the conventional IMF/Bank programs. Much of the available evidence here suggests that the multilateral response has been disappointed, with the result that the IMF and the World Bank are not making their best contribution. After more than 18 years of harsh stabilization and adjustment programs, the prospects for economic growth and development in Latin America are far from promising.

Conditionality, a term that describes the practice of attaching economic policy conditions and performance criteria to the provision of IMF loans, is not new in the relationship between the Bretton Woods institutions and Latin American countries, specifically between the IMF and the region. In fact, the region was the first visible target when the IMF invented the concept of conditionality in the mid-1950s. However, conditionality strictness fluctuates over time depending on the global macroeconomic and financial context. We have illustrated how the programs in Latin America have fluctuated over time, but we have also commented how the 1980s and 1990s have witnessed a dramatic increase in the number of agreements and in conditionality strictness. Besides that, despite that much of the discussion that we offer will be focused on the nature of conditionality, both the principle and the nature of conditionality can be criticized.

Between the mid-1950s and the mid-1970s, the objectives of the programs supported by the IMF were short-term in nature, emphasizing BOP and inflationary problems. Demand management techniques of fiscal and monetary restraint combined with exchange rate devaluation were essential elements of policy programs during that period. By the late 1970s stabilization programs came to be viewed with a longer-term horizon that included changes in the supply side of the economy. Trade and financial liberalization became part of the policy package endorsed by the IMF. This broadening of the "old orthodoxy" was reflected in certain new facilities created by the IMF during the 1970s and 1980s. The emergence of the debt crisis compelled Latin American countries to carry out orthodox programs of stabilization and adjustment supported by the IMF and the World Bank. But many years of severe stabilization and adjustment programs has hardly improved the performance of the region, which still remains poor in terms of the main economic and social indicators.

In the meantime, the World Bank, which was traditionally an institution whose resources were used for discrete development projects, has gradually changed its emphasis since the early 1980s to macropolicy-based lending. Specifically the Bank sees policies designed to promote the efficient use of resources as being a requisite to achieve greater economic growth. Stabilization of the orthodox type is also seen as a prerequisite for successful adjustment efforts. With respect to Latin America, the Bank's attention has been modest and conditioned upon previous agreements with the IMF.

Today the convergence of the IMF and the Bank in terms of functions and policy approach seems irreversible. That the two institutions together have become a sort of global capitalist authority for Latin American countries is also beyond question. Not only is the magnitude of the presence of these institutions (especially the IMF) in the region is striking, but the impact of their policy-based programs has also required a substantial sacrifice without much substantial signs of improvement. Admittedly, during the 1990s many countries in the region brought inflation under control and improved their foreign reserves position. However, overall, the external debt remains high, the current account deficit is increasing, and the short-term nature of financial inflows does not guarantee stability. Moreover, investment is still low and the rate of growth has failed to increase sufficiently. This contradicts the IMF/WB's much publicized objective of adjustment with growth.

In this perspective, the brief review we have presented in this chapter suggests the need for a fundamental rethinking of the IMF and World Bank's approach in their dealings with LDCs in Latin America. Some natural questions then arise: Why are stabilization and adjustment programs of the IMF/World Bank type so unsuccessful? Is there something wrong with the rationale of the underlying theoretical models used by these institutions? Is there any coherent alternative framework to these orthodox approaches? These are questions that we intend to address in the following chapters, but first we will try to explore the theoretical constructs of the IMF/Bank policy packages, an enterprise that we believe is still absent or incomplete in the literature, due perhaps to the variety and eclectic character of the models used by both institutions.

Notes

1. In the worst year of recession, 1982, Latin America export revenues fell by about 10 percent (see Pastor 1987, p. 154). Sutton (1984) reports a deterioration of the terms of trade of non-oil LDCs of 15 percent.

2. In the case of the IMF, the original Articles of Agreement established the mandate for surveillance and financing. Among other things, effective surveillance by the IMF should help to avoid or diminish the severity of general disturbances to the world economy. Through stronger surveillance, for instance, the IMF could eventually help to provide financial markets with the information that they need to form judgements concerning a country's creditworthiness, but also it could focus on the causes of general economic stress to the world economy and on the cooperative policies that will help to avoid it. However, no attempt is made here to evaluate and discuss the nature and extent of IMF surveillance. Rather, it is financing and the accompanying exercise of "conditionality" that concern us here.

3. In February 1989, after years of unsuccessfully rescheduling negotiations, Venezuela ended up signing an agreement with the IMF and the World Bank.
4. By around 1981, imports to the region were approximately $100 billion. In 1985 this figure had decreased to $57 billion (Foxley 1988).
5. The volatile nature of these resources was confirmed in 1994 when strong capital flight occurred in Mexico, Argentina, and Venezuela, undermining growth prospects.
6. According to World Bank (1994) classifications long-term private capital flows comprise foreign direct investment, portfolio equity flows, portfolio debt flows, and other debt flows.
7. In Mexico, the IMF signed an Extended Fund Facility for 3,729 million of SDRs in May 1989, and this was extended until May 1993.
8. Political events started in January 1994, when rebels occupied San Cristobal de las Casas and continued in March when the Institutional Revolutionary Party candidate, Luis Colossio, was assassinated. Elections took place in August, and in October, Institutional Revolutionary Party official Carlos Ruiz Massieu was killed.
9. Access to Fund credit usually has acted as a catalyst for increased inflows from other countries. In the 1960s, for example, U.S. aid programs were often conditional on previous signing of an agreement with the IMF by the recipient country. This type of linkage was very common in the 1960s in Latin America, when disbursements of loans from the Agency for International Development (AID) were frequently conditioned on the fulfillment of narrowly defined domestic policies (Griffit-Jones 1983). This was clearly illustrated by American aid to Chile in the period 1963–66. In the 1980s and 1990s, banks have frequently required a prior agreement with the IMF on some kind of policy program as a precondition for rescheduling negotiations of debt.
10. Peru also signed the first program in which conditions of borrowing were explicitly stated in a letter of intent (Scheetz 1986). Without doubt both innovations give Peru a rather dubious claim to fame.
11. A good account of the process of inception, blueprint, negotiation, approval, and monitoring of IMF-supported programs can be found in Mussa and Savastano (1999).
12. Mexico devalued its currency in 1948, 1949, and 1954.
13. The Chilean government hired a U.S. consulting firm to devise a stabilization program to deal with the alarming increase in inflation over the previous couple of years. The mission, known as the Klein-Saks mission, was strongly attacked by center and left-wing politicians, as well as by economists who argued that the program developed had detrimental effects on growth, employment, and wages, and failed to deal with the fundamental causes of inflation (Kay 1989).
14. For major studies that appeared in the 1970s on the significance of trade liberalization in spurring growth, see Kahler (1990, p. 40).

15. Killick and Sutton (1982) have distinguished between "conventional" or "old" programs, and the "new orthodoxy" programs, the former focusing on short-run stabilization while the latter adds a longer liberalization element.

16. It was not until 1979 when the IMF made the decision to extend the stand-by to three years where circumstances warranted.

17. The figures are taken from an excellent statistical compilation of Fund facilities collected by Peter Korner, Gero Maass, Thomas Siebold, and Rainer Tetzlaff in *The IMF and the Debt Crisis* (1986).

18. Under the Extended Fund Facility funds can be drawn in phases over three years and repaid between four and a half and ten years later. Conditionality is similar to that in upper credit tranches of the regular lending facility, but covers a broader range of policies, reflecting the fact that programs are longer and geared more to production.

19. Mussa (1997) indicates imperfect information, coordination problems, problems of enforcing loan contracts, and multiple equilibria as being important factors that cause these market imperfections to occur.

20. The policy of enlarged access was approved in 1981. Under this policy countries may borrow up to 450 percent of their quotas, a remarkable improvement with respect to 1974, when a country could purchase up to 165 percent under an EFF, and with respect to the previous period, when the maximum was 100 percent under a stand-by arrangement (Griffit-Jones 1983).

21. See for instance, *Accelerated Development in Sub-Saharan Africa—An Agenda for Action, 1981*; the *World Development Report, 1983*; and *Sub-Saharan Africa—From Crisis to Sustainable Growth: A Longer Term Perspective Study, 1989*.

22. World Bank, *Structural Adjustment Lending Progress Report*. Washington D.C., 1984.

23. John Willamson (1990) coined the term "Washington Consensus" to signify the set of orthodox policy prescriptions undertaken by Latin American economies during the 1980s.

24. Cross-conditionality has been a subject of wide analysis in Feinberg (1990).

CHAPTER 2

The Analytics of the Orthodox Approaches to Stabilization and Adjustment

2.1 Introduction

In chapter 1 we presented (among other things) a highly schematic description of IMF/World Bank policy prescriptions in Latin America. The description was a good starting point but needs amplifying since it does not tell us anything about the rationale for the use of these policies and the underlying theoretical models. Before we get any further into this discussion, a word of caution is required. For years it has been widely believed that that there is no such thing as a simple and unique IMF/Bank approach to economic policy. Khan and Knight (1982, p. 728), at the IMF, for instance, clearly state that "there is, of course no unique stand of thought underlying stabilization programs," and Katseli (1983) has emphasized that "a cursory review of recent documents and missions reports. . . . [R]eveals that often the same policy prescriptions are based on different analytical arguments. . . . [T]hat cast some doubt on the widespread acceptance within the IMF of a particular theoretical structure as a guideline for policy" (p. 359).

One of the main problems that we face is that the IMF approach to economic stabilization has been based largely on oral tradition (IMF 1987, p. 1). There is surprisingly little readily accessible written material on its theoretical underpinnings, in particular, on the interactions among various policy measures in achieving the ultimate objectives.[1] There are some presumptions that the analytical basis of the stabilization, and adjustment packages negotiated over the past four decades have been based, to a great extent, on the logical rationale of the developments of the macroeconomic theory for small open economies, and on the balance-of-payments adjustment theories (Khan and Knight 1982). Indeed, at some risk of oversimplification, it may be said that these theories are inextricably linked with the IMF/World Bank policy prescriptions. Crockett (1992) has lent support to this thesis[2]: "Influential thinkers in the IMF developed the underlying theory of external adjustment. . . . [A]nd this theory was put into practice in an increasing number of programmes of adjustment supported by the use of IMF resources" (p. 269).

The link between open economy macromodels and stabilization prescriptions is confirmed by Kahler (1990, pp. 36–37), who states, "both the absorption approach and the early monetary approach to the balance of payments owed their shape to the experience with stabilization programs in Latin America." Cardoso (1979, p. 58) complements this idea by saying: "popular models of stabilization in developing countries during the fifties and sixties relied on Meade (1951) and Swan-Mundell internal and external balance." We cannot deny then the fact that many elements of stabilization programs can be found in the absorption approach (as pointed out in Bacha 1990), in the Keynesian synthesis of the elasticity and absorption approach (Dornbusch 1982, Khan *et al.* 1982, and Cardoso 1979), in the monetary approach to the balance of payments (IMF 1987, Khan and Montiel 1989) and that sometimes the whole policy paradigm is based on an eclectic mix of Keynesian and Monetarist models for open economies (David 1985). In general these are the analytical constructs under which earlier plans, say those of the 1950s and 1960s, were based on. After all, short-term balance-of-payments and inflation targets were the main concern of IMF missions at that time. That implied that the system of protectionism, state intervention and control, and "financial repression" was left largely unaffected (Diaz Alejandro 1981). In the succeeding period, however, the scope of the orthodox packages gradually evolved and expanded. Today, even though the "new orthodoxy" still favors the manipulation of the demand side of the economy and the exchange rate as the keys for achieving stabilization, its recent emphasis on financial liberalization and supply-oriented programs are clearly built on new analytical models, in particular the McKinnon–Shaw hypothesis of "financial repression," and a relatively new synthesis of Polak and the neoclassical growth models respectively (Khan, Montiel, and Haque 1990). We have discussed in the previous chapter some of the reasons for this evolution in the formulation of economic management.

The purpose of this section is twofold. First, we will try to organize systematically, in a basic framework, the various theoretical approaches that lend support to the stabilization and adjustment programs. Thus, throughout the exposition, we will show how the various theoretical models are components of a much broader perspective within which they appear complementary. This means that though the various theoretical approaches can provide different analytical constructs with respect to the evaluation of a concrete situation, the instruments employed are to some degree complementary. As Blackwell (1978) has noted, the achievement of the complex set of economic objectives in most programs typically involves the use of a variety of instruments in an eclectic and reinforcing way. Second, we will attempt to show not only the interaction among typical policy measures in achieving the ultimate objectives, but also the essential elements and assumptions on which each model relies. We believe that this is an important way for the orthodox approach to be opened to scientific scrutiny.

In what follows, we will identify a set of macroeconomic policy-oriented models that have inspired for almost four decades the policy prescriptions of the Bretton Woods institutions. We initiate the exposition laying out a basic indeterminate framework that forms the common core of all models. Eventually we include auxiliary assumptions and slight changes in the specifications in order to eschew the questions at issue. The exposition follows closely an analytical order even though a chronological order through which these models has been digested into the orthodox literature is also possible.[3] We derive the monetary approach in its two main analytical versions (the Polak and Chicago versions) in order to help justify credit restraint as a stabilization measure to improve the balance-of-payments position. The targeted values for both the balance of payments and the rate of inflation can, however, be better understood by using the financial programming model, in which room is made for devaluation and credit restraint as instrumental variables. The absorption approach and the approaches' subsequent synthesis are carefully analyzed, as well as the implications that these models have with respect to the balance-of-payments position, and the level of real income. Exchange rate management and fiscal restraint are central policy instruments in these models. A simple synthesis of the Keynesian and monetary approaches is also presented to point out that the orthodox policy conclusions may be reconciled even in the context of a more eclectic framework. Finally, we show the way these developments have been followed by the flowering and absorption of new models that try to add a long-term perspective to stabilization. The basic framework allows an approach to linking growth-related elements with the basic financial programming model by incorporating the volumes of total investment and the capital–output ratio into the latter. The resulting model shows, among other things, the relationship between structural adjustment policies (given by such variables as total factor productivity and private savings) and growth. A further step would be to incorporate additional insights regarding the relationship between the saving rate, financial liberalization, and growth (the McKinnon and Shaw hypothesis).

2.2 An Overall Review of IMF/World Bank Policy Prescriptions

Before proceeding with the systematic review of the theoretical models, it will be useful to review briefly the main components of the IMF/Bank policy packages.

Regulation of the money growth rates is the cornerstone of the IMF approach to economic management. This is so because money is thought to play a pivotal role in both disturbances and adjustment. Accordingly, balance-of-payments deficits or surpluses are viewed as reflecting stock disequilibrium between demand and supply in the market for money. Under the assumption of a stable demand for money, and under a set of relationships, domestic credit expansion is linked to a decrease in reserves to the extent that it does not induce a similar increase in income (and therefore in the demand for money). Once a relationship is established between domestic credit creation and the BOP, it becomes possible to determine the domestic asset variation required to achieve a desired target for the BOP. Moreover, beyond full capacity utilization any increase in domestic credit will increase nominal income and therefore will give rise to inflationary pressures. A credit ceiling can therefore be linked to the BOP and inflation objectives (Buira 1983).

Devaluation is apparently the most common precondition in any policy package. From 1947 (inaugural year of the IMF) to 1971–73 (end of Bretton Woods), country members of the IMF made more than 200 devaluations, most of which were central components in IMF stabilization programs, particularly in Latin American countries (Meller 1987, p. 200). During the period 1970–76, there were 62 upper credit tranche stand-by arrangements approved by the IMF, 29 of them involving exchange rate action (Buira 1983, p. 122). Avramovic (1988, p. 9) reports that for the period 1980–84, about 55 percent of IMF conditionality included devaluation. Devaluation should, it is argued, produce an improvement in the balance of trade and an overall increase in output if the sum of import and export elasticities is sufficiently large, i.e. if the Marshall-Lerner condition holds. On the demand side, devaluation increases the relative price of imports in terms of exports, which tends to raise exports and decrease autonomous imports. The reason is that as the domestic currency devaluates, domestic goods become cheaper relative to foreign goods, and this tends to improve the trade balance. The overall effect of a devaluation on domestic absorption is supposed to be negative (Khan and Knight 1982). On the supply side, however, the effects of the devaluations are supposed to switch production from nontradeable to tradeable goods (Crockett 1981). Both demand and supply effects tend to reduce excess domestic absorption and the payments deficit.

The orthodox IMF/WB policy package suggests that both inflation and external deficits often have a common source in budget deficits (IMF 1987). IMF staff members think, for instance, that because of the limited availability of financing sources outside the banking system, it is frequently not possible for LDCs to achieve a significant deceleration in monetary growth without a reduction in government's overall deficit (Crockett 1981, Cline 1983). Avramovic (1988, p. 3) reports budget deficit reductions in 86 out of 94 IMF-supported programs during the period 1980–81. To achieve this goal, the IMF often calls for reducing or eliminating subsidies and capital expenditure (Harris and Kusi 1992, p. 79), and/or food subsidies and expenditures in different welfare schemes (Sarkar 1991). To reduce the budgetary burden of the government, state enterprises are also expected to cover their costs by raising the prices of their goods and services.

Most of the various policies described above and the economic models out of which policy actions were drawn were supposed to have a short-term impact, but new facilities and attitudinal changes occurred in the mid seventies. As we note in chapter 1, they led the Bretton Woods institutions to accept supply-oriented reforms and adjustment with growth.

One of the objectives that structural adjustment policies attempt to achieve is the liberalization of the financial system. In particular, interest rate adjustment typically forms part of any IMF/World Bank policy package.[4] The central argument is that financial repression, i.e. administratively determined real rate of interest below its equilibrium value, reduces the real rate of growth and the real size of the financial system thus retarding the development process (Shaw 1973). So, to the extent that they direct financial resources from consumption to saving, higher interest rates enable financial intermediaries to finance a higher volume of investment. Also, by discouraging low-yielding investment, higher interest rates may free resources for higher-return projects, thus improving the efficiency of aggregate investment.

At a general level it is widely believed that LDCs suffer from "distortions" that arise because of the propensity of governments to intervene in the pricing and allocation of resources, or because of a rigorous system of protection. In the words of Khan and Knight (1982, p. 704) the most common sources of distortions are "public sector pricing policies and government price controls, various types of taxes, subsidies, tariff and quotas; and certain industrial regulations." These distortions would lead to economic inefficiency and low productivity of factors. The IMF/World Bank answer is that the removal of distortions would permit greater efficiency and a far more rapid economic growth.[5]

2.3 The Basic Orthodox Framework of IMF/WB Models

An integrated system of accounts covering national income and expenditure, as well as financial flows and associated stocks, lies at the heart of the macroeconomic framework of IMF and World Bank models. For an adequate understanding of the operation of policies, the identities must, however, be complemented by relations that indicate the typical reaction or response of some of the variables included in the accounting framework to changes in other variables. The macroeconomic framework that we will present serves as a convenient starting point for a more detailed study of the various alternative transmission mechanism between the array of policies typically included in IMF/World Bank programs and the ultimate objectives of the BOP, price stability, and economic growth. It is noteworthy that while one may base models and programs on different theoretical relationships, we will show that this framework is wide enough to offer consistency among the different approaches.

The core of the orthodox macroeconomic framework can be summarized as follows:

$$CA = Y - A \qquad (2.1)$$ Current account balance (nominal terms)

$$Y - A = X - IM \qquad (2.2)$$ Overall national income account

$$\Delta R = X - IM + \Delta F \qquad (2.3)$$ Change in the stock of international reserves

$$\Delta F = e(\Delta F_g^* + \Delta F_p^* - INT^*) \qquad (2.4)$$ Change in net financial transfers

$$INT^* = INT_g^* + INT_p^* \qquad (2.5)$$ Interest payments to the rest of the world

$$X = eX^* \qquad (2.6)$$ Nominal exports

$$IM = ep^*(Z) \qquad (2.7)$$ Nominal imports

$$Z = \beta_0 + \beta_1 y + \beta_2(ep^*/p_d) \qquad (2.8) \quad \text{Volume of imports}$$

$$M_s = R + D \qquad (2.9) \quad \text{The money supply}$$

$$\Delta M_s = \Delta R + \Delta D \qquad (2.10) \quad \text{Change in the nominal stock of money}$$

$$\Delta D = \Delta D_g + \Delta D_p \qquad (2.11) \quad \text{Change in domestic credit}$$

$$M_d = pL(y, i \ldots) \qquad (2.12) \quad \text{Demand for money}$$

$$M_d = M_s = M \qquad (2.13) \quad \text{Stock equilibrium in the money market}$$

$$Y = py \qquad (2.14) \quad \text{Nominal output}$$

$$y = y_f \qquad (2.15) \quad \text{Real output}$$

$$p = (1 - \alpha)p_d + \alpha ep^* \qquad (2.16) \quad \text{General price level}$$

$$\Delta CD_g + \Delta F_g = pGSI - T + INT_g^* \qquad (2.17) \quad \text{Government budget constraint}$$

$$\Delta y = z_0 + z_1 \Delta k \qquad (2.18) \quad \text{Growth of GNP equation}$$

$$(SR_p - \Delta k) + (TR - G) = (\Delta R - \Delta F)/p_d \qquad (2.19) \quad \text{Accumulation balance of the economy in real terms}$$

The starting point is the economy-wide identity known from national accounts in which the difference between the value of domestic production, Y—which is equal to nominal income—and absorption, A, equals the balance of trade in goods and services or the current account, CA. Without loss of generality the model assumes that the current account is equivalent to the balance of trade, that is nominal exports, X, minus nominal imports, IM (equation (2.2)). From the balance-of-payments identity, equation (2.3) says that the change in foreign reserves, ΔR (in domestic currency) equals the sum of the surplus/deficit on the trade balance and other net non-trade related flows to the private sector and government, ΔF. The change in net financial transfers of the country, ΔF, is the sum of changes in the private sector's debt position in foreign currency (ΔF_p^*), in the public sector's debt position (ΔF_g^*), and in overall interest payments, INT^*, as given in equation (2.4). In (2.5) net interest payments to the rest of the world are split into public (INT_g^*) and private (INT_p^*) components. In (2.6) nominal exports are assumed to be determined exogenously, though we will relax this specification later on. Nominal imports in (2.7) are by definition the result of multiplying the nominal exchange rate, e, and the value of imports in foreign currency, p^*Z. The volume of imports, Z, could, for simplicity, be assumed to be a linear function of nominal output (as we will see in the Polak model), but a slightly more complicated linear import function, which makes imports dependent not only on real output, y, but also on changes in the real exchange rate, ep^*/p_d, as used in (2.8).

The monetary block starts with equation (2.9) which specifies the accounting identity expressing the money supply, M_s, as the sum of international reserves, R, and central bank domestic credit, D. If the central bank purchases government securities, domestic credit will increase. Moreover, a rise in reserves increases the money supply, and this will occur if the central bank purchases foreign exchange in order to stabilize the exchange rate. Thus, under a fixed exchange rate system, the money supply is partly endogenous in the sense that it changes according to changes in the balance of payments. Expression (2.9) can be written in terms of changes, as in (2.10) and "Δ" preceding a variable indicates a one period change. In (2.11) changes in domestic credit, ΔD, will consist of the changes in claims on the public and private sectors $(\Delta D_\mathrm{g} + \Delta D_\mathrm{p})$. In equation (2.12) the money demand, M_d, can be specified in a variety of ways, ranging from a relation reflecting a constant income velocity of money to a general function relating the nominal demand for money to variables such as domestic income, y, prices, p, the opportunity cost of money, etc. In any case the standard monetarist assumption of a stable demand for money function will be required. In equation (2.13) the money market is assumed to be in continuous equilibrium, where M is the money stock.

Nominal output, Y (in equation (2.14)) is given as real output, y, times the price level of the economy, p. In (2.15) real output is taken to be exogenous determined or at their full employment level, y_f. However, a change in aggregate expenditure (absorption) below the productive capacity of the economy may be allowed, as we will show later on (see IMF 1987, p. 6). The domestic price level, p, is introduced in equation (2.16) as a weighted average of the price for domestic goods, p_d, and the exogenous international price, p^* (measured in foreign currency) for imported goods. The share of imports in the price index is denoted α so the share of domestic goods is $(1 - \alpha)$. Note that when $\alpha = 1$, the "law of one price" holds. The government budget constraint is introduced in expression (2.17), whereby the government must finance any deficit in nominal terms $(pGSI - T) + INT_\mathrm{g}^*$ by either increasing its net borrowing from abroad, ΔF_g, or by increasing its net borrowing from the central bank, ΔD_g. The terms GSI stands for government spending without interest payments to abroad (in real terms), and T for a level of government revenues in nominal terms. This budget constraint contains an implicit assumption that there are no sales of government debt to the private (non-bank) sector.[6] Equation (2.18) formulates the expansion of capacity, Δy, as a linear function of real investment Δk. Finally, expression (2.19) shows that the difference between real savings $(SR_\mathrm{p} + TR - G)$ savings and investment Δk (in real terms) must equal the current account balance in real terms, $(\Delta R - \Delta F)/p_\mathrm{d}$.

The appealing potential flexibility that this basic framework poses will be illustrated in what follows. It will allow us to address a set of models that contain the whole array of policy measures that are linked to stabilization and structural adjustment issues.

2.4 Deriving the Monetary Approaches to the Balance-of-Payments

The fully developed monetary approach to the balance of payments stresses in its radical version this proposition: that the balance of payments is essentially a monetary phenomenon (Johnson 1976, pp. 282–283). Accordingly, a necessary condition for a deficit on the balance of payments is that current purchases by non-central bank domestic residents of goods, services, and assets must be larger than their total sales. This difference can only be financed by domestic residents, either running down their cash balances or selling assets to the central bank in exchange for funds to finance the difference between total purchases and sales. Now this purchase of assets by the central bank involves an increase in the central bank's creation of domestic credit. Therefore, a deficit on the BOP necessarily involves either dishoarding by domestic residents or increasing the central bank's creation of domestic credit. The difference between domestic residents desired holding of money balances from those currently in existence is subtracted from their cash balances through conversion into foreign money through the foreign exchange. Therefore, exponents of the monetary approach assume a stable demand or predictable demand for money function, that permits the divergence between the demand for money and the supply of money. As originally developed, the monetary approach focused on the determinants of the official settlements balance (under fixed exchange rates), and on the movements in the exchange rate (under flexible exchange rates).

Although the work of a group of economists led by Robert Mundell, Harry Johnson, and Jacob Frenkel, (who were primarily teaching at or trained at the University of Chicago),[7] is thought to have played a key role in the development of the approach, their work was preceded by the developments of J. Polak and others at the IMF in the late 1950s and early 1960s.[8] The argument here will proceed along the following lines: From the previous macroeconomic framework we will examine first the so-called Polak model, and after that we will present the main analytical constructs of the Chicago version. An eclectic and more pragmatic model of the monetary approach derives from financial programming. Common assumptions and key differences between these three analytical models are discussed, specifically the transmission mechanism through which a domestic credit expansion works.

2.4.1   The Polak Version of the Monetary Approach

The approach developed by Polak became known as the IMF version of the monetary approach.[9] Although naive and oversimplified in the extreme, the Polak version appears to have had rather profound effects on IMF policies toward deficit countries.[10] Even the more recent published writings by IMF staff in the general area of financial programming closely follow the directions set by this contribution (IMF 1987, p. 1).[11] This version begins with the standard monetarist assumption that the demand for money, M_d, is positively related to changes in the price level, p, and real output, y, and that the velocity of money, v, is constant. Polak and most proponents of the monetary approach claim that the demand for money is a behavioral equation derived from the equation of exchange. Therefore, using (2.12) we have;

$$M_d = py/v \qquad (2.12)$$

Nominal output, Y, is given by (2.14) as

$$Y = py \qquad (2.14)$$

and (2.12) can be rearranged as

$$Y = M_d v \qquad (2.19)$$

The money supply expression (2.9) can be expressed in term of changes as in (2.10)

$$\Delta M_s = \Delta D + \Delta R \qquad (2.10)$$

Presumably the change in domestic credit can be controlled by the monetary authority and may therefore be considered an autonomous or exogenous variable.[12] Now from expression (2.3) we know that the change in foreign exchange reserves depends on the balance of payments in nominal terms, that is,

$$\Delta R = X - IM + \Delta F \qquad (2.3)$$

Polak assumes that X and ΔF are given exogenously, so that both (2.4) and (2.6) apply. The second major behavioral assumption is that imports, IM, are directly proportional to nominal national income so that by combining expressions (2.7) and (2.8) we have,

$$IM = ep^*(\beta_1 y) \tag{2.20}$$

which is equal to:

$$IM = my \tag{2.21}$$

where $m = ep^*\beta_1$ can be thought of as the marginal propensity to import with respect to nominal income. In deriving his results, Polak lags imports by one period so at time t

$$IM = my_{t-1} \tag{2.21a}$$

This will give the model some sort of dynamic properties that will assure that the money stock will return to its original level after an initial change (as in any gold standard system). Combining (2.21a) and (2.19) and assuming money market equilibrium, we see that

$$IM = mvM_{t-1} \tag{2.22}$$

Hence imports are proportional to the money stock of the preceding period.[13] When combined with the level of autonomous exports and financial transfers (that include capital inflows and interest payments), the change in reserves (2.3) yields

$$\Delta R = eX^* - mvM_{t-1} + e(\Delta F_p^* + \Delta F_g^* - INT_p^* - INT_g^*) \tag{2.23}$$

Equation (2.23) is equivalent to what is called in the literature the "fundamental equation" of the monetary approach. From this expression it is clear that a balance-of-payments deficit implies an excessively large money supply (caused by an increase in domestic credit), whereas a surplus implies the opposite. The transmission mechanism through which an increase in domestic credit works is first to increase the money supply by the same amount (equation (2.10)). This increases income (equation (2.19)) as borrowers spend the whole amount. Most of the additional expenditure will be directed toward domestic goods and services, increasing real output (under excess capacity) or prices (under full employment). The increase in money income will, however, increase imports (equation (2.21a)), and the balance of payments will deteriorate (equation (2.23)) with a resulting fall in international reserves.

What Polak's model does is to focus on the links between changes in the domestic money supply and changes in the external account. If a BOP target (ΔR) is set, a corresponding maximum "permissible" expansion in domestic credit extended by the monetary system can be estimated. If credit expansion by the monetary system exceeds the value the economy can afford, the only consequence will be declining international reserves, that is, the target (ΔR) will not be met. *The policy conclusion is that improving the external balance implies domestic credit restraint.* Of course, if the credit expansion is discontinuous, the ongoing BOP deficit will require the monetary authority to sell foreign exchange. Since that reduces the money stock, the demand for imports declines and the BOP is then brought into equilibrium in a similar fashion to the price-specie-flow mechanism.

2.4.2 The Chicago Version of the Monetary Approach

The Chicago version of the monetary approach is very similar in its objectives and conclusions to that of Polak. Nevertheless, monetary phenomena are much more in focus and their importance is highlighted, even to the extent that output adjustments are neglected through the assumption that real output is exogenous. To illustrate the main differences from the Polak version, it is important to note that the domestic price level in the Chicago version is determined by foreign prices through purchasing power parity, so if the "law of one price" holds and real output is exogenous, the Polak model breaks down, as there is no mechanism to dispose of the excess money supply generated by a credit expansion. In the Chicago version, the transmission mechanism through which a domestic credit expansion works is much more direct and speedy. Unlike the Polak version, this version assumes the basic monetary relationship holds continuously.[14] Increases in domestic credit increase the money supply, but the demand for goods, services, and assets is stimulated directly and the exchange rate market reacts instantaneously.

Following the simple lines developed by Johnson and Frenkel (1975) the model may be summarized by using expressions, (2.9), (2.12), (2.13), (2.14), (2.15), and (2.16) of the general framework presented above:

$$M_s = R + C \tag{2.9}$$

$$M_d = pL(y, i) \tag{2.12}$$

$$M_d = M_s = M \tag{2.13}$$

$$Y = py \tag{2.14}$$

$$y = y_f \tag{2.15}$$

$$p = (1 - \alpha)p_d + \alpha e p^* \tag{2.16}$$

The model's main structure includes the liability of the banking system, a stable and conventional demand for money function, the equilibrium condition in the money market, the neoclassical assumption of real output at its full employment level, and the price level equation. By assuming that $\alpha = 1$, expression (2.16) yields the law of one price

$$p = ep^* \tag{2.24}$$

This implicitly states that competition between profit-making traders will lead toward equalization of prices. We further assume that the interest-parity theorem holds, that is

$$i = i^* + \hat{e}^e \tag{2.25}$$

An important implication of this latter relationship is that under flexible exchange rates, one cannot predict the direction of capital flows from interest rate differentials alone. The domestic interest rate, i, could be greater than the foreign interest rate, i^*, but still less than $i^* + \hat{e}^e$, i.e. a depreciation of the exchange rate is expected.

From the equilibrium condition of the monetary sector, equation (2.13) gives

$$R = pL(y, i) - D \tag{2.26}$$

Again this is the fundamental equation of the monetary approach, this time expressed in level form. It is apparent that an increase in the demand for money will result in a BOP surplus. Modern proponents of the monetary approach called the excess of the demand for money "hoarding." Hoarding is supposed to cause desired nominal expenditure to fall short of national income, which leads to a corresponding BOP surplus and an increase in international reserves. In absence of sterilization of reserves inflows, the gap between the demand for money and the money supply is filled up. It is important to notice that in all versions of the monetary approach a stable and predictable demand for money function is required. For a change in domestic credit to have a predictable effect on the balance of payments the public should not be willing to hold the additional money created.

If we totally differentiate equation (2.26) with respect to time, we get

$$\frac{dR}{dt} = L(y, i)\frac{dp}{dt} + p\frac{\partial L(y, i)}{\partial y}\frac{dy}{dt} + p\frac{\partial L(y, i)}{\partial i}\frac{di}{dt} - \frac{dD}{dt} \tag{2.27}$$

The term on the left-hand side is the rate of change of foreign reserves (in domestic currency). Now, if we divide both sides of (2.27) by the stock of money, M, and manipulate each term in the right-hand side of the equation, we get

$$\frac{dR/dt}{M} = \hat{p} + n_y\hat{y} + n_i\hat{i} - \frac{D}{M}\hat{D} \qquad (2.28)$$

A hat over the variable indicates growth rates, i.e. $\hat{x} = (dx/dt)/x$. Similarly, $n_y = [\partial L(y, i)/L(y, i)]/\partial y/y$ and $n_i = [\partial L(y, i)/L(y, i)]/\partial i/i$ are the income and interest rate elasticities of the demand for money, respectively.

In a fixed and fully credible exchange rate system the expected growth of the exchange rate is zero, so that $\hat{e}^e = 0$. Additionally, from the small open economy assumption, i^* is exogenous, so we can assume that it is fixed. All these transform the interest-parity theorem into $i = i^*$. Hence we can deduce that there is no growth in the interest rate.

Now, taking natural logarithms of both sides of the law of one price equation (2.24) and differentiating through with respect to time, we get

$$\hat{p} = \hat{e} + \hat{p}^* \qquad (2.29)$$

Under a fixed exchange rate regime, $\hat{e} = 0$. Therefore, the growth in the domestic price level must equal the growth in the foreign price level, so the domestic rate of inflation is constrained to equal the growth rate. Using these results to substitute into equation (2.28) we get[15]

$$\frac{dR/dt}{M} = \hat{p} + n_y - \frac{D}{M}\hat{D} \qquad (2.30)$$

Now, as $(1/D)(dD/dt)$ is equivalent to the growth rate of domestic credit we can multiply (2.30) by M and end up with the following expression

$$\frac{dR}{dt} = M(\hat{p}^* + n_y\hat{y}) - \left(\frac{dD}{dt}\right) \qquad (2.31)$$

If we assume for the moment that the foreign price, p^*, is constant and that the economy is stationary, then the term between the parentheses is equal to zero, and equation (2.31) reduces to

$$dR/dt = -dD/dt \qquad (2.32)$$

Under these circumstances any attempt by the central bank to increase the money stock through increasing domestic credit creation will be nullified by an exact shrinkage in the foreign reserve component of high-power money. Thus, a monetary expansion leads to a BOP deficit and loss of foreign reserves. *The way to solve the problem is to limit domestic credit expansion.* The Polak model (for the long run) reaches the same conclusion, but in that model the end of the state was reached through a process in which real income as well as prices might be affected in addition to the balance of payments.

In a case in which the foreign price level and the domestic real income are growing, so that the demand for money is also growing, we can see from (2.31) that the change in foreign reserves will be zero, provided that domestic credit increases at the same rate as the demand for high-power money. If the central bank exceeds (falls short of) this rate of increase in its expansion of domestic credit, then there will be a deficit (surplus) on the BOP and a loss (gain) in foreign reserves.[16]

2.4.3   Financial Programming: The Pragmatic Version

Both the Polak and the Chicago version of the monetary approach support a limit in domestic credit expansion as a way to solve an external imbalance. However, in practice, orthodox programs support both demand deflation, based on controlling domestic credit and the fiscal deficit, and devaluation. These policies will presumably reduce the rate of inflation and improve the BOP position. The financial programming model considers the exchange rate as an additional policy instrument (an aspect that is not considered formally in the Polak or the Chicago version) and attempts to find the values of policy instruments (domestic credit and the exchange rate) so that the desired values of the target variables (the reserve position and change in inflation) can be achieved. In practice the simple financial programming exercise involves mainly the manipulation of balance sheet relationships, with the demand for money being an important behavioral relationship to enter the picture (IMF 1987).

From the preliminaries we have described, the financial programming version can be constructed. A fairly schematic picture can, nevertheless, be put together from a review of IMF (1987), Chand (1989), Edwards (1990), Mill y Nallari (1992), and Tarp (1993). Here, equations (2.3) through (2.18) (from the basic macroeconomic framework) provide the bare bones of the financial programming approach. As we will show the model reduces to a set of two equations expressing the monetary and external equilibrium. The demand for money function takes the form derived from the equation of exchange

$$M_\mathrm{d} = py/v \qquad\qquad (2.19)$$

which in first differences gives

$$\Delta M_{\mathrm{d}} = (1/v)\Delta Y \tag{2.33}$$

The flow (or continuous) equilibrium in the money market is given by:

$$\Delta M = \Delta M_{\mathrm{s}} = \Delta M_{\mathrm{d}} \tag{2.34}$$

By substituting (2.34), (2.33), and (2.11) in (2.10), we have

$$\Delta R = (1/v)\Delta Y - (\Delta D_{\mathrm{g}} + \Delta D_{\mathrm{p}}) \tag{2.35}$$

which is a version, in first differences, of the fundamental equation of the monetary approach. It states that the balance-of-payments position can be expressed as the difference between the private sector's demand for money $((1/v)\Delta Y)$ and the flow of domestic credit $(\Delta D_{\mathrm{g}} + \Delta D_{\mathrm{p}})$.

In (2.14) for small changes in the general price level and in real GDP, the change in nominal income can be approximated by[17]

$$\Delta Y = \Delta p y_{t-1} + p_{t-1}\Delta y \tag{2.36}$$

where y_{t-1} is the previous period real income (observed), Δy is the change in real income (predetermined), p_{t-1} is the general price level of the previous period (observed), and Δp is the change in the general price level.

An important addition of the financial programming approach with respect to the Polak and Chicago versions is that prices are treated as endogenous. This opens the door for the impact that the flow of money has on the domestic price level. In the Polak model, for instance, it is nominal income that is treated as the endogenous variable, while in the Chicago version the law of one price and the constant level of real output assumptions leave no room for nominal income changes. Taking first differences in equation (2.16), we have

$$\Delta p = (1 - \alpha)\Delta p_{\mathrm{d}} + \alpha e \Delta p^{*} \tag{2.37}$$

We know also that $e = \Delta e + e_{t-1}$. Substituting (2.36) and (2.37) into (2.35) the latter can be rewritten as:

$$\Delta R = (1/v)[((1 - \alpha)\Delta p_{\mathrm{d}} + \alpha(\Delta e + e_{t-1})\Delta p^{*})y_{t-1} + p_{t-1}\Delta y]$$
$$- (\Delta D_{\mathrm{g}} + \Delta D_{\mathrm{p}}) \tag{2.38}$$

To the effects of financial programming, the velocity of money, v, is constant and predetermined; and the change in real income, Δy, and the credit ceiling to the private sector, ΔD_p, are also predetermined; while the previous period's real GDP, nominal exchange rate, and price levels (y_{t-1}, e_{t-1} and p_{t-1}) are observed. Equation (2.38) contains also two unknowns; ΔR and Δp_d, and two policy instruments; Δe and ΔD_g.

Specifying equation (2.3) further can create a second sub-system. In fact in equation (2.3), we have another expression relating the reserve position to exports, imports, interest payments, and capital flows. Substitution of (2.4), (2.5), and (2.6) into (2.3) yields

$$\Delta R = eX^* - IM + e(\Delta F_\mathrm{g}^* + \Delta F_\mathrm{p}^* - INT_\mathrm{g}^* - INT_\mathrm{p}^*) \tag{2.39}$$

This expression is similar to expression (2.23). However, instead of using Polak's special specification for the imports demand function, we will use the full specification given by equations (2.7) and (2.8) of the basic framework, that is

$$IM = ep^*(\beta_0 + \beta_1 y + \beta_2(ep^*/p_\mathrm{d})) \tag{2.40}$$

We may express nominal imports as $IM = IM_{t-1} - \Delta IM$. Furthermore, ΔIM is equal to the extra import payments due to the change in imported quantity plus the valuation change in the imports of the last period (as the exchange rate may change). The imported quantity change is

$$\Delta Z = \beta_1 \Delta y - \beta_2 \Delta e(p^*/p_\mathrm{d}) + \beta_2 ep^* \Delta p_\mathrm{d} \tag{2.41}$$

as $p_\mathrm{d} = ep^* = 1$, this expression equals to

$$\Delta Z = \beta_1 \Delta y - \beta_2 \Delta ep^* + \beta_2 \Delta p_\mathrm{d} \tag{2.41a}$$

This is the additional import cost in domestic currency for the extra units imported. The valuation change is equal to $IM_{t-1}\Delta ep^*$ as the foreign import price is assumed not to change. It follows that

$$IM = IM_{t-1} + \beta_1 \Delta y - \beta_2 \Delta ep^* + \beta_2 \Delta p_\mathrm{d} + IM_{t-1}\Delta ep^* \tag{2.42}$$

Which, rearranged, yields

$$IM = IM_{t-1} + \beta_1 \Delta y + \beta_2 \Delta p_\mathrm{d} + \Delta ep^*(IM_{t-1} - \beta_2) \tag{2.43}$$

Substituting (2.43) into (2.39) we obtain the following expression for ΔR as a function of Δp_d

$$\Delta R = -IM_{t-1} - \beta_1 \Delta y - \Delta ep^*(IM_{t-1} - \beta_2)$$
$$+ e(X^* + \Delta F_\mathrm{g}^* + \Delta F_\mathrm{p}^* - INT_\mathrm{g}^* - INT_\mathrm{p}^*) - \beta_2 \Delta p_\mathrm{d} \tag{2.44}$$

Recall that $e = \Delta e + e_{t-1}$, so (2.44) transforms into

$$\Delta R = -IM_{t-1} - \beta_1 \Delta y + e_{t-1}(X^* + \Delta F_g^* + \Delta F_p^* - INT_g^* - INT_p^*)$$
$$+ \Delta e[X^* + \Delta F_g^* + \Delta F_p^* - INT_g^* - INT_p^* - p^*(IM_{t-1} - \beta_2)]$$
$$- \beta_2 \Delta p_d \tag{2.45}$$

Now ΔR and Δp_d (both endogenous variables) appear together with a set of parameters and predetermined variables, as well as one policy instrument (Δe).

It follows that the two expressions in equations (2.38) and (2.45) give solutions for the values of the policy instruments ΔD_g and Δe (once the values for the targets ΔR and Δp_d, have been established). Once the change of credit to the government ΔD_g and the change in the nominal exchange rate have been calculated following this procedure, the corresponding fiscal balance can be found from equation (2.17), i.e.

$$(GSI - T) + eINT_g^* = \Delta D_g - e\Delta F_g^* \tag{2.17}$$

but $e = \Delta e + e_{t-1}$, so (2.17) can be rewritten as:

$$(GSI - T) = \Delta D_g - e_{t-1}(\Delta F_g^* + INT_g^*) - \Delta e(\Delta F_g^* + INT_g^*) \tag{2.46}$$

Given the change in government borrowing from abroad and the amount of interest payments to abroad, the size of the fiscal deficit (in nominal terms) will adjust according to the changes in government borrowing from the banking system and the exchange rate adjustment. Thus in a simple financial programming framework *fiscal policy played the role of constraining the government sector's demand for credit within an overall ceiling on total domestic credit expansion* (IMF 1987). For these reasons, changes in fiscal policy are often a key feature of stabilization programs.

Equations (2.38), (2.45), and (2.46) summarize the model. They are a fair representation of the monetary equilibrium, the external equilibrium, and the fiscal balance, respectively. Moreover, these expressions can be abbreviated to:

$$\Delta R = \rho_0 + \rho_1 \Delta e + \rho_2 \Delta P_d - \Delta D_g \tag{2.47}$$

$$\Delta R = \rho_3 + \rho_4 \Delta e - \rho_5 \Delta P_d \tag{2.48}$$

$$(GSI - T) = \rho_6 - \rho_7 \Delta e + \Delta D_g \tag{2.49}$$

where

$$\rho_0 = [(1/v)\alpha e \Delta p^* y_{t-1}] + (1/v)p_{t-1}\Delta y - \Delta D_p$$
$$\rho_1 = (1/v)y_{t-1}\alpha \Delta p^*$$
$$\rho_2 = (1/v)y_{t-1}(1 - \alpha)$$
$$\rho_3 = -IM_{t-1} - \beta_1 \Delta y + e_{t-1}(X^* + \Delta F_g^* + \Delta F_p^* - INT_g^* - INT_p^*)$$
$$\rho_4 = X^* + \Delta F_g^* + \Delta F_p^* - INT_g^* - INT_p^* - p^*(IM_{t-1} - \beta_2)$$
$$\rho_5 = \beta_2$$
$$\rho_6 = -e_{t-1}(\Delta F_g^* + INT_g^*)$$
$$\rho_7 = \Delta F_g^* + INT_g^*$$

It can be seen that equations (2.47) and (2.48) can be represented as straight lines in a $\Delta R - \Delta p_d$ space with respectively positive and negative slopes. They are depicted by the MM and BP lines in figure 2.1.

Turning to figure 2.1, if (as an example) the macroeconomic situation in terms of reserves position and inflation at point 'a' is unsatisfactory, the objective then may be to attain point 'b,' which signifies an improvement in the reserve position (balance of payments) associated with a lower inflation. The IMF approach would suggest the following strategy: *first, a ceiling on the expansion of domestic credit* will shift the MM line up toward point 'b,' *and*

Figure 2.1 Exchange Rate Adjustment and Credit Restraint in the Financial Programming Model

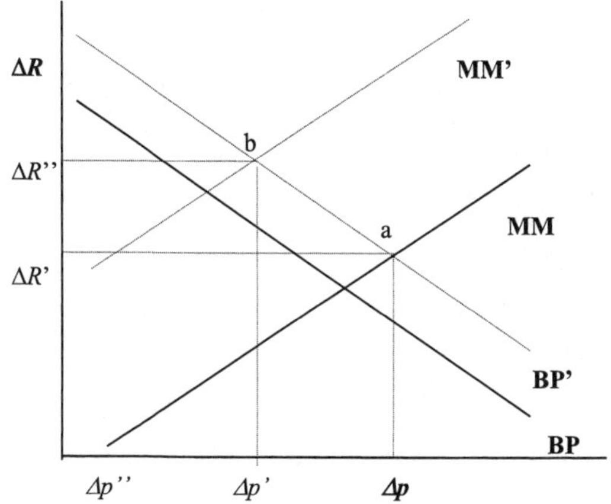

second, a devaluation will also shift both the MM and the BP lines upward toward point 'b.'

The financial programming approach has provided the IMF, especially in recent years, with a comprehensive framework that allows for the inter-relationships between the rate of exchange and the monetary and real sectors of the economy.[18] But it is important to note that even with the existence of an analytical framework integrating the relationship between the exchange rate and other policy variables, the benefits of an exchange rate adjustment are usually derived from some variety of expenditure switching mechanism. The direct effect of a switch in the composition of spending from foreign to domestic goods is at the crux of the so-called elasticities approach, whose fundamental theorem is best known as the Marshall-Lerner condition and is summarized by the expression

$$|n_\mathrm{x}| + |n_\mathrm{im}| - 1 > 0 \qquad (2.50)$$

where n_x and n_im are the exchange rate elasticities of the demand for exports and imports respectively. The theorem states that for a depreciation to lead to an improvement in the trade balance, expression (2.50) is required.[19]

In its many variants, the elasticity formula gives intellectual support to the notion of "elasticities optimism" that is usually emphasized by the IMF. As Thirwall (1988) has argued: "Most Economists seem to accept as axiomatic that the elasticities are 'right' for currency depreciation to do the trick, and governments and supra-national institutions like the International Monetary Fund proceed on that basis. All other assumptions that have to be satisfied for the policy to work are typically and conveniently forgotten" (p. 5).

It must be remembered, therefore, that the Marshall-Lerner condition applies under rather restrictive assumptions: the economy is small (in the sense that it does not have a major influence on the world economy), supply decisions react passively to demand at the fixed price level, and domestic prices are unaltered and unaffected by the exchange rate.

2.5 *Absorption*

One basic assumption underlying the IMF policy packages is that the balance of payments (BOP) disequilibria facing less developed countries are generally caused by unsustainable expansion in aggregate demand relative to aggregate supply, and that has typically manifested itself in BOP deficits. The restoration of macroeconomic equilibrium, therefore, involves either (1) the short stabilization or restructuring of domestic demand through the com-plementary use of monetary, fiscal, and exchange rate instruments (as we have seen), and/or (2) reducing domestic "absorption" in relation to income. We will focus now on the relevant analytical pillars supporting these complementary views.

The major purpose of the absorption approach, launched by Alexander (1952), is to integrate the balance of payments with the functioning of the total economy.[20] The balance-of-payments disequilibrium in the trade account is viewed as the outcome of the difference between decisions to produce and spend or save and invest.

We begin with the familiar Keynesian national income–expenditure identity (2.2) of the basic orthodox framework presented earlier

$$Y = A + X - IM \qquad (2.2)$$

where Y is national income (in nominal terms) or output, and A is domestic absorption as $A = C_p + C_g + I_p + I_g$, which is constituted by consumption and investment from the private and public sectors. Now, A is assumed to react to changes in income as expected in a simple Keynesian model when the economy is below full employment, i.e. $A = A(Y) + A_0$. Thus, rewriting (2.2), we can observe that net exports or the current account must equal the difference between national income and absorption; that is

$$CA = Y - A(Y) - A_0 \qquad (2.1a)$$

A deficit on the current account implies that current domestic absorption is greater than national income and that excess of expenditure over income is financed by borrowing abroad (selling existing assets to foreigners), or by running down foreign exchange reserves. The country in this case is "living beyond its means," that is, it is spending or "absorbing" more than its domestic savings or income potential. The expression (2.1a) also shows that any policy that will successfully eliminate the current account deficit must either increase national income more than it increases absorption, or else decrease absorption more than it decreases national income (which is the common IMF policy recommendation). If the economy gravitates around the full employment position, the external deficit can only be corrected by reducing the autonomous component of the absorption variable A_0. As Williamson (1987, p. 608) indicates, "Fund adjustment programs in principle fall in this category," even though the expression suggests four systems by which the current balance may improve.

Additionally, the absorption approach defines the macroeconomic balance in terms of an equilibrium between total savings, S, and total investment, I. Therefore, net exports, or the excess of income over absorption, is really a reflection of the overall gap between domestic savings and investment. In other words:

$$(X - IM) = (Y - C_p - C_g - I_p - I_g) = (S - I) \qquad (2.51)$$

Further, the savings–investment gap can be disaggregated into two components: a private component, $S_p - I_p$, and a public component, $T - GN$, where T is government total revenues and GN government total spending (in nominal terms), i.e. $G = C_g + I_g$.[21] Thus

$$(S - T) = (S_p - I_p) + (T - GN) \qquad (2.52)$$

Equation (2.51) can therefore be reformulated as follows:

$$(X - IM) = (Y - A) = (S_p - I_p) + (T - GN) \qquad (2.53)$$

Orthodox economists usually derive from this an order of causality whereby a permanent external imbalance is produced by a government deficit (Johnson and Salop 1980). In analytical terms, where the current account deficit ($IM > X$), or the excess of absorption over income ($A > Y$), corresponds to the private savings–investment gap ($I_p > S_p$), the imbalance can be rectified through an inflow of private capital. In a well-functioning world capital market, resources will flow into the developing countries that need external finance for investment as long as private investment yields a rate of return greater than the relevant world interest rate. Therefore, the resultant trade balance deficit is considered to be "temporary" and "reversible," and it is assumed to reflect a sustainable pattern of consumption within the nation (Salop and Spitaller 1981). If the origin of the imbalance is the government budget deficit ($GN > T$), then, at least in theory, there could be a transfer of resources from the domestic private sector and/or the external sector. However, the orthodox stabilization programs depart from the key assumptions that interest rates are determined internationally for the small open economy, so that savings and investment are thus unaffected by the budget deficit.[22] In this case the impact of the budget deficit is upon the trade balance through the increased demand for foreign liabilities. To solve the external imbalance the proposed solution is a reduction in government spending, GN, and/or an increase in government revenues, T.

With respect to devaluation the basic idea of the absorption approach is simple: any effect of devaluation on the trade balance can be explained by determining its effects on income, Y, and absorption, A. The trade balance

$$CA = Y - A(Y) - A_0 \qquad (2.1a)$$

and the effect of devaluation becomes

$$\frac{dCA}{de} = (1 - A_Y)\frac{dY}{de} - \frac{dA_0}{de} \tag{2.54}$$

where $0 < A_Y < 1$ is the marginal propensity to absorb. Devaluation analysis seems to turn on the effect of the exchange rate on (a) output, as reflected by dY/de, and (b) the level of absorption function as expressed by $(dA_0)/de$. Price elasticities seem to play no role. It was soon recognized, however, that this impression is misleading. Equation (2.1a) alone is insufficient to determine either Y or CA. As a consequence, Alexander's (1952) devaluation analysis did not progress beyond suggestive hints on the possible factors behind dY/de and dA_0/de. In order to obtain a determinate solution, another blade had to be added to the analytical scissors. It is provided by the export surplus $X - IM$, where IM is supposed to depend on national income. Thus using (2.6), (2.7), and a small variation of (2.8) the system becomes

$$CA = Y - A(Y) - A_0 \tag{2.1a}$$

$$CA = eX^* - ep^*(\beta_0 + \beta_1 y) \tag{2.14}$$

But if the law of one price holds ($p = ep^*$), then (2.14) may be expressed as[23]

$$CA = eX^* - ep^*\beta_0 - \beta_1 Y \qquad \text{or} \qquad CA = a - \beta_1 Y \tag{2.55}$$

where $a = (eX^* - ep^*\beta_0)$ corresponds to the autonomous part of the current account function.

This can be best seen in graphical terms. In figure 2.2, equation (2.12) is an upward-sloping curve that intersects the horizontal axis at the point where aggregate output is just enough to satisfy absorption. This curve alone is clearly not enough to determine CA, because it is not known at what point the economy finds itself. The missing element is provided by $CA = a - \beta_1 Y$. This curve must slope downward, because for a given foreign demand for exports, the demand for imports rises with income. The trade balance is determined jointly by Y, by the intersection of the two curves, so Y is the central mechanism of the model. The intersection of $(Y - A)$ with $(X - IM)$ (which corresponds to point 'q'), gives the level of balance Y'' in the goods market of the country's economy. This level of balance Y'' in the goods market is achieved with a deficit $Y''q$ in trade balance; for this deficit it is necessary that $Y - A < 0$, i.e. that the level of absorption is greater than the income level. In terms of figure 2.2, a currency devaluation would eventually shift the

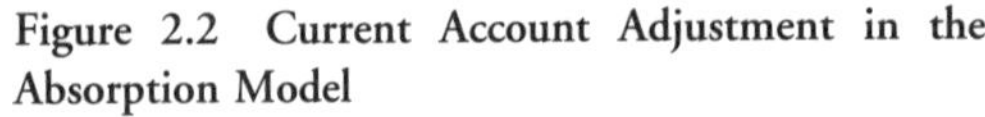

Figure 2.2 Current Account Adjustment in the Absorption Model

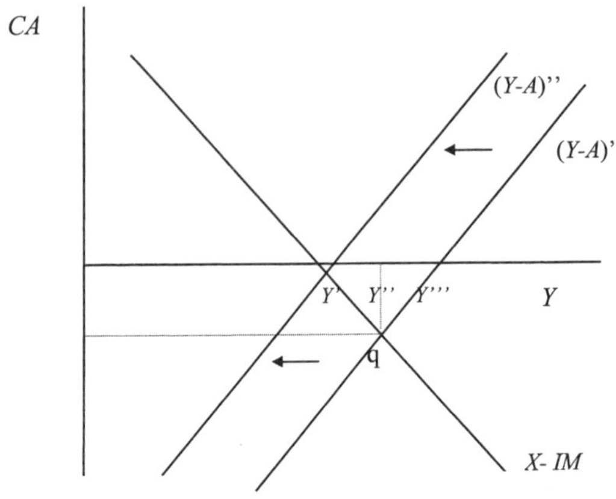

$(X - IM)$ schedule up (because X rises and IM falls) and improves the economy's trade balance if the nation operates at less than full employment to begin with (and if the Marshall-Lerner condition is satisfied). However, Alexander's point here is that the net final improvement in the nation's trade balance is less than the upward shift in the $(X - IM)$ schedule because domestic production rises and induces imports to rise, thus neutralizing part of the original improvement in the trade balance. If the goal is to eliminate the external deficit it will be necessary to reduce the level of absorption, A, by using contractionary fiscal and monetary policy; and in order to reduce A it will be necessary to reduce the income level Y. This would shift vertically upwards line $(Y - A)'$ in figure 2.2, so that it would cut line $(X - IM)$ at output level Y', introducing a higher level of unemployment than originally existed in Y''. Thus, any attempt to use expenditure policy to achieve external adjustment will increase unemployment.[24] From figure 2.2 it is clear that Y' and Y''' (the income level of full employment) cannot be reached simultaneously.

2.6 A Simplified Synthesis of the Expenditure Switching, Absorption, and Monetary Approaches

It has recently been claimed that different conceptions of the balance of payments are not necessarily inconsistent with one another. Rivera-Batiz and Rivera-Batiz (1985, p. 483), for instance, state that "no matter what the approach to the balance of payments is—elasticities, absorption, or monetary—it should be consistent with the other approaches. The difference between them lies in the way the balance of payments is looked at." Niehans (1984, p. 100) shares similar views when he says, "from the point of view of economic content, the monetary approach and the elasticity approach are largely equivalent, though with significant differences in emphasis and the choice of simplifications. The same can be said of the expenditure approach."[25] Yet the attempts to show this reconciliation lie in *ex post* identities. (see IMF 1987, Rivera-Batiz and Rivera-Batiz 1985, and Bacha 1990a). We will show very briefly that economic content can be given to the main identities so that a more complete picture of how economic variables interact can be given. The value of this sort of synthesis is that it allows us to derive further insight into the analytical basis of the orthodox position towards stabilization. Specifically, we will show that the popular complaint that the IMF model explains no real variables and that output variation is ignored (see for instance Tarp 1993, p. 76) can be easily dismissed. In fact, the merged Keynesian-monetary model that we derive from the basic framework does highlight the fact that IMF policy prescriptions still apply and can be enhanced in other frameworks in which output variation is allowed.

From the basic framework let us take expression (2.2) for the overall national income account (in nominal terms).

$$X - MI = Y - A \tag{2.2}$$

The current account must also be matched by changes in international reserves, ΔR, and net financial transfers, ΔF, as given by expression (2.3).

$$X - IM = \Delta R - \Delta F \tag{2.3}$$

Replacing ΔR by the intermediate expression (2.10), substituting (2.2) into (2.3) and regrouping terms, expression (2.3) may be written as:

$$X - IM = Y - A = \Delta M_s - \Delta D - \Delta F \tag{2.56}$$

Since ΔF is assumed exogenous, expression (2.56) states that absorption will exceed the sum of domestic resources (income) when the change in domestic credit exceeds the change in the money stock. Though these different orthodox conceptions of the balance of payments seem to be consistent with one another, the problem with these balance equations is that they do not amount to a model as no behavioral equations are specified. The identities do not give any clue as to how the adjustment process takes place and in some sense constitutes an empty framework. However, as Bacha (1990a, p. 751) has clearly stated, "such accounting identities are in fact the basis of the IMF's financial exercises."

As we just mentioned, for a better synthesis of the Keynesian (elasticity and absorption) and monetary approaches it is necessary to specify the causal links in the economy. In order to do that we now analyze a simple model of the determination of output, the balance of payments, the interest rate and the price level, which derives from the initial basic orthodox framework. We proceed along the lines suggested by Frenkel, Gylfanson, and Helliwell (1980) and Chen and Tsaur (1981). The equations of the model are as follows:

$$\Delta R = X(ep^*/p) - IM(ep^*/p, y) + \Delta F \qquad (2.3a)$$

$$M_s = D + R \qquad (2.9)$$

$$M_d = pL(y, i) \qquad (2.12)$$

$$M_d = M_s \qquad (2.13)$$

$$i = i^* \qquad (2.25a)$$

$$py = CA(ep^*/p, y) + A(py) + A_0 \qquad (2.1b)$$

$$y = y(p) \qquad (2.57)$$

Many of the elements of the present synthesis have already been discussed and can therefore be stated rather briefly. Equation (2.3) represents the external balance or the change in foreign reserves position as a result of the trade balance and the change in net transfers to abroad. The trade balance captures the elasticity-absorption synthesis. Expressions (2.9), (2.12) and (2.13) represent monetary equilibrium common to the monetary approaches. Expression (2.25a) is the interest parity theorem for the special case of a fixed and credible exchange rate regime (as in the Chicago version of the monetary approach). Equation (2.1b) comes from the income–expenditure identity (2.1), but now it combines elasticity and absorption arguments. Finally, equation (2.57) is a standard aggregate supply function, which can be derived from equilibrium conditions in the labor market.

We will deal first with a small open economy in which domestic output, y, is freely flexible, but its domestic currency price level, p, is fixed (equation (2.57) does not apply). Moreover, we will treat the domestic interest rate, i, as an endogenous variable in a Keynesian fashion (equation (2.25) does not apply). The model reduces to a three-equation model as described by

$$py = CA(ep^*/p, y) + A(py) + A_0 \tag{2.1b}$$

$$pL(y, i) = D + R \tag{2.26}$$

$$R = CA(ep^*/p, y) + \Delta F + R_{t-1} \tag{2.3a}$$

Equation (2.26) is the Chicago version of the fundamental equation of the monetary approach, which derives from the stock equilibrium in the money market. Additionally, $R - R_{t-1}$ has been substituted in (2.3a) for ΔR, where R_{t-1} denotes the stock of international reserves held at the beginning of the period. Differentiation of this system yields

$$\begin{bmatrix} p(1 - A_y) + m & 0 & 0 \\ p\dfrac{\partial L(y, i)}{\partial y} dy & p\dfrac{\partial L(y, i)}{\partial i} di & -1 \\ m & 0 & 1 \end{bmatrix} \begin{bmatrix} dy \\ di \\ dR \end{bmatrix}$$

$$= \begin{bmatrix} \dfrac{\partial CA}{\partial(ep^*/p)} d(ep^*/p) + dA_0 \\ dC \\ \dfrac{\partial CA}{\partial(ep^*/p)} d(ep^*/p) + d\Delta F + dR_{t-1} \end{bmatrix}$$

where $0 < A_y < 1$ is the marginal propensity to absorb; m is the marginal propensity to import; and $\partial L(y, i)/\partial y > 0$, $\partial L(y, i)/\partial i < 0$, and $\partial CA/\partial(ep^*/p) > 0$ if the Marshall-Lerner condition is satisfied. Furthermore, the determinant of the above matrix is $\Psi = [p(1 - A_y) + m] \times [\partial L(y, i)/\partial i] p\, di < 0$.

We can consequently solve for dy and dR

$$dy = \frac{\left[\dfrac{\partial CA}{\partial(ep^*/p)} d(ep^*/p) + dA_0 \right] p\dfrac{\partial L(y, i)}{\partial i} di}{\Psi}$$

$$dR = \frac{\left[p\dfrac{\partial L(y, i)}{\partial i} di \right] \left[(p(1 - A_y) + m)\left(\dfrac{\partial CA}{\partial(ep^*/p)} d(ep^*/p) \right) - \left(\dfrac{\partial CA}{\partial(ep^*/p)} d(ep^*/p) + dA_0 \right) m \right]}{\Psi}$$

For simplicity we have assumed that $d\Delta F = 0$ and $dR_{t-1} = 0$. By evaluating the impact of devaluation (expenditure switching) and expenditure reduction policies on the external balance we have

$$\frac{dR}{d(ep^*/p)} = \frac{\left[p\dfrac{\partial L(y,i)}{di}di\right]p(1-A_y)\dfrac{\partial CA}{\partial(ep^*/p)}}{\Psi} > 0 \quad \text{if} \quad \frac{\partial CA}{\partial(ep^*/p)} > 0$$

$$\frac{dR}{dA_0} = \frac{-\left[p\dfrac{\partial L(y,i)}{di}di\right]m}{\Psi} < 0$$

which confirm conventional results in terms of the balance of payments. We may then evaluate the effect of a change in autonomous expenditure on real income under the assumption that no action is taken on the real exchange rate $(d(ep^*/p) = 0)$. This gives

$$\frac{dy}{dA_0} = \frac{p\dfrac{\partial L(y,i)}{\partial i}di}{\Psi} > 0 \quad \text{since both} \quad \frac{\partial L(y,i)}{\partial i} < 0 \quad \text{and} \quad \Psi < 0 \quad (2.59a)$$

An expenditure reduction policy reduces real income as expected. If no action is taken on autonomous absorption $(dA_0 = 0)$ regrouping terms we have

$$\frac{dy}{d(ep^*/p)} = \frac{\left[\dfrac{\partial CA}{\partial(ep^*/p)}\right]p\dfrac{\partial L(y,i)}{\partial i}di}{\Psi} > 0 \quad \text{if} \quad \frac{\partial CA}{\partial(ep^*/p)} > 0 \quad (2.59b)$$

That is, a real exchange rate devaluation will unambiguously increase real income if the Marshall-Lerner condition is met. This is the so-presumed supply-side effect of devaluation (see IMF 1987, p. 38).[26] Notice that the results of this model reaffirm that the various components of IMF programs are complementary. In the words of Meller (1987, p. 201): "the IMF program is supposedly an indivisible package. . . . [T]he recessionary effect of a reduction of the fiscal deficit and of the money supply is offset by the expansionary effect of the devaluation."

Let us deal with the same small open economy model, but now take into account equation (2.57), which implies that the domestic price level is endogenous. Further, we assumed a full equalization of the domestic and the foreign interest rate, which implies that (2.25) applies.

To focus the analysis on output and the balance of payments, the model may be solved for y and R as follows. First the aggregate supply equation (2.57) is solved for p by writing

$$p = p(y), \qquad dp/dy > 0 \tag{2.60}$$

Assuming that the foreign price level, p^*, is fixed and equal to one and substituting equations (2.60) into the balance-of-payments equation (2.3a) gives the following relationship between R and y

$$R = \frac{dCA}{dy}y + \frac{dCA}{de}e + R_{t-1} \tag{2.61}$$

Now, the stock equilibrium condition in the money market $(M_s = M_d)$ implies that

$$pL(y, i) = D + R \tag{2.62}$$

Substituting (2.60) and (2.25a) into (2.62) gives a second relationship between R and y.

$$R = \frac{\partial L}{\partial p}\frac{dp}{dy}\,y - D \tag{2.63}$$

where, as conventionally stated, $dCA/dy < 0$, $dCA/de > 0$, and $\partial L/\partial p > 0$. The two relationships are shown in figure 2.3. It should be noted that the

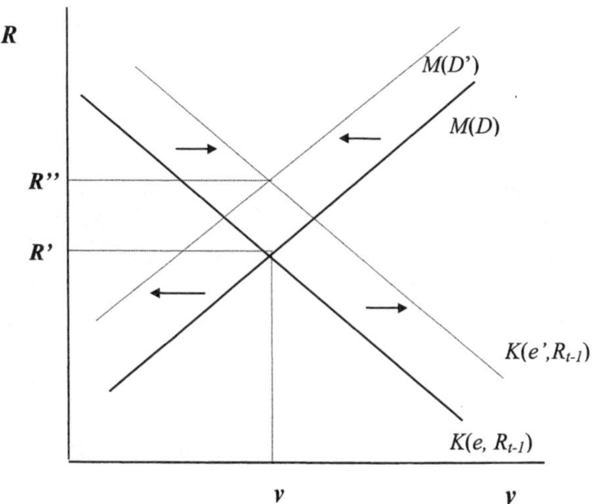

Figure 2.3   Stabilization Policy in the Keynesian and Monetary Synthesis

Table 2.1 Effects of Changes in e and D on Y, R, and p

	de	dD
dY	+	+
dR	+	−
dp	+	+

slope of the two schedules (i.e. the signs of dCA/dy and $[\partial L/\partial p][dp/dy]$) reflect not only the effects of income changes on the current account and the demand for money, respectively, but also the price effect.

The analysis implies that an increase in the exchange rate induces a rightward shift of the K-schedule sufficiently large so as to improve the balance-of-payments position and increase output. The price level increases through equation (2.60). However, by using contractionary monetary policy, the domestic credit reduction shifts the M schedule to the left, improving the level of reserves further and reducing output and the price level. The short-run comparative-statics properties of the model are summarized in table 2.1.

2.7 *The Integrated IMF/WB Model: Stabilization and Adjustment with Growth*

Earlier in chapter 1 when we analyzed the nature and evolution of conditionality, we pointed out how by the mid-1970s the concentration on demand management techniques and exchange rate manipulation in stabilization programs changed so as to be viewed with a longer-term horizon. In fact, the introduction of SAL programs moved the World Bank to the promotion of adjustment with growth in which supply-side transformation is required to complement demand management of the IMF type. In recent years, the desire to develop a macroeconomic framework for growth-oriented adjustment has led IMF staff to formulate an "integrated" or "merged" model that contains a growth block and a monetary block. It is in this direction that the work of Khan and Knight (1985); Corbo, Goldstein, and Khan (1987); Khan and Montiel (1989); and Khan, Montiel, and Haque (1990) have offered analytical support to the relatively new emphasis on growth.

The two main building blocks of the integrated IMF/WB model are the monetary approach to the balance of payments (as developed by Polak) and a simple version of the neoclassical growth model (in which the economy is assumed to be open). The advantage of this framework is that, among other things, it permits us to calculate both the effects of structural policies that alter private savings and the efficiency of investment on the rate of growth of the economy.

The first element in the simple growth block is the equation for the expansion of capacity, Δy, which comes from expression (2.18) of the basic framework

$$\Delta y = z_0 + z_1 \Delta k \qquad (2.18)$$

in which y is real output and Δk is the variation of the capital stock (or investment). The coefficient of investment, z_1, is the marginal product of capital, and the constant term, z_0, captures the combined effects of increases in total factor productivity and the change in the size of the labor force.[27]

The second element in the simple growth block is the identity (2.19), which relates aggregate investment to aggregate savings. In our framework this is written as

$$\Delta k = SR_p + (TR - G) + (\Delta F - \Delta R)/p_d \qquad (2.19)$$

where SR_p, TR, G, and $(\Delta F - \Delta R)/p_d$ are the real values of private savings, taxes, government spending, and net foreign interest payments, respectively, measured in units of domestic goods. The first term in equation (2.19) is, therefore, real private saving, the second is real public saving, and the third is the real current account deficit (that is, real foreign saving). Assuming that real private saving is a proportion s of real disposable income, equation (2.19) can be rewritten as:

$$\Delta k = s(y - TR) + (TR - G) + (\Delta F - \Delta R)/p_d \qquad (2.64)$$

We assume that TR, G, and ΔF are exogenous in real terms. Finally, because $y = y_{t-1} + \Delta y$ and $p_d = p_{dt-1} + \Delta p_d$, and using the growth equation (2.18), we can derive the following relationship between real output growth and changes in the price level:

$$\Delta y = (1 - sz_1)^{-1} \left\{ z_0 + z_1 \left[s(y_{t-1} - TR) + (TR - G) + \frac{\Delta F - \Delta R}{p_{dt-1} + \Delta p_d} \right] \right\} \qquad (2.65)$$

Equation (2.65) basically implies that investment and growth are saving-constrained. It can be seen that an increase in the private savings rate, government savings, or exogenous component of the current account deficit would increase real output growth, in each case by increasing aggregate savings and, therefore, investment. Since it contains three endogenous variables, Δy, ΔR, and Δp_{d}, two additional restrictions on these three variables are necessary to close the model.

The monetary block is summarized by equation (2.38), which we derived previously within the frame of the financial programming approach

$$\Delta R = (1/v)[((1-\alpha)\Delta p_{\mathrm{d}} + \alpha(\Delta e + e_{t-1})\Delta p^*)y_{t-1} + p_{t-1}\Delta y] - \Delta D \tag{2.38}$$

but now, instead of assuming Δy as a predetermined variable, we will assume this as endogenously determined in the model. Again, the velocity of money, v, is constant and predetermined, and the credit ceiling to the private and public sector sector, D, is also predetermined; while the previous period's real GDP, nominal exchange rate, and price levels (y_{t-1}, e_{t-1} and p_{t-1}) are observed. Rearranging (2.38) we have

$$\Delta y = \frac{v(\Delta R + \Delta D) - [(1-\alpha)\Delta p_{\mathrm{d}} + \alpha(\Delta e + e_{t-1})\Delta p^*]y_{t-1}}{p_{t-1}} \tag{2.66}$$

Equation (2.38) contains three unknowns, ΔR, Δy, and Δp_{d}, so two additional restrictions among these endogenous variables are required to close the system.

Because both the growth equation and the monetary equation are incomplete as they stand, they are supplemented by an additional relationship common to both models. The additional relationship is the already-known balance-of-payments identity (2.3).

$$\Delta R = CA + \Delta F \tag{2.3}$$

We will assume that the trade balance in domestic currency, CA, is a linear function of changes in the real exchange rate and income. Therefore

$$CA = CA_0 + z_3(e/p_{\mathrm{d}} - 1) - z_4\Delta y \tag{2.67}$$

In other words, the trade balance, CA, improves when the real exchange rate depreciates ($e/p_{\mathrm{d}} > 1$), and deteriorates when real output, y, increases. These are quite conventional assumptions derived from the elasticity and absorption synthesis. The coefficients z_3 and z_4 stand for the impact of the real exchange rate and real income on the trade balance.

Substituting (2.67) into (2.3), the equation for ΔR will be

$$\Delta R = CA_0 + z_3(e/p_d - 1) - z_4\Delta y + \Delta F \tag{2.68}$$

This equation can now be used to close the growth and monetary block. We can use equation (2.8) to eliminate ΔR from the growth equation (2.65). The result is

$$\Delta y = \left(1 - sz_1 + \frac{z_1 z_4}{p_{dt-1} + \Delta p_d}\right)^{-1}$$
$$\times \left\{ z_0 + z_1 \left[s(y_{t-1} - TR) + (TR - G) + \frac{-CA_0 - z_3(e/p_d - 1)}{p_{dt-1} + \Delta p_d} \right] \right\} \tag{2.69}$$

Combining the balance-of-payments equation (2.68) with the monetary equation (2.66), and assuming that the change in real output is exogenous, we can solve the monetary for ΔR and Δp_d.

$$\Delta y = \frac{v(CA_0 + z_3(e/p_d - 1) + \Delta F + \Delta D) - [(1 - \alpha)\Delta p_d + \alpha(\Delta e + e_{t-1})\Delta p^*]y_{t-1}}{(p_{t-1} - vz_4)} \tag{2.70}$$

Because the growth equation (2.69) assumes exogenous prices and the monetary equation keeps real output exogenous, a natural alternative closure for the two models is to dispense with the ancillary assumptions made for each equation (about the respective exogeneity of Δp_d and Δy) and to combine the two models to solve for Δp_d and Δy simultaneously.

The implicit solutions for Δp_d in the growth and monetary equations are:

$$\Delta p_d = \frac{z_1[CA_0 + z_3(e/p_d - 1) + z_1 z_4\Delta y]}{z_0 + z_1[s(y_{t-1} - TR) + (TR - G)] - (1 - sz_1)\Delta y} - p_{dt-1} \tag{2.71}$$

$$\Delta p_d = \frac{v(CA_0 + z_3(e/p_d) + \Delta F + \Delta D) - (vz_4 - p_{t-1})\Delta y - \alpha(\Delta e + e_{t-1})\Delta p^* y_{t-1}}{(1 - \alpha)y_{t-1}} \tag{2.72}$$

Equation (2.71), corresponding to the growth part of the model, traces a positively sloped locus in the $\Delta p_d - \Delta y$ space (labeled GG).

The slope of GG is

$$\left.\frac{d(\Delta p_d)}{d(\Delta y)}\right|_{GG} = \frac{z_1 z_4 z_5 + (1 - s z_1) z_6}{(z_5)^2} > 0 \qquad (2.73)$$

where

$$z_5 = z_0 + z_1 [s(y_{t-1} - TR) + (TR - G) - (1 - s z_1)\Delta y$$

and

$$z_6 = z_1 [CA_0 + z_3(e/p_d - 1) + z_1 z_4 \Delta y$$

The expression above is positive on the assumptions that $CA_0 \geq 0$ and that the Marshall-Lerner condition holds $(z_3 > 0)$.[28]

Equation (2.72), which relates to the monetary part of the model, traces out a negatively sloped locus, labeled LL in figure 2.4. The slope of LL is given by

$$\left.\frac{d(\Delta p_d)}{d(\Delta y)}\right|_{LL} = \frac{-(v z_4 + p_{t-1})}{(1 - \alpha) y_{t-1}} < 0 \qquad (2.74)$$

The resulting "integrated model" is described graphically in figure 2.4. The integrated model can be used to determine the impact of

Figure 2.4   The Integrated Model Effects of a Change in the Savings Rate and in Total Factor Productivity

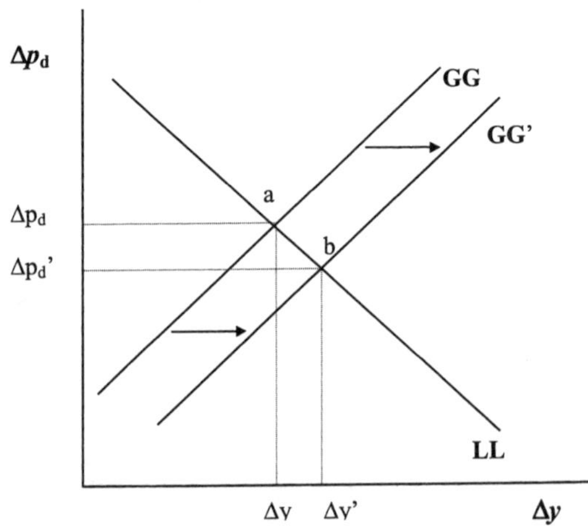

demand-management policies, exchange-rate policies, and structural policies (policies to increase savings and total-factor productivity) on the BOP, the rate of growth of the economy, and the rate of inflation. With respect to demand-management and exchange-rate policies the results of the model "turn out to be broadly consistent with widely held belief" (Khan and Montiel 1989, p. 281).

In the case of structural policies or supply-oriented policies the model is very interesting since it is able to address issues that are not usually tackled in stabilization models. In fact, the supply-side case is difficult to analyze because mere models cannot capture the forces involved. However, Khan and Knight (1982) provide us with a simple characterization of what orthodoxy means by supply-oriented policies. These can be divided in two broad categories: (1) policies designed to increase the total flow of current output by improving the efficiency with which the factors of production are allocated, and (2) measures to increase the total domestic saving and investment. A change in any of these two categories is precisely captured in the integrated model by a change in the parameters z_0 and s.

An increase in the saving rate, s, for example, increases domestic saving, thereby creating an excess of saving over investment. The increase in s can be achieved through, for example, an increase in interest rate or financial deepening (via the McKinnon and Shaw hypothesis). As investment rises output will increase, which leads to a further increase in private saving, shifting the GG in figure 2.4 to the right. All this is captured in equation (2.71). Assuming further that the increase in savings is matched by investment and does not go into hoarding (leaving the LL unaffected) there will be a higher rate of growth and a lower rate of inflation, as the increase in output must be accompanied by a decrease in prices to clear the flow money market.

An improvement in total factor productivity, that is, an increase in z_0 will mean a larger amount of output at the original level of investment. As we have mentioned before, the removal of distortions as tariff, imports licensing, food subsidies, price controls, etc. permits, according to the IMF and the World Bank, greater efficiency gains and higher factor productivity. This higher productivity implies that the economy will experience an incipient excess of saving over investment. This new saving would be channeled into investment, and output will rise still further. The GG schedule will shift rightward, as in figure 2.4, and once again, the LL schedule would be unaffected. Thus, a rise in total factor productivity, like an increase in saving, constitutes in effect a positive supply shock. Again, the increase in output exerts downward pressure on prices.

2.8 Financial Repression: The McKinnon and Shaw Hypothesis

Within the orthodox framework, in general, the goal of stimulating higher levels of investment, and thus higher output growth, usually relies on measures to increase domestic savings. In contrast to measures that attempt to improve the efficiency with which scarce resources are allocated among competing uses, these policies are intended to increase the rate of growth over the medium term. Though in the integrated model an increase in the private savings rate affects investment positively, the way in which this increase in the private savings rate could be brought in is unexplained. However, an important literature developed since the 1970s has taken shape in which the arguments concerned with appropriate financial policies to increase savings and investment in LDCs are paramount. McKinnon (1973) and Shaw (1973) first took direct issue with this phenomenon by claiming that financial repression leads to the withdrawal of funds from the banking sector, and lowers actual investment—and therefore economic growth—in LDCs. Because of the complementarity of savings and investment in financially repressed economies, the policy recommendation is to free interest rates, and to liberalize the financial sector. As a matter of fact, establishing high real interest rates has become a standard part of the policy advice given to LDCs by external experts, ranging from the visiting academic economists to emissaries of the IMF and the World Bank (see Fry 1982, Van Wijnbergen 1983, IMF 1987, Polak 1989, and Bagchi 1990).

McKinnon (1973) and Shaw (1973) do not offer a rigorous formulation of their ideas but the financial repression case is usually illustrated with the help of figure 2.5. Domestic and foreign savings, $S(g)_0$, at the rate of growth g_0, are a function of the real rate of interest $(i - \pi^e)$, which is the difference of the nominal interest rate, i, and the expected rate of inflation, π^e. Investment is an inverse function of the real interest rate. Financial repression, taken here to consist simply of an administratively determined nominal interest rate, holds the real interest rate below its equilibrium level. At the institutional real interest rate, $(i - \pi^e)_0$, the actual investment is constrained to I_0 because of the limited saving that is available.

If the monetary authorities decide to ease the financial repression and raise the real rate from $(i - \pi^e)_0$ to $(i - \pi^e)_1$, both domestic and foreign savings will rise, and this in turn will increase private investment. Potential investors must accumulate money balances prior to their investment. The more attractive the process of accumulating money, i.e. the higher the $i - \pi^e$, the greater the incentive to invest. Moreover, the low-yielding investment that is supposed to be the result of the safest and simplest modes of finance when

**Figure 2.5   Financial Repression: The McKinnon
and Shaw Model**

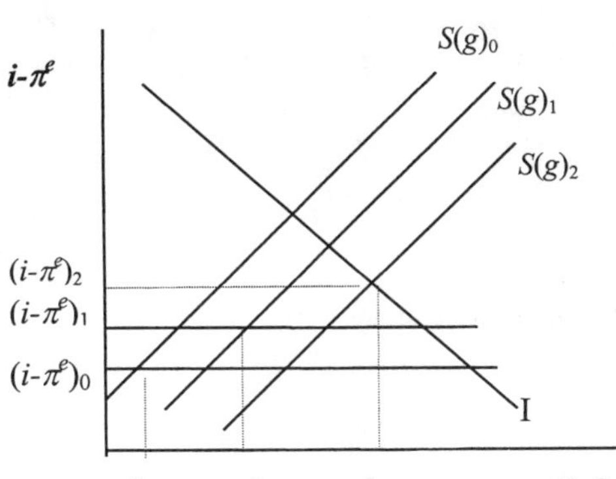

interest rates are administrated will be eliminated, and the overall efficiency of investment will increase. This will lead to a rise in income and saving, and hence the saving curve will shift right to $S(g)_1$. Actual investment will rise to I_1. If the monetary authorities are bold enough to abolish financial repression altogether, then the level of actual saving and investment will rise further, leading to a further expansion in the rate of growth (the impacts on growth are multiplicative).

The model thus implies that an increase in the real interest rate will induce savers in the LDCs to save more, which will enable more investment to take place, raising the rate of growth of the economy. In this context, the McKinnon-Shaw hypothesis contends that saving, investment, and financial intermediation would be suboptimal when the real interest rate is arbitrarily fixed at a point that is lower than its equilibrium value.

An impressive theoretical work on formal model building of the financially repressed economy has been undertaken (for a good summary see Fry 1982). Since we are dealing with small open economies, here we construct a simple model of a financially repressed economy following the lines of Cardoso (1979). To illustrate the workings of the model and to underline the claim that orthodox approaches towards the issue of stabilization and structural adjustment complement one another, we maintain the same basic equations of the growth block of the integrated model. Actual investment is limited to the amount of domestic and foreign saving. In addition, we abandon the assumption of an exogenous saving rate and embrace, instead, the assumption that the saving rate, s, is a positive function of the real deposit interest rate, $i - \pi^e$. We have left aside the government sector in order to focus on the private-sector behavior. To evaluate financial liberalization claims we establish that nominal interest rate ceiling hold the real interest rate below the level at which saving and investment are equalized.

Leaving aside the government sector, we know from identity (2.19) that investment, Δk, is equal to savings, SR_p, plus the current account deficit.

$$\Delta k = SR_p + Z - X \tag{2.19}$$

where Z and X stand for imports and exports in real terms. A simplified version for the equation of expansion of capacity (2.18) is

$$y = uk \tag{2.18a}$$

where u represents now the output–capital ratio (z_0 in 2.18a is assumed to be zero). The assumption of a constant u will imply that financial liberalization will affect the volume but not the quality of investment.

The output growth rate, g, equals the growth rate of capital, $\Delta k/k$.

$$g = \Delta k/k \tag{2.74}$$

The model now assumes that the saving rate is a positive function of the real deposit interest rate. Therefore

$$s = s(i - \pi^e) \tag{2.75}$$

If we further assume that imports are proportional to investment we can write

$$Z = z(ep^*/p)\Delta k \tag{2.76}$$

where z is the share of imports in income Z/y, which is assumed to be a decreasing function of the real exchange rate ep^*/p, and the share of exports in output X/y is a positive function of the real exchange rate

$$X/y = x(ep^*/p) \tag{2.77}$$

By dividing (2.19) throughout by k, we obtain an expression for the growth rate of output and capital

$$g = \Delta k/k = (SR_p + Z - X)/k \tag{2.78}$$

By multiplying top and bottom by y, and applying common factor y/k, we get

$$\frac{\Delta k}{k} = \frac{y}{k}\left(\frac{SR_p}{y} + \frac{Z}{y} - \frac{X}{y}\right) \tag{2.79}$$

Substituting (2.75), (2.76), and (2.77) into (2.79) we have

$$\frac{\Delta k}{k} = \frac{y}{k}\left[s(i - \pi^e) + z(ep^*/p)\frac{\Delta k}{y} - x(ep^*/p)\right] \qquad (2.80)$$

or

$$\frac{\Delta k}{k} = \frac{y}{k}[s(i - \pi^e) - x(ep^*/p)] + z(ep^*/p)\frac{\Delta k}{k}$$

Gathering $\Delta k/k$ terms and using expression (2.18a) we finally get

$$g = \frac{u[s(i - \pi^e) - x(ep^*/p)]}{[1 - z(ep^*/p)]} \qquad (2.81)$$

$$g = f(i - \pi^e, ep^*/p)$$

For a given interest rate $(i - \pi^e)$, we can represent equation (2.81) by a downward-sloping schedule, as in figure 2.6.

By imposing the restriction that imports must equal exports we can derive a second expression for the growth rate from the current account. In that case (2.80) will transform into

$$\frac{-y}{k}[x(ep^*/p)] + \frac{\Delta k}{k}[z(ep^*p)] = 0 \qquad (2.82)$$

Figure 2.6   **Growth in a Financially Repressed Open Economy**

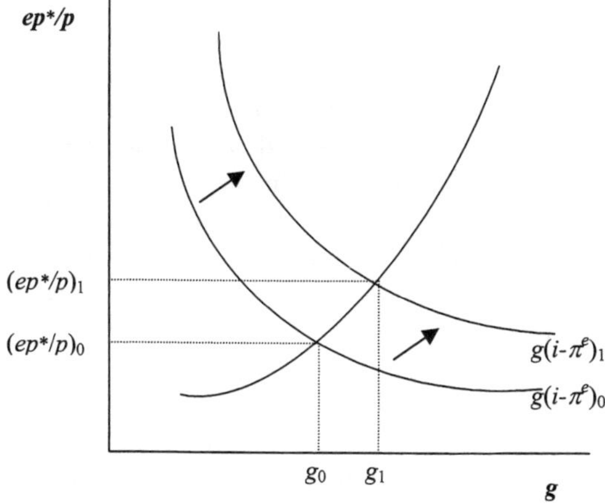

Solving for $\Delta k/k$, we get

$$g = \frac{u[x(ep^*/p)]}{z(ep^*/p)}$$

$$g = g(ep^*/p)$$

which we represent by the upward-sloping schedule of figure 2.6.

If the real exchange rate falls below $(ep^*/p)_0$, the growth rate determined by the current account is binding and we sit to the left of g_0, because at the going exchange rate the economy cannot afford to import the goods it needs to grow faster. When the real exchange rate equals $(ep^*/p)_0$, both constraints are binding and the "repressed" economy grows at the rate g_0. Keeping the real interest rate constant and increasing the real exchange rate would do no good since the economy cannot grow by foreign inputs only, but needs the domestic investment (savings) to build the infrastructure for the inputs to operate. However, a higher interest rate would shift the schedule $g(i - \pi^e)$ to the right, and if combined with a higher real exchange rate, would induce faster growth. This is precisely what McKinnon (1973, chap. 11) and Shaw (1973, chap. 7) advocate. Both view a crawling peg policy and interest rate liberalization as the crucial elements in the optimal financial liberalization program.

2.9 Concluding Remarks

Our full and fair representation of the conventional stabilization and adjustment models seeks to accomplish at least two ends. First, it shows that most of the models that have served as inspiration to the IMF/World Bank policy prescriptions can be embedded in a basic framework. In fact, from the basic framework we have derived different approaches and considered the different instruments of stabilization and adjustment. The analysis shows how most of these approaches complement one another and how occasionally a synthesis emerges among them. In all cases conventional results have been derived. Second, the exposition has permitted us to distinguish the essential elements and assumptions on which each model relies. We believe this is a key means through which the orthodox approach can be opened to scientific scrutiny.

The monetary approaches to the balance of payments, with their explicit links between the monetary and external sector, their emphasis on Walras law and a stable demand function, and the critical assumption that real output is constant, lead to the familiar posture that the balance-of-payments deficit is the result of excess domestic credit. In the Polak version of the monetary approach, nominal and real variables are not separated; therefore, an increase in domestic credit increases nominal income and imports and deteriorates the balance of payments. In the Chicago version nominal and real variables are separated explicitly through the introduction of the domestic price level, so once the extreme assumption of perfect competitive markets, law of one price, and interest rate parity are invoked, the same implications are derived, though the transmission mechanism through which a domestic credit expansion works is much more direct and speedy. The IMF, however, stress the control of inflation as an additional stabilization target. It is the financial programming model, a pragmatic application of the monetary approach, that helps reconcile domestic credit ceilings and exchange rate devaluation as the key instruments to achieving external balance and low inflation. The way the nominal exchange rate is introduced as a policy instrument is assuming that the domestic price level is a weighted average of the price for domestic goods and the exogenous international price. The benefits of an exchange rate adjustment are usually derived from some variety of expenditure-switching mechanism. It is in this sense that the Marshall-Lerner condition becomes crucial.

The absorption approach indicates a complementary way of improving the external balance by reducing income and the level of employment. It also imposes a very popular order of causality from the budget deficit to the current account by assuming that the saving–investment gap has a self-adjusting nature. A flow-of-funds identity justifies the popular assertion that the only way to spend more than one earns is to get credit from someone else: it specifies that to any difference between domestic absorption over income there needs to be a similar difference between foreign-plus-domestic credit expansion and money demand. But, as we noted, perhaps identities are not very meaningful.

In order to give a full reconciliation between the absorption approach (and its income mechanism) and the expenditure-switching mechanism and the monetary approach, we have taken a look behind the identities in order to see what the implicit assumptions and mechanisms are. When combined in this sense, the resulting model serves to validate the assumed expansionary effect that devaluation has on national income. Two versions of this model are explored: a fixed-price/endogenous-interest-rate version and an exogenous-interest-rate/endogenous-price version. Both versions validate in principle the idea that the widespread policy mix of expenditure reduction and devaluation works to restore the external balance without inducing any recessive impact. The latter version allows us to take price level variations as an endogenous variable (driven by output) so that output variations are determined with one eye on reserves variation and the other on inflation.

The IMF/World Bank emphasis on adjustment with growth has been analyzed through a specific derivation of the single basic framework. The resulting model is similar to the integrated IMF/WB model. A growth block in which growth is saving constrained is combined with the fundamental equation of the monetary approach, and supplemented by a balance-of-payments equation similar to the one used in the Keynesian and monetary synthesis. The interesting aspect of the integrated model is that it permits us to visualize the impact of IMF/WB supply-side policies on growth. Supply-side policies as trade liberalization, and the removal of price distortions that try to achieve greater efficiency gains and higher productivity are captured by changes in a parameter representing total factor productivity. Financial liberalization is implicitly captured also by changes in the saving rate. In both cases the results support the case for supply-oriented reforms of the orthodox type.

A specific treatment of the McKinnon and Shaw hypothesis is also derived. In this case, the analysis presented shows how that the presumed good results of financial liberalization rest upon two crucial assumptions: (1) that savings respond positively to real interest rate changes, and (2) that investment is saving constrained. We have shown within the confines of the basic framework how the analysis of the McKinnon–Shaw hypothesis may be reduced to two expressions of the rate of growth of the capital stock. Growth requires both an increase in the real interest rate and an exchange rate adjustment.

Notes

1. There have been some recent attempts to present written material on the IMF/ WB analytical frameworks, but all these representative works are in some sense far from complete and comprehensive (see Khan and Knight 1981; Khan, Montiel, and Haque 1990; Mills and Nallavi 1992; and Tarp 1993).
2. A former advisor of the IMF and after that an executive director of the Bank of England.
3. A chronological exposition would allow us to observe that the policy prescriptions of the Bretton Woods institutions are strongly tied to the development of the macroeconomics for open economies.
4. See, for instance, the World Bank (1989) report on development and financial structure.

5. In response to criticism, the IMF has acknowledged that stabilization and adjustment packages can have strong effects on the distribution of income and social equity and welfare. Steward and FitzGerald (1998) point out that from 1988, each IMF country mission was required to report on the poverty implications of country programs. They also argue that safety nets measures introduced in association with the programs shows that "they are rather ineffective, reaching only a small fraction of those in need" (Steward and FitzGerald 1998, p. 19).

6. For most LDCs this is not a particularly restrictive assumption to make since in these countries markets for government securities are nonexistent or very thin (IMF 1987). Nevertheless, in a number of LDCs, especially in Latin America, we need to take into account the fact that certain controlled, or "captive," nonbank financing sources—such as social security and pension funds, public enterprises, and local government—may provide a substantial portion of government resources.

7. Frenkel subsequently became research director at the IMF.

8. The most important works on the monetary approach are Polak (1957), Mundell (1968), Johnson (1975) and (1977), Frenkel and Johnson (1975), IMF (1977), and IMF (1987).

9. Polak was director of the IMF research department from 1958 to 1979 and also economic counselor to the executive directors.

10. In reference to Polak's original paper, Lance Taylor has said: "Since this paper has guided the practice of IMF missions in scores of country interventions, it is one of the most important pieces of macroeconomics done after Keynes" (Taylor 1987, p. 33).

11. In the words of Polak (1997, p. 4): "the model that the Fund introduced in the 1950s ... appeared to be still very much alive 30 or 40 years later."

12. As Darby (1980) as clearly pointed out, domestic credit exogeneity is one of the key assumptions that provides the monetary approach with its empirical teeth.

13. It is interesting to note that Tsiang (1957), while working at the IMF, pointed out in a study of the Peruvian experiment with floating exchange rates, that the volume of Peru's imports was remarkably closely correlated with the money supply of that country.

14. Monetary flows are in equilibrium at all times, and any excess supply of money is constantly eliminated.

15. We can verify expression (2.28). Total differentiation of (2.26) with respect to time gives us expression (2.27), and after dividing this throughout we get

$$\frac{dR/dt}{M} = \left[\frac{L(y,i)(dp/dt)}{M}\right] + \left[\frac{p\partial L(y,i)}{\partial y}\right]\frac{dy/dt}{M}$$

$$+ \left[\frac{p\partial L(y,i)}{\partial i}\right]\frac{di/dt}{M} - \frac{(dD/dt)}{M}$$

Monetary equilibrium implies that $M = L(y, i)p$. Substituting this into the previous expression we get

$$\frac{dR/dt}{M} = \frac{dp/dt}{p} + \left\{ \left[\frac{\partial L(y, i)}{L(y, i)} \right] \Big/ \partial y \right\} \frac{dy}{dt} + \left\{ \left[\frac{\partial L(y, i)}{L(y, i)} \right] \Big/ \partial i \right\} \frac{di}{dt}$$
$$- \frac{(dD/dt)}{M}$$

Now multiplying top and bottom of the three last terms of the right-hand side by y, i and D respectively, and rearranging terms

$$\frac{(dR/dt)}{M} = \frac{(dp/dt)}{p} + \left[\frac{(\partial L(y, i)/L(y, i))}{(\partial Y)/y} \right] \frac{(dy/dt)}{y}$$
$$+ \left[\frac{(\partial L(y, i)/L)(y, i))}{(\partial i)/i} \right] \frac{(di/di)}{i} - \frac{D}{M} \frac{(dD/dt)}{D}$$

which can be written as (2.28).

16. Under flexible exchange rates the monetary model is identical to the one we set out, with the only difference being that the exchange rate, e, adjusts to respond to market forces. Under a clean float the BOP is zero and the stock of foreign exchange reserves remains constant, so that $dR/dt = 0$. As a consequence the central bank gains complete control over the nominal money stock, as there are no induced reserve flows to alter the money stock from the level set by the central bank through its open market operations. Changes in the exchange rate and the domestic inflation can be analyzed by setting equation (2.28) equal to zero and rearranging terms

$$\hat{p} = (D/M)\hat{D} - (n_y\hat{y} + n_i\hat{i})$$

From this expression it is clear that domestic inflation accelerates when the rate of growth in domestic credit exceeds the rate of growth in the demand for money due to real income and interest rate changes (the term in brackets on the right-hand side of this equation). This result follows directly from the exogeneity of the money stock.

From (2.29) we know that exchange rate changes are given by

$$\hat{e} = \hat{p}^* - \hat{p}$$

Substituting the previous expression into this equation and assuming constant interest rates, we get

$$\hat{e} = \hat{p}^* - (D/M)\hat{D} + n_y y$$

This final expression shows that under flexible exchange rates the behavior of the exchange rate depends on the domestic country's inflation rate *vis-à-vis* other countries, and this in turn depends on domestic monetary policy.

17. We are ignoring second-order terms.

18. Buira (1983) points out that, at least until the early 1980s, decisions on devaluations were of an ad-hoc character.

19. In its simplest form, the elasticities approach is based on some variant of the following oversimplified model. From accounting expressions (2.1) and (2.2) the balance of trade or the current account CA in domestic currency may be expressed as

$$CA = pEX(ep^*/p_d) - ep^*Z(ep^*/p_d, y)$$

where the volume of exports, EX, is now sensitive to changes in the real exchange rate or relative price of traded goods. Assuming that $\partial p/\partial e = 0$ and that $\partial y/\partial e = 0$, we may determine the impact of a change in e on CA as

$$\frac{\partial CA}{\partial e} = \frac{p\partial EX}{\partial e} - p^*e\frac{\partial Z}{\partial e} - p^*Z$$

$$= \frac{pEX}{e}\left(\frac{e}{EX}\frac{\partial EX}{\partial e} - \frac{p^*e^2}{pEX}\frac{\partial Z}{\partial e} - \frac{ep^*Z}{pEX}\right)$$

If we assume initial payments equilibrium $pEX = (ep^*)Z$, then

$$\frac{\partial CA}{\partial e} = \frac{pEX}{e}(|n_x| + |n_{im}| - 1)$$

A rise in e indicates, then, a depreciation of the domestic currency. If $\partial CA/\partial e > 0$, it is required that $n_e + n_{im} - 1 > 0$.

20. Alexander, in 1952 a staff member of the IMF, widely criticized the elasticity approach because it ignored the income–expenditure effects of exchange rates movements. He pointed out that devaluation, for instance, tended to increase production in exports and import-competing industries. Devaluation, therefore, tends to raise national income and the demand for imports.

21. We have assumed away government interest payments to abroad.

22. "The monetary approach to the balance of payments" resembles a similar picture. When the budget deficit is financed by increases in the money supply that exceed the demand for money, and insofar as interest rates are determined internationally, private savings and investment are not affected by the deficit.

23. The law of one price is used here for reasons of analytical and notational simplicity and does not bias the nature of the results.

24. James Meade (1951) gathered monetary and fiscal policies in one category, expenditure policy.

25. Early attempts to reveal the complementary character of the elasticity and absorption approaches can be found in the works of Johnson (1958), Alexander (1959), and Brems (1957). Attempts to combine the elasticity, absorption, and monetary approaches have been made by Chen (1975) and Shieh (1981).

Frenkel, Gylfanson, and Helliwell (1980) provide a synthesis of the monetary and Keynesian approaches to the balance of payments.

26. The IMF, however, recognizes that since devaluation increases the world price level in domestic currency terms, demand-side effects may exist as a consequence of a reduction in real wealth and expenditure (see again IMF 1987, p. 38).

27. In empirical analysis of growth in LDCs, an even simpler form of equations (2.18) is sometimes used, in which z_0 is set equal to zero. The result is the familiar "incremental capital–output relationship" (ICOR).

28. It has also been assumed that the factor $(1 - sz_1)$ is greater than zero, a condition that is unlikely to be violated empirically.

CHAPTER 3

A Critical Appraisal of IMF/World Bank Economic Reasoning

3.1 Introduction

The merit of making explicit the nature of the models upon which stabilization and adjustment policies are based is that it aids the task of criticism. A close look at these models and the observable effects of the policies derived from them provokes in us a sense of insecurity. At least the impetus for subscribing to the conventional policy package is severely diminished, and doubts abound. We argue in this chapter that there are various grounds for questioning the appropriateness of the typical stabilization and adjustment package. As we see it, the weaknesses of economic models can arise basically from three different sources. First, there are theoretical weaknesses that are intrinsic to the models. Second, there are weaknesses that are a result of erroneous premises and assumptions. Finally, weaknesses can be observed at the empirical level when the theory is subject to the historical test.

On the basis of this broad characterization of the potential weaknesses of economic models, we intend to challenge the underlying assumptions and the analytics of the models described earlier, and indicate the practical shortcomings of many components of the orthodox strategies in Latin America. The dominant approaches (with all the changes and substitutions made in them) have been developed in relation to the economic situation of industrial countries, so the perception of reality is distorted by the analytical constructs. Balance-of-payments adjustment, inflation control, and growth (just to mention the ultimate objectives of the orthodox programs) are not amenable to the restrictive vision that has characterized successive generations of dominant macropolicy-oriented models for open economies (upon which stabilization and adjustment are based). The fact of the matter is that these models are extensions of neoclassical macroeconomic theory, in which the historical, institutional, and structural context of LDCs is usually ignored. These differences have major implications for the efficacy of orthodox policy prescriptions. As we will also stress in this chapter, the consideration of the specific characteristics of Latin American economies will often mean that the application of orthodox stabilization and adjustment measures have undesirable and perverse effects. Moreover, as we will also show, the vast experience with orthodox packages in Latin America reveals that these efforts have not achieved any sustained success in terms of explicit and implicit goals.

3.2 Discovering the Pitfalls of the Monetary Approach

3.2.1   The Assumed Dependence upon Walras's Law

The core of the monetary approach is found in its Walrasian belief that an excess demand for money must be matched by an excess supply of something else, namely goods and services, and securities in the aggregate, and that this supply is expressed in a balance-of-payments surplus. Conversely, a balance-of-payments surplus, supposedly reflecting an excess supply of goods and services and securities, must be matched by an excess demand for something else, namely money.

The central criticisms of the monetary approach must be leveled against its dependence upon Walras's Law, i.e. against the claims that excess demand and supplies may exist in each market but are balanced off by other markets. In the real world, theoretical difficulties arise with Walras's Law. These difficulties become relevant when we examine the way in which Walrasians define money and the excess demand for money.

For proponents of Walras's Law, goods (and labor included) are indistinguishable from money as sources of effective demand. Money is not seen as a special commodity with special qualities. But of course it does have special qualities.[1] In a monetary economy (in contrast with a barter economy), no exchange is possible in the market without going through the crucial intermediate step of exchange conduction (where money plays a central role). This general intermediation of money in exchange breaks the link of simultaneity between sale and purchase, so transactions are not simultaneous and expenditures are not synchronized. Since purchases out of money can be postponed to a later date, it makes money not only a medium of exchange but also at least a temporary abode of purchasing power. Consequently, money acts as a medium of not only temporal but also intertemporal exchange. It is in this role of conducting intertemporal exchanges where money acquires its further attribute as a store of value, and not, as orthodox economists suppose, in the context of the Walras's Law. Under Walras's Law the demand for money means the demand for money to hold as an asset after reaching the desired level of demand for commodities and bonds. This is Lange's interpretation of the demand for money under the Walras's Law, which was also passed on to Patinkin and handed down to the Chicago monetarists (Tsiang 1977). As such, Walrasians and followers of the monetary approach not only eliminate the demand for money to spend (which is a basic function of money), but also misunderstand the essential property of money as a store of value by confusing it with an asset value.[2] This unfortunate imprecision with respect to the peculiarities of money has confused the modern monetarists into thinking that an increase (decrease) in the demand for transaction balances would, just like any increase (decrease) in the speculative or asset demand for money, necessarily imply the withholding (or the addition) of a corresponding amount of income from spending.

Treating transaction balances as well as asset balances equally as "money to hold," and referring to any increase in the demand for money balances as "hoarding" is very unfortunate indeed. Defined in this way, any excess demand for money would actually lead to a shortfall of spending compared with income, which in turn will bring about a surplus in the balance of trade. However, if we alternatively consider the demand for money to spend, an excess demand for money (to spend) would generally imply an attempt to spend more than one's income. For in a modern monetary economy, incomes are normally received embodied in the form of money (so are sales receipts of firms). There is therefore no need for any economic agent to seek additional money to spend unless s/he (or it) intends to spend more than her/his (or its) income. So, the fundamental problem is that only a narrow definition of money is particularly suitable to be fitted into the Walras's Law relation.

Walras's Law in the monetary approach can also be confronted by counterexamples. Indeed, counterexamples that refute the identification of payments surplus with an excess demand for money and a payments deficit with an excess supply (this is the central theorem of the monetary approach) are plausible. For example, in countries suffering both a depression at home and a balance-of-payments deficit, the initiating disturbance might be a drop in the foreign demand for the affected country's goods that drains money out of circulation through the payments deficit. Moreover, Rabin and Yeager (1982) present a simple model showing that the link between imbalances in the money market and imbalances in the balance of payments does not hold when nontradeable goods appear in the analysis and disequilibrium in this market prevails. They claim that the monetary approach overlooks the distinction between goods, services, and securities that are internationally traded and those that are purely domestic and not traded, including factors of production. Thus, an excess demand for or supply of money holdings need not be matched by a corresponding imbalance in the market for internationally traded goods, services, and securities, but by an imbalance in the market for nontradeables.

Rabin and Yeager's claim can be easily illustrated by adapting a figure from Mundell (1976). Three equilibrium schedules express the locus combinations of the relative price of nontradeable goods, P_n/P_t, and the money supply, M_s, that result in money market, balance-of-payments and nontradeable market equilibrium. P_t is assumed to be exogenously given by the world level of tradeable goods prices. The line LL is the line along which the demand for money is equal to the supply of money. The curve is upward sloping because an increase in the money stock will be associated with an increase in P_n so that real balances may be maintained at an equilibrium level. The BB line shows that the balance-of-payments equilibrium and its slope are negative because an increase in the money supply will normally be associated with a deficit. To correct the deficit, P_n must be decreased to shift the domestic demand from foreign products to domestic goods. Finally, the NN line is the locus along which there is equilibrium in the market for nontradeable goods. An increase in the money supply creates an excess demand in nontradeables that can be eliminated by an increase in P_n.[3] Figure 3.1 illustrates six possible zones, two of which invalidate the fundamental equation of the monetary approach. In zone 6 there is a balance-of-payments surplus, along with an excess supply of money, while in zone 3 there is a balance-of-payments deficit, along with an excess demand for money. In the depression-and-deficit dilemma (zone 6), for example, an excess demand for money is matched not by excess sales abroad of traded goods but by an excess supply of (or deficient demand for) domestic goods and factors of production. The fundamental equation of the monetary approach is valid if one assumes that the market for nontradeable goods is always clear (the economy will always be on the NN line). By making this assumption, we can eliminate from consideration the two zones where the strong version is invalid.[4]

Rabin and Yeager's (1982) exercise allows us to understand that it is the way in which the underlying structure of the model is formulated, and not the approach per se, that determines how the balance of payments will respond to disturbances in the monetary sector. In the same vein Sau (1992)

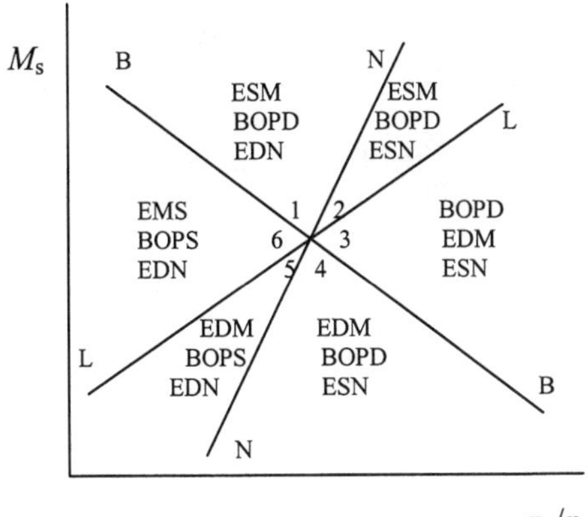

Figure 3.1

ESM = Excess Supply of Money

EDM = Excess Demand for Money

BOPS = Balance-of-Payments Surplus

BOPD = Balance-of-Payments Deficit

ESN = Excess Supply of Nontradeable Goods

EDN = Excess Demand for Nontradeables

shows that if we make some minor changes to the underlying structure of the model, we can refute the central theorem of the monetary approach as well.[5] Sau assumes an endogenous determination of the domestic interest rate (as an equilibrating saving–investment mechanism), and introduces direct foreign investment as an argument of the import demand function. By making direct foreign investment a function of interest rate differentials he shows that a fall in domestic credit increases the domestic interest rates and reduces the level of income. Depending upon coefficients, the effect on the level of imports (and on the change of foreign reserves) that a fall in income can cause may be swamped by that of a rise in the domestic interest rate, leading to a fall in foreign reserves. Thus, a credit reduction can cause a deficit in the balance of payment.

These arguments reveal some of the internal inconsistencies of the monetary framework. In general the proposition that a balance-of-payments deficit implies either dishoarding (by the residents) or credit creation (by monetary authorities) is not necessarily correct. To complement this criticism we can illustrate these inconsistencies by using a simple example. Let us assume an economy with one good, one primary factor, and money. Let us denote the excess demand for goods E_g. In an open economy where there are two sources of demand, foreign and home, exports represents foreign demand, and imports home demand. Suppose additionally for simplicity that wheat is the only commodity that is produced and internationally traded (no capital movements). Let land be a primary factor and a significant component of the agents' wealth, and let there be a given amount of "outside" money circulating in the economy. There are three markets in this economy: wheat, land, and money. By Walras's Law the excess demand in these three markets must match the trade surplus, so that

$$E_g + E_l + (M_d - M_s) = (X - IM) \qquad (3.1)$$

where E_l and $(M_d - M_s)$ denote excess demand for land and money, respectively. It follows that the monetarist assertion that

$$(X - IM) = (M_d - M_s) \qquad (3.2)$$

(i.e. that a balance-of-payments deficit has to be matched by an excess supply of money) is true if and only if $E_g + E_l = 0$. It is evident that this condition is fulfilled only if there is full employment in the economy. If there is, for example, less than full employment, the excess supply of goods will not match any excess demand for land. Therefore, $E_g + E_l > 0$. In this case the Walras's Law can hold, i.e. (3.1) holds, but (3.2) is not true anymore. A trade surplus and/or an excess supply of money matches the deficient demand for wheat and land.

3.2.2 Assessing the Assumed Specification, Stability, and Independence of the Money Demand Function

Additional difficulties derive from the definition of the demand for money used in the monetary approach. It is not just that the demand for money as defined by Walrasians is inconsistent with the conventional definition of the demand for money used by the proponents of the monetary approach; it is also the definition and the presumed stability of the demand for money function itself that can be the target of criticism, especially when we consider the peculiarities of LDCs.

In the Polak version and the financial programming version of the monetary approach, it is conventional to assume a constant velocity of circulation. So long as the velocity of circulation can be postulated to be constant, the equation of exchange (2.25) can be interpreted as being a theory of the demand for money. The idea that money is demanded basically for transactions fits in well with the traditional versions of the quantity theory, and allowed early proponents to formulate a functional relationship between the quantity of money demanded and the nominal income. This relationship was supposed also to be highly stable. In the Chicago version, the demand for money is formulated as a function of real income and the interest rate. The relationship is also presumed to be highly stable. This is indeed a widely accepted form of the money demand function, but strictly speaking it is also unsatisfactory for several reasons that we will describe here.

It is clear that there are some serious problems with assuming velocity to be constant.[6] In fact, this seems to be an article of faith because velocity, at least in Latin American economies, varies over the business cycle, with changes in collective payments, with financial innovation, with social habits (over longer periods), and with the effects of sociopolitical instability. Scheetz (1986) does a 31-year time series analysis of velocity in Peru (from 1950 to 1981), and he does not find the stability that is claimed by followers of the monetary approach. Using GNP/M1, Scheetz finds yearly variations in velocity as high as 25.9 percent,[7] and even using a more stable indicator (national income to M2), the changes found are as high as 13.3 percent. An interesting finding in Scheetz' figures is that instability increases with economic and political problems, just when the IMF steps in. If velocity is not constant, the relationship between money and nominal income becomes uncertain and less predictable, and the setting of monetary targets in stabilization programs (based on any chosen velocity) has to be seriously questioned.

The traditional overprediction of real balances for both developed and less developed countries that show periods of "missing money" has been recently attributed to financial innovation. Recent studies by Arrau, de Gregorio, Reinhart, and Wickham (1991); Melnick (1991); and Copelman (1996) show that ignoring financial innovation is the principal aspect of the stability issue in the money demand equation. Copelman, in particular, estimates the long-run demand for money in Bolivia and Venezuela using cointegration methods with quarterly data from 1980:1 to 1991:4. By introducing a proxy for financial innovation, she shows not only that in the long-run the demand for money shifts down, but also that in the short run the effect of financial innovation has been to increase the speed with which people adjust their actual money holdings to their desired money holdings.[8] This leads to the conclusion that the money demand in these countries was basically unstable.

The specification of the demand for money does not seem to be relevant in the context of LDCs either. First, the view that the demand for money as a medium of exchange is directly related to income is a misleading simplification. This problem derives from Keynes's (1936) tendency to emphasize the demand for money as a medium of exchange solely from the householder's position. Orthodox economists have been misled by this cursory treatment in *The General Theory*, and have specified the transactions balance function as planned household expenditures that depends on income. Keynes himself tried to remedy this misunderstanding by explicitly formulating the "finance motive" (1937). The finance motive strongly suggests that the demand for transaction balances should be related to the amount of expenditure that the public plans to make in a future period, rather than to the total income received or output produced. The introduction of the finance motive concept involves relating the demand for transactions balances to planned, contractual, or expected spending propensities of investors and consumers during the period (Davidson 1978). This means that the demand for money is subject to frequent exogenous and unpredictable disturbances. Total income will affect the transactions demand for money as long as it affects aggregate demand. But if consumers and investors decide to spend more (less) at any flow of income, then there will be an increase (decrease) in the demand for money for the purchase of goods at each level of output.[9]

Secondly, it is certainly not correct to assume that in small open economies so long as national income remains the same, the aggregate volume of trade, expectations of exchange rate changes, expected level of inflation, and financial innovation have no effect on the demand for money, which is what the conventional demand for money function clearly implies. Gathak (1981), Dornbush (1987), Arestis (1988), and several empirical studies of the demand for money in LDCs (Deaver 1970, Campbell 1970, Hynes 1967) lend support to the belief that it is the expected rate of inflation and not the interest rate that is the best proxy for the opportunity costs of holding money. This is motivated by the limited array of financial assets in LDCs, which in turn results in a limited degree of substitution between money and financial assets, and in a high margin of substitution between money and real assets (houses, stocks of foods, durable goods, machinery, etc.). Thus, when inflation is chronic and expected to continue, the increased cost of holding money leads to a reduction of real money demand and to substitution of money for real assets. Tsiang (1977) argues that the volume of trade creates a demand for transaction balances, in addition to income that is not captured by the aggregate level of income of domestic residents. He suggests that changes in the volume of trade relative to national income must have some influence on the demand for money. Arestis (1988) points out that expectations of changes in the exchange rate induce wealth owners to change the composition of their portfolios between foreign and domestic currency, and argues that the demand function will involve currency substitution considerations.[10] As Giovannini and Turtelboom (1994, p. 417) have pointed out, "for Latin American countries, most studies find significant currency substitution." It is important to note that the perceived instability in velocity and money demand functions has led some authors to attribute it to currency substitution.

Here it is important to distil two important implications of this critical analysis of the conventional demand for money. Neither the specifications nor the presumed stability of the demand for money seems to be relevant in the context of LDCs. The recognition of the finance motive prepares us to understand that there is no reason to expect a constant relationship between the demand for money for transaction purposes and the level of output. Additionally, interest rates are not a good proxy for the opportunity cost of holding money. On the other hand, when the demand for money function is assumed to respond to variables such as the planned aggregate expenditure (finance motive), the share of the volume of trade in national income, the expected changes of exchange rate, and expected inflation, it will be an error to expect it to be stable.

In all versions of the monetary approach it is assumed that the demand for money is independent of changes in domestic credit. The conditions for making this assumption are quite stringent since an expansionary open market operation by monetary authorities, for instance, must have no effect on domestic interest rates, spending decisions, or the exchange rate. In addition, it is not possible to assume that the variables that affect the demand for money, particularly real income, are independent of changes in domestic credit unless the period taken as reference is the long run. In the short run, changes in domestic credit can influence output and thus cause shifts in the demand for money since there is no presumption that individuals will be continually on their demand schedules. In other words, if there is a change in any of the variables that influence money holdings, there may be a significant lapse of time before money balances actually adjust to the new level. If there are such lags in adjustment, then assuming continuous equilibrium when projecting the demand for money in the course of an orthodox program would lead to errors that could have significant impact on the credit ceilings. Chandrasekhar (1995) goes even further and illustrates how the equilibria that suggest an inverse relation between fiscal deficit and the change in external assets of the central bank are not the only ones compatible with money market equilibrium.[11] The reason is that the demand for money is not a given. To illustrate this we can use identity (2.10) depicting the balance sheet of the central bank, namely

$$\Delta R = \Delta M_s - \Delta D \qquad (2.10)$$

Since the government's fiscal deficit is financed either by domestic or external borrowing, expression (2.17) applies.

$$(GSI - T) + eINT_g^* = \Delta D_g - e\Delta F_g^* \tag{2.17}$$

Hence,

$$\Delta R = (T - eINT_g^* - GSI + e\Delta F_g^*) + (\Delta M_s - \Delta D) \tag{3.3}$$

It should be clear that a reduction in the fiscal deficit would be accompanied by a reduction in the borrowing of the government, either from the central bank or from the public. If the monetarist assumptions with regard to full employment output and prices do not hold, this could affect the demand for money in two ways: first, the reduction in government expenditure could adversely affect the level of real income; and second, a cut in the government's borrowing from the public could reduce the rate of interest. The two mechanisms have contrary effects on the demand for money. If the interest rate elasticity of the demand for money were low, the net effect would be a decline in the demand for money. This implies that, if money market equilibrium holds, money supply would be lower than it would have been without the cut in the fiscal deficit. In addition, lower interest rates would raise domestic credit to the public. Both these effects, by reducing the second term on the right-hand side of (3.3), could more than neutralize the increase in the first term, consequent to the fiscal deficit cut, and therefore result in a decline in net foreign assets, ΔR.

3.2.3 Full Employment, Exogenous Money Stock, and the Law of One Price

The monetary approach can additionally be assailed for having the unrealistic assumptions of full employment, exogenous domestic money stock, and the law of one price.

The tendency to move toward full employment equilibrium is a unique characteristic of the allocative mode of activity on which neoclassical economics rests. In particular, the allocative mechanism in the labor market ensures a tendency toward full employment equilibrium, while the aggregate price level adjusts to ensure the sufficiency of aggregate demand. Money wages will adjust, in the light of the aggregate price level, to ensure the market-clearing level of real wages in the labor market. This assumption of equilibrium with full employment used in neoclassical economics and passed on to the monetary approach, where the supply side is quietly ignored and prices and wages are assumed to be flexible, is by no means justifiable. Mark-up pricing and rigid wages are not even considered to be possibilities. However, the most significant consequence of the behavior of the industrial sector in capitalist economies is that it creaes a utilization problem for industrial capital, and unemployment of the labor force. Moreover, in the context of LDCs, it is price inflexibility and sluggish demand that develops a tendency for excess capacity (Bharadwaj 1979).

In all models of the monetary approach, money in its domestic (or inside) component is considered to be exogenous, fully under the control of the monetary authority. The monetary approach allows money endogeneity only when variations in the level of international reserves are not perfectly sterilized by the monetary authority. It is the assumed exogeneity of the domestic component of the money stock that ensures the effectiveness of credit restraint. This is nevertheless an extreme position, because the function of central banks is to operate as the bankers' bank, so financial institutions will deal with the central bank only if the latter is sufficiently accommodating. It is not possible, within the space limits of this broad critique of the monetary approach, even to summarize the abundant academic commentaries on the problem of assuming exogenous money. However, it is important to note that the core of the endogeneity thesis is that even in an open economy the domestic money supply is determined by the demand for bank lending, and that this in turn depends upon the level of nominal output. Since the monetary authorities have no alternative but to supply reserves to validate the lending, varying the level of interest rates is the only instrument of monetary control available to the central bank.

As for the purchasing power parity (PPP) theorem, there are sound analytical and empirical reasons for skepticism about the propositions that it must hold. The existence in all countries of nontraded goods and services whose prices are not linked internationally allows systematic deviations from the theorem represented in equation (2.35). International differences in consumption patterns will also impose significant impediments to the PPP theorem if national price levels do not place the same weights on the prices of different goods. Imperfectly competitive market structures that involve discriminatory pricing do not favor the PPP theorem either. In fact, the combination of product differentiation and segmented markets leads to departures from the law of one price. All these elements undermine the belief that, in a fixed exchange rate system, competition of profit-maximizing firms (or traders) leads to price equalization. At the empirical level there has been considerable dissatisfaction with the PPP. Years ago Williamson

(1983, p. 60) summarized most of the empirical scrutiny in this way: "The hypothesis... has probably been rejected more decisively by empirical evidence than any other hypothesis in the history of economics." In a recent review article Rogoff (1996, p. 650) concludes: "commodities where deviations from the law of one price damp out very quickly are the exception rather than the rule."

There have been relatively few econometric evaluations of PPP for Latin American countries. As far as we know only McNown and Wallace (1989), Liu (1992), Leon and Oliva (1992), Mahdavi and Zhou (1994), and Liu and Burkett (1995) have tested PPP using multicountry data from Latin America. Liu, employing nonstationary and cointegration tests, accepted the PPP as the Johansen test results show that there is at least one cointegrating relationship among the price indexes and the nominal exchange rate for all nine countries involved.[12] Similar results are obtained by McNown and Wallace's time-series analysis of monthly data for Argentina, Brazil, Chile, Mexico, Peru, and Uruguay. Mahdavi and Zhou (1994) have applied cointegration tests and error correction models to five Latin American countries using quarterly data for the modern floating exchange rate era, with results supporting long-run PPP in all five cases. These general affirmative results contrast with those obtained by Leon and Oliva (1992) and Liu and Burkett (1995). Leon and Oliva (1992) use the variance ratio statistic to gauge the stationary component in the real exchange rate, as well as the real exchange rate dynamics after a shock occurs. The nominal exchange rate and/or the internal price index does not fully adjust to the inflation differentials since the results show that the real exchange rate can be modeled as a quasi-stationary process with a significant mean-reverting component that cancel out part of the shock. Thus, short-run deviations from PPP are not completely offset in the long run.[13] Liu's and Burkett's concern is that even assuming a long-run PPP relationship to the short-run concerns of policymakers depends not only on the average time of adjustment toward this relationship, but also on how unstable this speed of convergence is in the short run. Based on time-varying parameter estimates of error correction models and using quarterly data for Argentina, Chile, Colombia, and Mexico vis-à-vis, the United States, the study revealed extreme instability in short-run PPP adjustments. Parameter estimates have rather high variances and appear to have directly contradicted the PPP hypothesis during a substantial number of quarters. Since a conclusive answer to the validity of the PPP has never come up, a better approach would be to investigate what determines the price in each country's own currency.[14]

3.2.4 The Impact of Credit Restraint

The monetary approach suggests that, in the long run, a reduction in the level of domestic credit (in a small open economy) will be completely offset by international reserve flows that restore the money stock to its initial level, so that such a policy has no effect on the equilibrium level of output. This proposition is rather difficult to swallow. It is hard to imagine a situation, short of full employment, in which expansion or contraction of credit has no impact on production and income in the economy. The problem is that this adjustment process frequently operates through a reduction in the rate of capacity utilization and a rise in unemployment. The Chilean experience during 1981–82 is illustrative. In 1981, tight money and high real interest rates were used in an attempt to correct the external imbalance. Real GDP fell by approximately 15 percent in 1982–83, investment collapsed, and open unemployment rates climbed to almost 20 percent (Solimano 1993). Moreover, the recent awareness of the importance of working capital in LDCs has seeped into the theoretical models of stabilization, and has produced results that are contrary to the standard view.[15] For instance, a fall in the money supply will cause a rise in the interest rate, and hence an increase in the amount of interest cost on working capital. The normal business response would be to cut back on activity and attempt to pass higher interests on through higher prices.[16] It is instructive to note, then, that the orthodox credit restraint policy, as often imposed by the IMF, can be counter-productive with respect to both output and inflation.

There is a further aspect in which the underlying dynamic adjustment process of credit restraint does not permit any improvement in the initial excess demand gap of the economy but a higher price level. Bhaduri (1992), for instance, points out that a restriction on domestic credit availability will affect both the demand and the supply side simultaneously through different routes. According to Bhaduri, it is reasonably well understood that credit restriction and a sharp reduction of government deficit will typically lead to contraction of aggregate demand. However, it is not always understood that credit restraint may also reduce supply. Current and potential production of the economy can be reduced due to reductions of credit for working capital, for financing inventories (which constrain supply less directly by creating more frequent bottlenecks), and for fixed investment. Thus, starting from an initial position of excess demand, which a stabilization scheme presumably tries to control, if, as a result of credit restraint, supply falls more steeply that demand, the excess demand gap will worsen. The argument can be demonstrated by using conventional aggregate demand and supply function in which domestic credit, D, is included as an argument. Thus, in equilibrium

$$AD(p, D) = AS(p, D) \tag{3.4}$$

Total differentiation yields

$$AD_{\mathrm{p}}\, dp + AD_{\mathrm{D}}\, dD = AS_{\mathrm{p}}\, dp + AS_{\mathrm{D}}\, dD \tag{3.5}$$

Rearranging terms we have

$$\frac{dp}{dD} = \frac{AS_{\mathrm{D}} - AD_{\mathrm{D}}}{AD_{\mathrm{p}} - AS_{\mathrm{p}}} \tag{3.6}$$

Under "normal" market conditions, the denominator of the above expression is unambiguously negative, since $AD_{\mathrm{p}} < 0$ and $AS_{\mathrm{p}} > 0$. We have also assumed that $AS_{\mathrm{D}} > 0$ and $AD_{\mathrm{D}} > 0$. Thus, if the numerator is positive, meaning a higher response of the aggregate supply function to domestic credit restraint, greater credit restriction must imply a higher market clearing price level.

Monetary restraint can also affect income distribution over the medium and long terms, through changes in the distribution of assets. In many cases, credit restraint strengthens the position of large relative to small enterprises, since the former depend more on retained profits than the latter. Most often credit restraint discriminates in favor of larger enterprises, forcing their smaller counterparts into the informal credit market, where higher interest rates prevail. Moreover, the largest companies may be able to meet their financing needs through international capital markets, and on more favorable terms than those prevailing in domestic markets may. Larger enterprises would be placed at an advantage, with bankruptcy among smaller units leading inevitably to increasing asset concentration.

3.2.5 The Devaluation Case: The Trade Balance, Inflation and Income Distribution

Reference was made in the frame of the financial programming model to the key importance attached to exchange rate policy. The BP line will exhibit a negative slope in the $\Delta R - \Delta p_{\mathrm{d}}$ if the Marshall-Lerner condition holds. It is the dichotomy between exportable and importable goods that allows the exchange rate to become the mechanism for altering their price ratios. In this case, if the sum of the demand price elasticity of imports and exports is greater than one, devaluation is supposed to improve the trade balance (and the Marshall-Lerner condition is met). However, there are reasons to believe that some of the assumptions and the theoretical conditions (such as the Marshall-Lerner condition) are not met by Latin American countries, specifically in those low-income primary exporting countries such as the Central American countries, as well as Bolivia, Ecuador, Paraguay, and Guyana in South America. In these countries, primary exports may respond only slowly, if at all, to price incentives if the gestation period between decisionmaking and output is long (Knight 1976), or if it takes several years before investments in agriculture or mineral extraction produce increases in output (Loxley 1986).[17] The availability of land, the system of land tenure, and the lack of access to funds and technical knowledge impose serious constraints on the expansion of agricultural exports. In some countries the existence of sources of exploitable raw materials can increase the uncertainties concerning the response of exports (Crockett 1981). For example, in countries where crude petroleum constitutes the main source of foreign earnings (such as Venezuela, Mexico, or Ecuador), devaluation has no impact on the volume of exports. Thus, the usual assumption that exports supply will react passively to demand usually does not apply.[18]

Thirwall (1988) has argued that demand elasticities have a time dimension, and that it can take time for demand to adjust sufficiently to changes in relative prices (and the sum of the elasticities will not be greater than unity). Even if the sum of demand elasticities is greater than one, Thirwall argues, currency devaluation (or depreciation) may still not be effective because supply elasticities also matter as determinants of the terms of trade. As demonstrated by Stern (1973), if the product of the supply elasticities of exports and imports exceeds the product of the demand elasticities, the terms of trade will decline with a devaluation, real income will fall, and the balance of payments will worsen (if expenditure does not fall by as much as real income). This makes the Marshall-Lerner condition much more stringent, if devaluation is interpreted as one that improves the trade balance without real income's being reduced.

Additionally, the demand for exports may be a derived demand and therefore fairly inelastic with respect to price; thus, a devaluation would not generate greater demand for the product exported (Meller 1987). Protectionism in industrial countries (the main market for Latin American exports) will also contribute to a low elasticity of demand for exports. Better profitability for domestic export producers will mean a threat to employment with specific "safeguard actions" on the part of industrial countries. Sarkar (1991) has argued that the demand for LDCs' exports is a function of economic development in industrial countries in whose case demand will be insensitive to price changes.

On the other hand, the demand for imports can be inelastic with respect to price if imports consist mainly of essential foodstuffs, noncompetitive capital, and intermediate inputs for which it is difficult to find substitutes in the production process. There is some econometric evidence that shows that devaluation had no effect on import demand in Jamaica (Gafar 1982). Furthermore, where all nonessential imports have already been curtailed, imports will not be discouraged by devaluation (Singh 1986).

In the presence of intermediate imports in the production of domestic goods, the increase in the cost of production of domestic goods might prevent the expected increase in the ratio of internal prices to external prices.[19] Even in the absence of intermediate inputs, full nominal wage indexation is sufficient to prevent a change in relative prices. If nominal wages are tied to the consumer price index, then devaluation will increase nominal wages and the price of domestic goods by the full amount of devaluation. This will happen where organized labor predominates so that it is possible that responses on the part of unions to maintain real wage levels will erode the nominal devaluation and reduce the extent of expenditure switching. Many observers, such as Kaldor (1983), drawing largely on the Latin American experience, maintain that devaluation cannot usually change critical wage–price relationships, which are the outcome of social and political forces. Thus, the presence of imported intermediate inputs and upward nominal wage flexibility imposes severe limitations to exchange rate adjustments.

The connection between devaluation and inflation is also well known.[20] An easy way to show this connection is to assume that the price of home goods is determined by a markup on unit cost. If intermediate imports are required for the production of home goods, then the devaluation-induced rise in intermediate imports prices will increase output prices. This is a logical enough outcome when we consider that, to maintain a constant markup or a desired level of profitability, firms must increase their output price. However, if nominal wages remain fixed, firms need not increase output price as rapidly as the increase in import costs. But since devaluation reduces the real wage of the working class, it inevitably leads to compensating wage demands. Such demands, if they are not met, will produce political conflicts; on the other hand, if they are met, this will fuel inflation and thus require even more nominal devaluation, and the process will then repeat itself. As Thirwall (1989, pp. 13–14) has correctly pointed out, the orthodox recipe "would imply that continuous currency depreciation is necessary to raise permanently the growth rate of exports or to reduce permanently the growth rate of imports." If pursed for any length of time, then, devaluation becomes the route to high inflation, as the experience of many Latin American countries clearly demonstrates.[21]

But these are not the only channels through which devaluation can induce output price increases. Foxley (1983) has argued that once oligopolistic firms anticipate the inflationary consequences of devaluation, overcompensation will "overshoot" output prices. We can also mention that devaluation can exert upward pressures on prices by raising the domestic currency price of exports. To the extent that local currency prices of exports are raised as a result of devaluation, increases in the prices of competing commodities, such as foodstuffs, can be expected to follow.

Thus, it is not an accident that the orthodox programs of devaluation in many LDCs have led to a worsening of inflationary conditions and serious political conflict.

More recently, and based on the experience of stabilization in Latin America, structuralist economists have pointed out that if a devaluation creates expectations of further devaluations, the trade balance will deteriorate, making the elasticities approach irrelevant (see Arellano 1986). Based on the same experience, Sarkar (1991) points out that IMF/World Bank programs suffer from a type of "fallacy of composition." Within IMF/World Bank programs each country in the region is expected to increase its exports by devaluation. This will lead to a spiral of competitive devaluation among countries producing the same type of exports. If the expansion in exports occurs, the result will be a price crash. Sarkar cites the examples of Peru, Chile, Zambia, and Zaire, two Latin American and two African countries whose major export is copper; Devaluation of their domestic currencies under IMF pressure in 1975 produced over-production and a price crash.

In economies with abundant inflationary experience and organized urban workers (and such is the case in several Latin American countries), indexation forms part of the labor contracts in the modern sector, and is part of the wage policy employed by the government. If indexation exists, then one could argue that the fall in real wages is transitory. However, this is not entirely correct. Since nominal wages are adjusted periodically and not instantaneously, what matters is not the adjusted real wage but the average real wage between the periods of adjustment.[22] Under inflationary conditions the average real wage (between periods of adjustment) will be lower than the periodically adjusted real wage. Therefore, in either case it is apparent that the real wage will decline in most instances of "successful" devaluation, causing a reduction of the standard of living of the working class.

This regressive income distribution also has some further effects. Regressive income distribution may undermine labor intensity and hence productivity due to the declining real wages and increased social conflict. Moreover, as van der Hoeven (1987, p. 141) asserts, "extremely low wages are matched by low worker morale, low efficiency and rapid expansion of second jobs to supplement falling incomes, setting in motion a downward spiral of lower wages and lower productivity."

The effects of devaluation on income distribution can be even more complex. Demery and Addison (1987) have pointed out that if exchange rate adjustment has its major impact through reduced absorption, the income distribution implications of expenditure switching would be of only marginal relevance. Devaluation reduces absorption at a high cost in unemployment and rapid inflation. The direct effects of devaluation on domestic absorption arise by way of a number of possible mechanisms, among which the most important are: (a) reductions in real incomes, resulting from higher price levels that constrain household consumption levels, leading to reduced aggregate demand;[23] (b) income redistribution from wages to profits, which results in a fall in the level of aggregate expenditure; and (c) the domestic cost of servicing foreign debt denominated in foreign currency. All things considered, then, the effect of devaluation on absorption and income distribution is likely to be extremely negative.

In general the arguments just mentioned raise serious doubts about the effectiveness of devaluation in the conventional elasticities framework, and indicate the potentially severe inflationary and income distribution consequences of exchange rate adjustments.

Empirical studies that appear to be in conflict with the "pessimist" view of the effects of devaluation on the trade balance concentrate their attention on the value of the elasticities (Kahn 1974); the price ratio between tradeables and nontradeables (Cooper 1971, Cannoly and Taylor 1976); and export performance (Bhagwat and Onitsuka 1974). The findings in each of these studies are very much influenced, however, by the presence in the sample of countries with significant industrial capacity and established export markets (Loxley 1986). In Khan's study all but one of the 15 countries studied have manufacturing sectors that, as early as 1960, contributed between 12 and 20 percent of GDP. Bhagwat and Onitsuka themselves use in their sample countries with highly developed manufacturing sectors. Cooper's study (of 24 devaluations in 19 countries) includes 11 of the 15 countries sincluded in Khan's study, but Cooper also includes industrial countries and some major exporters of manufactures.

Brailovsky (1981) collects information from 13 countries with the purpose of analyzing the relationship between exchange rate movements and external competitiveness. He distinguishes between "developed" and "underdeveloped" countries, even though he includes in the second category four of the so-called NICs (new industrialized countries); Hong Kong, Korea, Brazil, and Singapore. By focusing on the relative share of each country in the market for manufactured goods, he finds that for four cycles of the world economy between 1960 and 1977, devaluation did not improve the relative share of any of these countries. Moreover, in countries where the exchange rate appreciated in at least two subsequent periods (like Korea and Hong Kong), increasing market share for manufactured goods was observed. On the other hand, in countries like the United Kingdom the relative market share sharply declined, even though the pound in real terms depreciated in two of the four periods of study.

Thirwall (1988) claims that the historical evidence between 1977 and 1985 shows that massive nominal exchange rate realignments have not rectified payments disequilibrium. He uses data of current account balance and changes in exchange rates from six industrial countries. The record seems to demonstrate that countries remained remarkably impervious to large changes in exchange rates. However, Thirwall's evidence is subject to some of the same criticisms raised earlier. He focuses on industrial countries, and he does not determine the significance of his results.

A more recent study by Sarkar (1991) attempts to examine whether a higher percentage rate of real devaluation is associated with higher rate of growth in export volumes. For a selected group of 29 countries, covering all the highly indebted countries, data were collected between the two periods 1980–82 and 1983–86. Simple regression analysis finds no statistically significant relationship between the percentage rates of real devaluation and the percentage changes in export volumes.

Gylfason and Radetzki (1991) use a sample of 12 LDCs (mostly African countries) and find that devaluation can be an effective tool for rectifying current account deficits.

Thus, with regard to the effects of devaluation on the trade balance, some scholars suggest modest short-term improvement in the current account while others argue that there is no improvement at all. In general, the findings of these studies are subject to considerable variation due to the different criteria employed when choosing the relevant variables, the sample of countries, the time period, and the statistical method.

A number of cross-countries empirical studies have been undertaken to assess whether the IMF-supported programs have led to an improvement in balance of payments and current account balances. These studies use a variety of methodologies and cover different country samples and time periods.[24] Using the before–after approach Reichmann and Stillson (1978), for instance, examined a total of 79 Fund-supported programs implemented during 1963–72. Using nonparametric statistical tests they found that a significant improvement in the balance of payments was achieved in only about a quarter of programs. Connors (1979), Killick (1984), and Zulu and Nsouli (1985) conducted similar analyses, and their results show no statistically significant effects of Fund-supported programs on the balance of payments or the current account. In another cross-country study, Pastor (1987) uses data from 18 Latin American countries. He analyzes the current account as a percentage of GNP in both countries under Fund-supported programs and those that were not. He finds no significant improvement in the current account ratios after an IMF program (for the period 1965–81). Pastor also finds that the change in the current account ratio is larger (more positive) for program countries than for nonprogram countries, but the overall significance level of this result is very weak (at 0.402). Killick, Malik, and Manuel (1995) updated and extended the earlier Killick (1984) study. In examining the effects of programs in 16 countries over the period 1979–85, they found an improvement in the balance of payments.

To overcome the inability of the before–after approach to distinguish between program and nonprogram determinants of macroeconomic outcomes Donovan (1982) uses the with–without approach and finds a little positive impact of Fund-supported programs on the current account. He investigates the movements of the balance-of-payments position during Fund-supported stabilization programs between the years 1971 and 1980. Donovan focuses on the current account deficit as a percentage of GNP, finding that in eight of the ten years considered, countries experienced larger average reductions (or smaller increases) in their deficits than did all non-oil less-developed countries. But he uses no statistical method to determine the significance of the results. Gylfanson (1987) also uses a version of the with–without approach and finds that program countries experience statistically significant improvements in the ratio of the balance of payments to GDP.

Problems with the before–after approach has led to the development of an empirical approach that uses a nonrandom selection of program countries, identifies the specific differences between program and nonprogram countries in the pre-program period, and then controls for these differences in initial positions in the comparison and subsequent economic performance. The evidence of the impact of Fund-supported programs on the trade balance (and other target variables) using this methodology is rather inconclusive. Goldstein and Montiel (1986) found that program countries systematically demonstrated no significant improvement in the current account and balance of payments. Kahn (1990), using a much larger sample, found that there was an improvement in the balance of payments, but this improvement was statistically significant only when the period of evaluation took place at least two years after the inception of the program. Conway (1994) applied a modified generalized evaluation estimator for a sample of 217 programs implemented during 1976–86 and found that the current account improved in the context of a Fund-supported program.

Of course, the results obtained are not exempt from criticism and limitations. It should be remembered, for instance, that not all IMF programs under study recommended devaluation and that eventually current account movements might well respond to other types of demand management policies. In fact these cross-country empirical studies of Fund-supported programs make no distinction between programs that implement a currency devaluation and those that do not.

3.2.6 Devaluation and Output Contraction

Orthodox theoretical treatments of currency devaluation generally conclude that it stimulates economic activity. This prevailing view is clearly drawn from the analysis of the elasticity-absorption synthesis (as we saw in the previous chapter). This expansionary output effect of exchange rate devaluation leads IMF/World Bank scholars to believe that it tends to offset the deflationary consequences of restrictive demand-management policy.

The conventional conclusion that, by itself, devaluation is likely to be expansionary has come under attack from both orthodox and structuralist economists.

On the orthodox side, Dornbusch (1973), among others, has pointed out that in a small open economy, where the domestic price level is determined entirely by the outside world (through the purchasing power parity equation), an exchange rate change can affect only the purchasing power of assets denominated in local currency. By reducing the real money stock and increasing the interest rate (which in turn lowers investment) devaluation has a deflationary impact. Cline (1983) argues that recession can come from decreased consumption through the real balance (Pigou) effect. But Johnson (1972) argues that since currency devaluation improves the trade balance, the real money stock will be reestablished in the long run. Therefore, this sort of criticism will ultimately apply in the short run.

In a more structuralist vein, currency devaluation can be contractionary for several reasons. Here we can distinguish between demand side and supply side effects. On the demand side, if the country is in deficit and the increment in import spending is greater than the export revenues, then real income and output will decline (Hirschmam 1949).[25] In certain circumstances devaluation may also redistribute income from workers to capitalists, causing output contraction. To detail this process, recall that if imported inputs are an important component of cost, devaluation will mean higher domestic prices. If money wage rates stay constant, then the purchasing power of labor income declines and the income distributions shift toward profits. If the saving rate from profit income exceeds that from wages, then consumption demand declines and the familiar trade improvement by economic contraction follows (Diaz Alejandro 1963, Krugman and Taylor 1978).[26] Redistribution could be contractive when the government has a unitarian propensity to save in the short run and income is transferred from the private to the public sector (Krugman and Taylor 1978). A third contractive redistribution from local to foreign capitalists can take place when export and import competing industries belong to foreign capitalists and a devaluation increases the transfer of profits abroad (Barbone 1984). Devaluation can also have financial effects, which in turn can affect the amount of domestic investment. If, as a result of a currency devaluation, firm liabilities in foreign currency increase more than the value of the capital stock, then the access to credit can be affected, as can the level of investment (Easterly 1985). In sum, the demand effects of the impact of a devaluation on the level of economic activity offer a variety of transmission mechanisms (real income fall, income redistribution, or financial effects) in which the main result can be output contraction.

On the supply side we find at least three important reasons to believe that devaluation will not be expansionary. First, the greater the share of imported inputs in the production of tradeables and nontradeables, the lower the impact of an exchange rate devaluation on the level of output (Bruno 1979). Second, in the case in which the consumption basket of workers contains either final imported goods or goods whose inputs are imported, devaluation will decrease the real wage. If nominal wages are adjusted the result will be output contraction (Solimano 1986b). Finally, the recent awareness about the importance of working capital in LDCs has raised doubts about the validity of standard theorems. A devaluation can reduce the real volume of credit available to finance working capital, which in turn will reduce output (Sau 1988). Thus, the most important conclusion of the analysis of the impact of devaluation on the supply side is that it can be equivalent to an adverse supply-side shock.

Additionally, longer-term effects of devaluation in output may include a further output loss and import saving as investment demand falls off in response to lagging economic activity. The decrease in capital formation may be especially sharp if firms have borrowed heavily abroad and the cost of their dollar-denominated debt is sharply increased by devaluation. But devaluation can also depress private investment in nontradeable activities if the import content is high, and if the real cost of inputs in terms of domestic goods increases (Branson 1986). We should note that this seems to be the case for highly indebted countries in Latin America. A third channel through which devaluation may affect investment is by its impact on aggregate demand. If devaluation is contractionary then the slump in economic activity is likely to form the basis for investors to cut investment spending (Serven and Solimano 1993).

The empirical evidence on the contractionary effects of devaluation is not abundant, but it is more conclusive. One of the first empirical studies on this topic is Diaz Alejandro (1965). In particular, this author focuses on the Argentinean episodes of devaluation during the period 1955–61. Diaz Alejandro finds that the effects of devaluations were highly consistent with the view that emphasizes contraction coming from income redistribution (from wages to profits).[27] A few years after the Diaz Alejandro study, Cooper in his 1971 study of 19 industrial and less-developed countries concludes that devaluations were followed by reductions in the level of economic activity.

More recent studies including Edwards (1986); Solimano (1986a); Kamas (1992); and Nazmi, Samaniego, and Lafuente (1998); tend to confirm the contractionary effects of devaluation. Edwards estimates an output equation whose arguments are the real exchange rate, the terms of trade, and variables for fiscal and monetary policy. He selected data from a sample of 12 LDCs between 1965 and 1980, and his results show that devaluations have a contractive effect in the short run, a slight expansionary effect in the "medium term," and a neutral effect in the long run. Solimano uses a macromodel with dynamic adjustments of import and export flows combined with supply mechanisms (such as wage indexation and the presence of imported input in the production of tradeables). The model is simulated for the Chilean economy and shows that a devaluation, *ceteris paribus*, will be followed by output contraction. Kamas specifies a macroeconomic model for Colombia (1967–89) and then simulates the impact of devaluation for given estimates of the parameters and elasticities of the model. While the simulations suggest that devaluation is expansionary, her results indicate that it is possible that for countries with larger shares of primary exports or imported inputs, or with smaller export price elasticities, devaluation could be contractionary. Nazmi, Samaniego, and Lafuente (1998) use time-series analysis and annual data from the economy of Ecuador over the period 1965–95 to test for the impact of the real exchange rate on private investment. They use a four-variable vector autoregressive model (VAR) and find that within the right cointegrating vector the exchange rate has a negative and significant impact on private investment. The short-run error correction representation finds the same impact (with one lag) on the rate of growth of private investment.

To our knowledge, Gylfason and Schmid (1983) is the only empirical study that emphasizes dominant expenditure switching effects. These authors employ a macromodel that combines supply and demand mechanisms. They try to study the impact that devaluation has on the level of economic activity by focusing on a sample of ten industrialized and semi-industrialized countries. The empirical evaluation of the main parameters of the model seems to indicate that devaluation will increase real income in eight of the ten countries.

In sum, the empirical evidence can contradict the traditional belief that devaluation is regarded as an expenditure-switching measure (which could be combined with an offsetting expenditure-reducing policy). What we have seen is that devaluation itself may have an output- or expenditure-reducing effect.

3.3 *The Inappropriateness of Absorption Analysis and Fiscal Restraint*

The simple model implicit in the fundamental equation of the monetary approach can also be put in a more general framework by explicitly considering income and expenditure relationships. The absorption approach states that the gap between income and absorption is equal to the current account. From the way the model is presented, however, the unfortunate impression is given that it is plans to produce that are causal in the explanations of trade imbalances or deficits, whereas in practice this may not be the case. Sometimes it is very tricky to infer causation from identities.

The absorption approach implies that $(X - IM)$ is identically equal to $(Y - A)$; that is, a deficit implies that absorption exceeds the money value of national income, or that $I > S$ (that total investment exceeds total saving). In other words, the economy would be "overheated" and demand deflation would be required. Clearly, however, an autonomous fall in exports, an autonomous rise in imports, or an autonomous secular or cyclical deterioration in the real terms of trade may have caused the trade deficit in the first instance. Therefore, the deficit confronting LDCs might be misperceived. It is precisely in this case that the absorption approach, based on an identity, could be partly responsible for a bad diagnosis.

Bacha (1983), in his critique of the IMF stabilization program signed by Brazil in 1982, argues that the Brazilian balance-of-payments crisis did not correspond to an excess demand, as the IMF claimed at that time. Exports declined because of the global recession in 1982 and not due to excess demand. However, the IMF recommended economic contraction in order to reduce the external deficit. The cost of this bad diagnosis was extremely high. In order to improve the trade balance by $5.2 billion (between 1982 and 1983), the required fall in output had to be three times greater, which implied a reduction in domestic demand to intolerable levels. This is the typical example of "overkill" a term that refers to a greater loss of output than is necessary to achieve adjustment.

Eatwell and Singh (1981) analyze the Mexican case of external desequilibrium (before the debt crisis) to conclude that the orthodox interpretation that points to excess demand (generated by the oil boom) as the unique cause of external deficits is incorrect. Against the "overheating thesis," Eatwell and Singh argue that the trade balance deterioration was attributed to the fall in Mexican exports in the late 1970s (of 8 percent) as a consequence of the contraction of American imports and to the general contraction in foreign markets.

That the IMF has put too much emphasis on internal adjustment via demand deflation for eliminating balance-of-payments deficit is beyond any doubt. The IMF's deflationary policies in Latin America are abundant. In Argentina, for instance, at the end of a five-year stabilization period, 1958 to 1963, the country's GDP was 2 percent lower than its initial level (Sarkar 1991). Some other countries, such as Chile and Peru, faced similar declines in their per-capita incomes during the period of IMF stabilization programs (Korner *et al.* 1984). In general, these policies lead to short-term adjustment in the balance of payments at the cost of increasing unemployment and reduction in growth rates or even an absolute reduction in GDP.

Once the appropriate degree of improvement in the balance of payments has been decided upon, and the associated reduction in net domestic absorption determined, the question arises of how this aggregate result is to be achieved. The IMF's answer rests on fiscal and monetary restraint. We will concentrate our attention first on fiscal restraint, since we have already discussed the matters of monetary restraint.

From identity (2.53) we know that orthodoxy assumes that an external imbalance is the consequence of the government budget deficit. Using this kind of argument, the IMF, and to some extent the World Bank (in its structural adjustment lending facilities), believes that what has to be done to solve the problem of external imbalance is to eliminate the fiscal deficit.[28]

Nevertheless, the relationship between fiscal deficit and trade balance deficit in either developed or less-developed countries is not uniform. Econometric tests for Latin America do not evidence a statistically significant association between government deficits and current account problems (Pastor 1987 and 1989).[29] Bhattacharya (1991) shows that there is no systematic relationship between the public sector saving-investment gap and the current account deficit in India during the 1980s. FitzGerald (1980), in an interesting analysis of the accumulation balance in Mexico, demonstrates that the effect of an increase in aggregate demand resulting from a budget deficit is to raise private savings, leaving private investment and the trade balance unaffected in the short run. Therefore, the preliminary lesson to be learned is that a zero fiscal deficit does not guarantee a zero trade account deficit, and similarly a balance external account does not automatically imply zero fiscal deficit.

The association between the external and the fiscal gap can also be misleading if causality is assumed from the fiscal to the external front (as orthodoxy does). For example, it is possible to have an economy, even with a fiscal surplus, in which the external imbalance originates in a sudden worsening of the terms of trade; and in this case, it is the deterioration in the trade balance that could transform a fiscal surplus into a fiscal deficit through a decline in tax collection generated by a loss of earnings in the exports sector. This could have been the case for the major primary exporter countries in Latin America during the 1980s. For example, in countries like Venezuela and Ecuador, where government revenues depend heavily on taxes from oil earnings, a steady fall in the price of oil from $35 to almost $12 between 1981 and 1986 severely damaged government finances. It is also possible that the maturity pattern of the government debt and the volatile behavior of foreign interest rates might increase the size of the public deficit. Somehow, the whole region faced this problem in the late 1970s and early 1980s, when a strong shift in the maturity pattern of government external debt, plus a dramatic increase in interest rates (and interest payments), imposed a severe burden on the budgetary position of the public sector.[30]

In the two cases mentioned above the budget deficit is a direct consequence of the balance-of-payments constraint (Singh 1986), and though a relaxation of that constraint will improve the budgetary position, the converse unfortunately is not necessarily true.

Steindl (1985) has advanced a similar point of view on the endogeneity of the fiscal deficit in capitalist economies. Steindl argues that while it is possible, in principle, to control the volume of government spending or taxation, the same is not true for the budget deficit. The budget deficit is not an active element incurred on purpose by the government, but "it is likely to play a passive role, and to be dominated by other sectors" (p. 161). Consequently any attempt to reduce it through retrenchment are mostly doomed to failure. The reasons are straightforward. In countries where the foreign balance takes large values the budget deficit will be largely determined by the amount of private investment and the foreign balance. An increase in taxation or a decrease in government spending leads, through a decline in income and employment (automatic stabilizers), to smaller household net lending and higher budget deficits and net foreign demand.[31]

If the orthodox view prevails, however, countries will have to reduce their fiscal deficits. Even assuming that fiscal retrenchment improves the trade balance picture, the improvement will probably be at the cost of recession. To appreciate this point we can go back to expression (2.53) and rearrange it as follows:

$$S_p = I_p + (GN - T) + (X - IM) \tag{3.7}$$

Equation (3.7) indicates that the private sector's assets can take the form of physical capital or financial claims on the public sector or on the rest of the world. If the fiscal deficit is reduced, there is an incipient excess of private savings over the uses of savings on the right-hand side of the equation. In effect, the economy starts to save more than needs to be saved, and aggregate demand goes down. The result is a reduction in economic activity, as the public spends less. In LDCs, as we have argued, imports are largely used as inputs in the production process. With less production, fewer imports will be required and the trade deficit will decline. As Lance Taylor (1987, p. 39) has stated, "the improvement comes from recession, not from relative price shifts or accounting magic, as maintained by the IMF." Thus, fiscal restraint would improve the trade balance, but the impact on the rate of capacity utilization, level of unemployment, and possibly rate of growth of capacity output (i.e. the overall development process of the economy), can be severe.

Structuralist economists argue that the alternatives open to the state for creating and financing the public sector deficit will influence the behavior and spending possibilities of the private sector. Specifically, inflationary-financed public investment will increase economic growth and profitability, and thereby stimulate private investment. This complementarity between public and private investment (crowding-in) is also argued from the point of view that public sector investment behavior in LDCs is usually oriented toward the removal of production bottlenecks, increasing private sector profitability. Several empirical studies have attempted to shed light on the relationship between public and private investment. The results obtained by Blejer and Khan (1984) from cross-country data indicate that public investment in infrastructure is complementary to private investment. More recently, Grenne and Villanueva (1991), using a panel of 23 LDCs, find complementarity. Serven and Solimano (1993), in a study of 15 LDCs, find that public investment has a positive effect on private investment. Musalem (1989) finds evidence of complementarity between private and public investment in a time-series study of investment in Mexico. An estimation of the real private investment function in Argentina between 1961 and 1982 carried out by Morisset (1993) suggests that complementary relationships between public and private investment dominate. It looks, then, like fiscal restraint carried out through reduction in public investment may have a negative impact on private investment.

There is no doubt that the specific means by which an overall fiscal reduction is achieved matters for the implications that it has on capacity utilization, employment, investment, and growth. It is also clear that measures affecting taxation, public revenues, and public expenditure have potential implications for income distribution, which in turn bear on the social and political acceptability of the orthodox recipe. The Bretton Woods institutions often argue that judgements on these aspects of economic measures must be left to the authorities directly involved; however, it is clear that the specific measures that enable these fiscal objectives to be attained are an intrinsic part of the programs. To curb the size of government deficits there may be room for the authorities to reduce real expenditures rather than collect higher real revenues. Capital expenditure on education and health services are among the first to be chopped (Polanyi 1992). Investment in the economic infrastructure (such as transport, power, irrigation, drainage) and labor-intensive public works will be targeted as well (Eshag 1989). Hicks (1991) reports this behavior for 11 Latin American countries for the period 1979–85. Harris and Kusi (1992) confirm the same results for 12 African countries involved with the IMF for the period 1977–87. As regards current expenditure, it is on the whole politically easier to restrain the growth of outlays on health, education, and welfare schemes in general, that primarily benefit the poorer groups of the community, than to dismiss employees in the public sector or reduce their wages and salaries. Thus, cuts in government expenditures would impact directly on employment and would adversely affect living standards of low-skilled urban workers, the lower middle class, and the poorer segments of the population. Rural incomes will come under pressure as the contraction in urban incomes reduces the demand for food and the flow of remittances from urban to rural areas (Demery *et al.* 1987).

If the attempts to reduce fiscal deficits come from price liberalization of public services (energy, electricity, water, public transportation, etc.), low-income groups will suffer more because expenditure on such goods and services accounts for a larger share of the income of the poor. Additionally, the price increase in these activities will increase government revenues but will cause an increase in the cost of production in other sectors the economy.

3.4 Some Inherited Weaknesses of the Expenditure Switching, Absorption and Monetary Synthesis

The simplest model of the elasticity-absorption-monetary synthesis was obtained by combining an income–expenditure equation, the stock equilibrium equation from the money market, and the external balance. The resulting model leaves the domestic price level fixed, but it endogenizes the domestic interest rate in a Keynesian fashion. As an alternative, we may assume complete capital mobility (full equalization of domestic and foreign interest rates). The domestic price level thus becomes an endogenous variable so that the impact that conventional stabilization policies have on domestic inflation can be evaluated.

In principle, this synthesis can be subject to much of the same criticism attributed to the monetary and absorption approaches and to the expenditure switching mechanism. Exchange rate adjustment will not restore external balance and will not improve the output level if the supply and demand for exports responds slowly to price incentives, if the demand for imports consists of essentials (with no substitutes), if there are expectations of further devaluations, if intermediate imports are used in production, if the fallacy of composition applies, if indexation of factor incomes exists, etc. Devaluation can also be inflationary, and in fact this is what happens when the assumption of constant domestic prices does not hold. Consequently, the synthesis depends on contractionary monetary policies to keep inflation under control, and this can have a severe recessive impact if devaluation does not do the work. On the other hand, a number of compromises have to be made in the process of presenting the monetary side. The demand for money has to be stable, predictable, and independent of changes in domestic credit, and the credit component of the money supply must be assumed to be exogenous.

The synthesis models take as their point of departure the conventionally constructed analysis of the simple Keynesian model. It is precisely this method of commencing with some broad Keynesian accounting and then introducing the fundamental equation of the monetary approach through ad hoc assumptions on a pragmatic basis that undermines the Keynesian-monetary model and any subsequent development. Indeed, by ignoring

Keynes's profound analysis of money and finance, the Keynesian-monetary synthesis has succeeded in reducing Keynesian ideas to banalities. First, the synthesis lacks a serious analysis of how investment and finance are related. This is because it does not offer a basis for modeling investment in a manner that allows interest rates and finance a fundamental role. When monetary effects are allowed to work, for instance, it is not through the interest rate impact on investment [as in the IS-LM extension developed by Tsiang (1961)]. In fact, one is struck by how many aspects are jettisoned by this approach: the low sensitivity of absorption to interest rate changes, the trivialization of the monetary sector, the absence of sterilization, and so on. Second, as in most orthodox models, income distribution and supply-side aspects are extremely simplified. This is important not only because income distribution can be severely affected by the adjustment process of the model, but also because money income of different classes is relevant to the determination of the money wage, output prices, profitability, and the general behavior of the current account in capitalist economies. In addition, an important distinguishing characteristic of production in LDCs is that imported intermediate inputs are extremely important in industrial production. Since they are an important element of cost, so is the exchange rate. As the price of foreign exchange goes up, *ceteris paribus*, we would expect the price of imported inputs to go up, and hence the price level to increase (in the case in which the price level is an endogenous variable). This means that the aggregate supply function (2.60) should include the exchange rate as an important element. Finally, the capital account plays no role in the Keynesian-monetary synthesis, and the way it came into prominence later, with the formal extensions of Mundell and Fleming, did not take into account the implications that mounting foreign debt has on the domestic economy and on the future imbalances of the current account.

3.5 Structural Adjustment and Growth: An Assessment

It was in response to the worsening performance of LDCs during the 1980s that adjustment lending with emphasis on growth was intensified by the Bretton Woods institutions. Indeed, it is this greater emphasis on growth that distinguishes the structural adjustment programs of the 1980s and 1990s from their predecessors. The adjustment component of the typical package is intended to expose the economy to international competition through trade liberalization, and give free reign to the play of market forces through deregulation. The latter usually means privatization, reduction of state intervention, and elimination of "price distortions" (such as subsidies or price controls). The emphasis in these measures, along with the already-studied case for financial liberalization, is mainly obtaining a more efficient sectoral allocation of resources, and an increased amount and efficiency of private investment.

In the integrated model the effects of such measures are assumed to be reflected in changes in the saving rate, s, and/or by changes in the total factor productivity coefficient, z_3. Nevertheless, neither the theoretical content of the integrated model nor the causal link between supply-oriented measures and growth are free of difficulties.

In fact, the integrated model retains many of the limitations of some of the models that we have previously criticized. The monetary block in equation (2.83), for example, still retains a narrow definition of money, the dependence on Walras's Law, and the controversial assumption of a constant (and stable) income velocity of money. The balance-of-payments equation (equation (2.84)), which is a relationship common to the two main blocks, is based in the Marshall-Lerner condition. Similarly, the growth block (equation (2.82)) is based on misleading accounting, since growth is alleged to support causality running from the right to the left. Instead, savings are determined by the level of net income resulting from the level of employment produced by the decisions of entrepreneurs to carry out investment projects (Kregel 1977), or in a more Kaldorian spirit, investment would determine savings through endogenous changes in the distribution of income between profits and wages. Moreover, right-to-left causality imposed on the accounting has the additional problem of a possible wrong association between higher government savings $(T - G)$ and more rapid output growth (other parameters unchanged). This correlation need not be (indeed, probably is not) observed in LDCs (Taylor 1989).

The causal link between supply-oriented policies and economic growth (at least in the way in which is conventionally formulated) is not straightforward and deserves some discussion. As we will suggest, the arguments that support financial liberalization to increase the willingness to save and invest are rather ill founded. Financial liberalization might not have the assumed impact on the saving rate and investment, and as shown by Massad (1991), investment and growth are not constrained by savings in Latin America. Having said this, the benefits of a structural adjustment strategy would have to come from internal deregulation and trade liberalization, i.e. from policies that are supposed to affect positively the total factor productivity coefficient.

In theoretical terms the case for such strategies is not as unambiguous as its proponents claim. The elimination of price distortion is no guarantee of avoiding inefficiency, which can be caused by numerous factors, such as poor management, excessive scale, lack of labor motivation, etc. Prices, on the other hand, are not the only instrument that contributes to organizing and legitimating markets in LDCs (Stein 1994). Markets are the result of a broader array of appropriate institutions. To a large extent these institutional structures are not designed to allow economic participants to induce and respond to changes in price "signals" in order to organize production and demand. Furthermore, as economists have long recognized, Adam Smith's invisible hand, which is commonly thought to guide the market allocation of resources, cannot perform its magic when there are significant spillover effects. In addition, a number of practical difficulties are present in any attempt to eliminate price distortions. First, if labor and capital are not very mobile between different activities, major changes in the pattern of resource allocation may necessitate an extended period of adjustment during which some factors may be unemployed. The fact that some of the incumbent's costs are sunk means that the incumbent cannot leave the market and recovers its cost. Thus, sunk costs are actually a barrier to exit and allow the established firms to prevent entry. Structural market characteristics, which impede the mobility of factors, can then be used to the benefit of established firms, so the beneficial implications of trade liberalization become a matter of discussion. If weaker firms cannot respond to the inducements of resource allocation, they may simply face bankruptcy. In the absence of potential entrants capable of buying the physical assets of defunct firms, bankruptcy may simply imply the loss of the productive power of physical equipment that is potentially profitable, as well as the dispersion to lower marginal product activities of workers with accumulated industry-specific skills (Pack 1993). Additionally, the abrupt realignment of prices and the slow adjustment of investment allocation can be counterproductive if the resulting inflationary pressures are not balanced via short-run increased efficiency. Second, many government programs that create price misalignments are designed to achieve objectives other than economic efficiency (for instance, health programs, food subsidies, etc.) have important implications from the point of view of equity, so that equity considerations may have a large influence on decisions.

The virtues of trade liberalization as an instrument for eliminating the inefficiencies of an inadequately protected domestic market are not self-evident and are often wildly overstated. Trade liberalization is supposed to lead to an outward orientation and, as a consequence, to a greater overall efficiency. The causative link is thus twofold: from trade liberalization to export orientation, and from export orientation to increased productivity and growth. This is the strategy so beloved by orthodox economists and held to be responsible for the recent industrial surge of several countries in East Asia (see, for instance, Balassa 1981, Krueger 1985, and World Bank 1993). Suffice it to say that many historically fast-growing economies did not follow liberal policies. For example, the United States was very protectionist until the 1930s and had massive state interventions, such as subsidies given to railway companies, through the nineteenth century. Japan typically followed a protectionist import policy and gave strong incentives to exporters. Two of the four East Asian new industrialized countries (NICs), South Korea and Taiwan, which in terms of population and spatial structure are comparable to medium-sized Latin American countries, have not abjured the use of protection to promote industrialization (Wade 1988 and 1990, Amsden 1989, and Luedde-Neurath 1988). Both South Korea and Taiwan, until the early 1970s, made extensive use of quantitative controls over imports (Fajnzylber 1981). Moreover those industries that were more exposed to import competition received levels of protection in Taiwan and South Korea that were higher than in countries like Colombia or Mexico (Jenkins 1991). This suggests that what appears to be a strong outward orientation in these countries is in fact the result of some industries' being highly competitive internationally and others' being heavily protected. The East Asian experience also suggests that trade policy instruments cannot be ranked in terms of efficiency independently of the institutional context within which they are applied. For example, in the South Korean case, in which highly selective quantitative controls have been important, the potential for rent-seeking behavior has not materialized, partly because of the relative autonomy of the state and of the role of a strong national development ideology in countering these effects (Evans 1990).

Within the Latin American context, the Chilean experience contrasts sharply with that of most of the Asian NICs. Between 1975 and 1979, Chile implemented a drastic trade liberalization, eliminating all quantitative restrictions, reducing tariffs to a uniform 10 percent in four years, and eliminating the government's role in promoting exports or defining external sector strategies (Edwards 1989). The major costs of this liberalization effort were a reduction in output and employment, and a lag in investment.[32] Expectations based on preconceived views are not adequate for explaining the important discrepancies found in the growth experience of Latin American countries. Thus, based on data collected between the mid-1950s and the late 1970s, de Paiva Abreu *et al.* (1990) show how Brazil, much more protected than, say, Argentina, had, together with Mexico, a far better record in terms of growth.

Widespread trade liberalization does not necessarily provoke a beneficial effect on expenditure-switching incentives, and it can sometimes lead to reverse import substitution. It is important to note in this sense that arguments that stress the importance of the liberalization of imports see this policy as beneficial due to the short-run promotion of exports where key intermediate imports have been restricted. However, if export intensive industries are not intensive in imported inputs, but mainly use domestic resources, then these industries may not benefit much from the external liberalization policy.[33] In this case the imports of inputs will be used mostly by industries that produce for the domestic market, to increase domestic sales. Moreover, if the import intensity of import-substituting industries is low and the amount of competitive imports is high, the import-substituting industries will suffer substantially from trade liberalization. All these elements indicate that a careful analysis of the import content, the final destination, and the structure of the productive sector are required before trade liberalization is to be adopted.

Trade liberalization presents a country's economy with a number of dilemmas, especially if the country is exposed to various kinds of stabilization measures. A contractionary devaluation, for example, will reduce the level of imports and will improve the trade gap. However, several analyses indicate that indiscriminate trade liberalization can rapidly drive import propensities up (Singh and Ghosh 1987) and increase substantially the import content of raw materials and spares (Siddharthan 1989).[34] In this case the short-run improvement in the trade balance could vanish in the medium term, worsening the trade gap even under conditions of low output growth. Reducing tariffs could reduce distortions but also will adversely affect government finances. As Edwards (1989) points out, most theoretical and policy discussions on trade liberalization assume, along the lines of traditional trade theory, that tariff proceeds are handed back to the public. In reality, however, this is not the case. Governments use tariff proceeds to finance their expenditures. This is particularly true in many poorer LDCs, where, for various institutional reasons, taxes on international trade represent a high percentage of government revenue. Hence, the reduction of the magnitude of the fiscal deficit, which is a crucial objective of any stabilization program, will not be achieved, because an important trade-off exists between tariff reduction and the achievement of the fiscal objective.

In trying to determine how growth rates are affected by the removal of price distortions and trade liberalization, the orthodoxy postulates a relationship between liberalization and productivity, and between productivity and growth.[35] As we mentioned earlier, the total productivity index aids in the specification of the efficiency-augmenting factors (see equation (2.82) of the integrated model); however, the whole definition of the total factor productivity resembles much of the neoclassical analysis, and for that reason it runs into trouble.

Being equivalent to the Solow residual, the productivity index, z_3, can be expressed as

$$z_3 = Q/(K^{w_1} L^{w_2}) \qquad (3.8)$$

where the usual assumption is that the elasticities of output Q with respect to the factors L and K (i.e. w_1 and w_2), are equal to the factor shares, so that constant returns to scale and competitive pricing applies. But none of these assumptions seems to apply in the manufacturing sector of LDCs. Moreover, expression (3.8) leaves the calculation of z_3 vulnerable to the critique of Shaikh (1980), in the sense that it would be measuring technical progress, as it often described. Instead, z_3 would reflect distributional changes.

The direction of causality that goes from trade liberalization and deregulation to a higher total factor productivity factor contradicts most of the evidence of some East Asian NICs, where small domestic markets and high protection levels went hand in hand with rapid growth in total factor productivity.[36] This view does not resist an adequate historical test in Latin America either. The studies that find strong correlation between total factor productivity and growth in these countries usually refer to periods of time when the industrial sector was highly protected (Ocampo 1991). In fact, these findings can be interpreted under the assumption that the relationship between the rate of growth of productivity and the rate of output growth is induced by the growth of output itself so that the result can be consistent with the so-called Kaldor's (or Verdoorn's) Law. From this viewpoint, it is the rate of growth of manufacturing output that determines the rate of growth of productivity in several nonmanufacturing sectors, as well as in the manufacturing sector. There are a number of a priori reasons for expecting such an induced relation, the most obvious being that output growth induces capital formation and this embodies technical progress. Learning by doing and by using and other externalities also play a part.

In empirical terms, the links among structural adjustment policies, economic efficiency, and rapid growth cannot be strongly established. On the one hand, most studies that restrict the attention to the growth effects of either IMF- or World Bank-supported programs seem to indicate that a positive relationship between structural adjustment and growth does not exist. The cross-countries empirical studies mentioned earlier using the before–after approach, such as Reichmann and Stillson (1978), Connors (1979), Killick (1984), Zuluc and Nsouli (1985), Pastor (1987), and

Killick *et al.* (1995), find either no discernible effects on growth or a reduction in the growth rate in Fund-supported programs. No better results are found in Donovan (1982), Gylfanson (1987), Goldstein and Montiel (1986), Khan (1990), and Conway (1994), which use the with–without approach and the generalized evaluation estimator.

In addition, a study by Mosley *et al.* (1990) shows that structural adjustment loan conditionality, in conjunction with IMF demand-related conditionality, has given rise to a decline in the adjusting country's invest-ment as a share of the GDP. This is confirmed by a more recent study by Corbo and Rojas (1992) on the effectiveness of adjustment lending by the World Bank in 25 developing countries, and it contradicts much of the publicized objective of adjustment with growth. Evans and Aghazadeh (1988), using data from the 1983 World Bank study of a sample of over 30 countries, found that the indexes of price distortions variables have no impact on microeconomic efficiency. Their empirical findings give more weight to non-price variables than appears in the mainstream accounts. Fani *et al.* (1991) constructed a set of performance indicators for 93 "developing" countries, among which 41 did not receive any IMF/World Bank adjust-ment loans during the period 1982–86. The results showed that participa-tion in IMF/World Bank programs does not appear to affect output growth in a significant manner. The same study investigated long-term sustainability by analyzing aggregate investment and aggregate output during adjustment, for a group of 13 countries that were intensive recipients of IMF/World Bank adjustment loans. The results suggested a sizeable output loss because of lower aggregate investment during the period of adjustment. It is important to note that two Latin American countries experienced the worst output losses (Mexico 23 percent and Chile 17 percent). In a recent study, Noorbakhsh and Paloni (1997) investigated whether World Bank-supported structural adjustment programs have in practice played any role in improving program countries' export performance and growth. They use a large set of cross-section data that includes 21 Latin American and Caribbean countries, and they analyze the main issues employing the "before–after," the "with–without," and the "modified control group" approaches over the period 1981 to 1995. They find that structural adjustment programs do not seem to have had a lasting or significant impact on supply capacity and diversification of production. In addition, export growth, output growth, and the share of manufacturing in GDP all fell in program countries during 1991–95. Finally, Doroodian (1993) attempts to gauge program effectiveness by incorporating a control group of countries in three semi-reduced forms. The study included 43 countries, of which 27 borrowed heavily from the IMF.

The period of observation was 1977 to 1983. The statistical results show that the IMF adjustment policies, in general, improve the inflation rate moderately and the BOP significantly. These policies, however, do not have much impact on the level of economic activity.

On the other hand, broad studies linking trade reform or "openness" to long-run growth are surprisingly fragile. Even though the round of very recent empirical research is generally credited for having yielded strong results on the beneficial consequences of openness (and its influence in policy circles has been considerable), recent studies dispute these conclusions. Problems have been found in the robustness of the exercises, the quality of the data and the measures of openness. Sala-i-Martin (1997) finds that the only openness measure that is robust in all these studies is the one constructed by Sachs and Warner (1995). However, Harrison and Hanson (1999) demonstrate that the Sachs and Warner composite index of openness fails to establish a robust link between more open trade policies and growth. An in-depth examination of the most influential papers on openness and growth has been carried out by Rodriguez and Rodrik (1999), and they demonstrate and conclude that "there has been a tendency in academic and policy discussions to greatly overstate the systematic evidence in favor of trade openness" (p. 39).

The impact of trade reforms on economic performance in Latin America has been examined directly by Bleaney (1999). He uses an annual panel data set of ten Latin American countries over the period 1979 to 1995, when trade policy represented one of the most intensive areas of reform. He finds a disappointing response, with most measures of real performance, such as GDP growth, investment, and exports, showing no significant improvement or in some cases a significant decline.

If one of the main objectives of orthodox growth-oriented programs is to restore growth, one must ask what causes this poor growth performance in countries under IMF/World Bank adjustment lending. The logic would ascribe much of the fall in output to the fall in private investment. This leads us to unexplored areas of analysis since the behavior of private investment requires the study of adjustment routes and the relationship between the short and the long term. In particular, the widespread belief that short-run stabilization is a prerequisite for the success of structural adjustment policies becomes suspect once we recognize the possible perverse effects that orthodox short-run shocks have on private investment. Short-run pain does not lead to long-run gain, and we suggested many of the reasons for this when we dealt with the impact of devaluation and demand restraint on the level of economic activity.

As we have mentioned in this chapter, in increasing the cost of the dollar-denominated liabilities of domestic firms, devaluation can directly affect capital formation. But devaluation can also depress private investment in nontradeable activities if the import content is high, and if the real cost of inputs in terms of domestic goods increases (Branson 1986). Additionally, devaluation may affect investment by its impact on aggregate demand. If devaluation is contractionary, then the slump in economic activity it is likely to provoke forms the basis for investors to cut investment spending (Serven and Solimano 1993). A fiscal restraint policy will also reduce the amount of private investment, if the fiscal adjustment takes the form of reduced public investment in infrastructure and other forms of public spending that tend to be complementary for private investment. Monetary restraint and financial liberalization will probably have an impact on investment through induced increases in the opportunity cost of retained profits—a major source of investment finance in LDCs. In light of these considerations, it may be very difficult to expect any success for the reform process in the long run.

An additional issue that begins to draw the attention of scholars is the key role of uncertainty in investment decisions during the process of stabilization and adjustment. The prevailing degree of uncertainty about the economic conditions will favor the option to wait for new information, which in turn will affect the desirability or timing of investment (Serven *et al.* 1993). The lack of credibility in the adjustment programs, perhaps mostly because of the size of the required adjustment, or perhaps also because of overambitious reforms in an unsettled macroeconomic environment, will increase the degree of uncertainty and lead many private investors to postpone their investment decisions (Fani *et al.* 1991). Therefore, the critical issue in this discussion is that countries affected by structural adjustment programs may not be successful with respect to their growth prospects, because of the short-run cost of stabilization (which undermines investment), the degree of uncertainty, and the failure of structural change itself.

3.6 *On the Vulnerability of the McKinnon–Shaw Hypothesis*

The weaknesses of the McKinnon and Shaw approach and the IMF/World Bank supply-side policies in favor of interest-rate liberalization lie in their misunderstanding of the functioning of finance in LDCs. The arguments that higher interest rates induce faster growth rates can only be plausible if either domestic or foreign savings are found to be a positive function of interest rates, and if investment and growth is assumed to be saving constrained. Raising interest rates to positive real levels is unlikely to raise savings in LDCs. At a theoretical level, we can argue that it is the distribution of income, the state of the government's budget, and the reinvestment (or remittance abroad) of profits, that might better explain the behavior of savings, and each is considered to be relatively insensitive to interest rates (except perhaps government savings). While there is evidence that positive rates increase savings held in financial form, sometimes this simply means a movement from an informal financial market to a more formal one, and not an increase in real savings (Van Wijnbergen 1982). Indeed, there are grounds to believe that under the circumstances prevailing in many LDCs, the link between interest rates and savings will not work. Empirical work by Giovannini (1983, 1985) casts doubt on the view that the interest elasticity of savings is significantly positive in LDCs. Similarly, Cho and Khatkhate (1990) and Gonzalez Arrieta (1988) also find no relationship between interest rates and savings in data from Asian and Latin American and other developing countries. In country studies in Latin America, De Melo and Tybout (1986), Werneck (1986), and Warman and Thirwall (1994) also find no evidence of a significant positive effect on aggregate savings in Uruguay, Brazil, and Mexico respectively.[37] Moreover, Werneck (1986) conducts some simulations in the case of Brazil that suggests that high interest rates may have a negative impact on domestic savings. Very recently, Bandeira *et al.* (1998) provide empirical examination (cointegration analysis) of the total effect of financial reform on aggregate private savings based on eight case studies (which include two Latin American countries: Chile and Mexico). They obtain a continuous financial liberalization index for each country and estimate an econometric relationship, expressing the private saving ratio as a function of the index and the real interest rate, along with income, inflation, and the savings of the public sector. The results confirm that there is no strong reliable interest rate effect on savings.

The analysis of the stimulation of foreign capital flows (foreign savings) in response to changes in interest rates disregards differences in the geopolitical and the overall economic situation of different countries as possible havens for capital. The same rise in the interest rate from the same levels would not, for example, attract the same inflows of capital into Brazil and the United States. The degree of response of foreign inflows of capital to changes in interest-rates is very different today from what it was in the 1970s in Latin America. It is true that positive interest rate policies were successful in some Latin American countries in attracting inflows of funds; however, since 1982 the end of private banks' voluntary lending made international capital inflows entirely insensitive to interest-rate differentials. Recent flows of foreign capital to the region seem to be caused by exogenous factors affecting the external opportunity cost of funds (Calvo, Leiderman, and Reinhart 1993). Moreover, high interest rates could have only a temporary effect on capital inflows due to different velocities of adjustment in goods and assets markets. For instance, high interest rates may attract capital flows in the short run, but once interest costs on working capital are translated into higher domestic prices, the real exchange rate loses value, leading to fears of an impeding maxi-devaluation, and setting off a huge capital flight. Something like this happened in Argentina during the liberalization experiments of the 1970s.[38] Nevertheless, if liberalization of the domestic financial system is associated with capital inflows, those large capital inflows can result in complex short-term macroeconomic consequences. For instance, there may be associated changes in the availability and cost of credit, revised expectations of income growth, and increases in financial wealth, especially caused by upward movements in property prices; and all this may lead to consumption booms and to a fall in the saving rate (Bandiera, Caprio, Honohan, and Schiantareli 1998).

Massad (1991) has reported on the recent evolution of savings and investment as a percentage of GDP in Latin America. If we look at the relationship between saving and investment from 1980 to 1989, it can clearly be seen that saving as a percentage of GDP continued to rise during the 1980s. From 23 percent in 1980, savings reached the highest proportion of the whole period in 1988, over 25 percent. However, investment declined from 24 percent in 1980 to 15 percent in 1983, and its recovery was only modest, so that by the end of the period it had only reached approximately 17 percent a year. This surplus of saving over investment during the 1980s finds no explanation in the McKinnon–Shaw framework, because in it "growth in a financially repressed economy is constrained by savings" (Fry 1982, p. 733). The fact of the matter is that, if these economies had been financially repressed during the 1980s, the expected result would have been the opposite, i.e. a deficit of saving over investment. On the other hand, financial liberalization would have been reflected in a significant increase in investment, which was not the case either. The explanation for this enigma of the saving–investment surplus may lie in the conventional mechanisms for funding investment in LDCs. Firms borrow short, hoping to repay by playing Ponzi games, i.e. by borrowing (to repay) until their investment matures and begins to produce additional cash inflows. Once the interest rate is liberalized, banks' liquidity preference rises, and this prevents financial institutions from expanding their lending activities.[39] Even if they did lend, banks would almost certainly prefer to lend short (toward the financing of consumption and/or speculation, for example). Additionally, savings may be poorly correlated with investment due to the impossibility of many Latin American countries' increasing the level of imports under conditions of external constraints. Since capital goods are a quite important proportion of imports in these countries, it is not sufficient to increase savings in order to increase the level of investments. In a recent study, Sinha and Sinha (1998) investigate the long-run relationship between saving and investment for a group Latin American countries. The results show that saving-and-investment ratios are cointegrated for only four out of ten countries.

There are still other problems associated with the way in which the McKinnon–Shaw hypothesis envisages investment behavior. In the McKinnon–Shaw framework, the possibility that higher interest rates can cause a more unequal income distribution, depressing the level of effective demand and, hence, the propensity to invest, is ignored. Moreover, as Lewis (1954) long ago pointed out, retained profits (that is, enterprise savings) are an important source of investment finance in LDCs, and these are not positively affected by interest-rate changes.[40] An increase in interest rates could eventually have a negative effect on the final destination of these financial resources if portfolio shifts occur from capital goods into monetary assets (saving and financial assets). This is a widely documented phenomenon in Mexico, Chile, and several other Latin American countries.[41] Moreover, an increase in the price of credit may discourage investment in small-scale industrial and agricultural enterprises since these sectors do not have the market power to generate additional investment funds. Additionally, since these are sectors where, for reasons of cost, risk, or reputation, the formal private financial institutions are reluctant to lend, a policy of financial liberalization may well reduce the funds available to them.

Even the complete abolition of government control of bank interest rates may not achieve the objectives hoped for by the advocates of financial liberalization because of credit rationing. Under credit rationing the real interest rate will rise, but it will still be below the interest rate that will equate supply and demand.[42] As Keynes (1935) put it in a famous passage, "lending does not . . . take place according to principles of a perfect market" (1935, p. 212). Banks face informational problems that do not allow them to know how the money they lend is being invested. Bank rationing, which seeks to eliminate high-risk borrowers by allocating credit on the basis of collateral, credit standing, and reputation, is liable to discriminate against smaller, poorer, newer, and more enterprising borrowers, among whom there may be many who would make good use of credit, and be able and willing to service their debts. The problem is that those who are willing to pay higher interest rates are likely to be higher-risk borrowers, so that as interest rates rise, the average riskiness of those who borrow increases. Stiglitz and Weiss (1981) call this the "adverse selection effect." In addition, they describe the so-called "incentive effect," which refers to the fact that higher interest rates reduce the return on projects that succeed, and are likely to induce firms to undertake projects with lower prospects of success but higher payoffs when successful. Thus, the assumption that financial liberalization and high interest rates promote the "efficiency" of investment is by no means necessarily true.

Concerns about the consequences of financial liberalization have grown with the explosion of banking crises around the globe in the last two decades. Stiglitz (1998a) and Demirguc-Kunt and Detragiache (1998) note the role played by premature financial liberalization in these episodes, especially where regulation, supervision, and other parts of the infrastructure that would support incentive-compatible behavior are absent. McKinnon (1993) himself argues that much of the financial disarray has arisen because the proponents of liberalization have not followed an optimal sequence of liberalization, including ensuring macrostability before financial deregulation. There is a widespread agreement that financial liberalization in the midst of macrostability greatly exacerbates any economic dislocation.[43] Under conditions of instability (or some future threat), financial liberalization boosts the level of interest rates, leading to disintermediation and causing problems of credit stringency for medium-size and small firms. Even discerning private bankers will gravitate toward short-term lending activities or to the certainty of government paper. Though macrofactors and institutional failure are common factors in bank insolvency in Latin America, premature liberalization could be cited in virtually all cases of financial crisis in the region (see table 3.1). Demirguc-Kunt and Detragiache (1998) gauge the effect of

Table 3.1 **Major Experiences of Financial Liberalization in Latin America**

Country	Financial Liberalization	Financial Crisis
Argentina	1976–1980	1980–1982
Chile	1974–1978	1981–1982
Uruguay	1974–1980	1982
Bolivia	1985–1987	1987
Colombia	1978–1981	1982
Venezuela	1989–1993	1994–1995
Guyana	1991–1995	1993–1995
Mexico	1991–1992	1995

financial liberalization on financial fragility, constructing a financial liberalization dummy variable for 53 industrial and developing countries covering 1980–95. They estimate the probability of a banking crisis using a multivariate logit model and test the hypothesis that the dummy variable significantly increases the probability of a crisis when other factors are controlled. Their findings are clear. Financial liberalization has an independent and negative effect on banking sector stability.

3.7 Concluding Remarks

The objective of this chapter has been to evaluate the validity of the models that underlie the typical stabilization and adjustment package. Intrinsic theoretical weaknesses and inconsistencies, erroneous premises and assumptions, and empirical inconsequences plague the orthodox framework.

In the monetary approach, the central belief that any excess supply of money must be matched by an excess demand of something else is not necessarily correct. In reality, transactions are not simultaneous and expenditures are not synchronized since money acts as a medium of not only temporal but also intertemporal exchange. We have noted that in a depression-deficit dilemma case, an excess demand for money is matched not only by excess sales abroad of commercial goods but by an excess supply of domestic goods and factors of production. We have also pointed out that in general the Walras law holds only when a full-employment situation is assumed.

The definition and stability of the demand for money function is subject to criticism. If the demand for money is not stable, the setting of monetary targets in stabilization programs is questionable. Moreover, if sterilization by monetary authorities has effects on domestic interest rates, spending decisions, or the exchange rate, then the demand for money can not be assumed to be independent of changes in the money supply. We have also argued that changes in domestic credit can influence output and thus cause shifts in the demand for money since there is no presumption that individuals will be continually on their demand schedules. Thus, assuming continuous equilibrium when projecting the demand for money in the course of an orthodox program would lead to errors that could have significant impact on the credit ceilings. Additionally, if the monetarist assumptions with regard to full employment output and prices do not hold, a reduction in the fiscal deficit could cause a decline in the demand for money, and this implies (if money market equilibrium holds) that the money supply would be lower than it would have been without the cut in the fiscal deficit. The cut in the government's borrowing from the public could also reduce the rate of interest, which in turn would raise domestic credit to the public. The lower money supply and the higher domestic credit would result in a decline in net foreign assets. Therefore, when the demand for money is not independent of the money supply, a reduction in the fiscal deficit does not imply an unambiguous improvement in the balance of payments.

In the process of presenting monetary models, a number of additional compromises have to be assumed. Monetary models rely on the unwarranted assumption of full employment, flexible prices, and exogenous credit money. Market imperfections and real wage resistance are not even considered as possibilities. The supply side is virtually ignored, making these models virtually irrelevant to the reality of LDCs. When the PPP theorem is invoked (as in the Chicago version), no possibility is allowed for nontraded goods, product differentiation, and segmented markets. The presence of these latter factors may explain why the PPP theorem, in the post-Bretton Woods era, by and large has failed to stand up to the empirical scrutiny.

The effectiveness of credit restraint cannot be guaranteed if the domestic component of the money supply is endogenous. But even assuming an exogenous domestic money supply, it is rather difficult to suggest that a reduction in the level of domestic credit has no effect on the equilibrium level of output. Instead, the adjustment process frequently operates through a reduction in the level of economic activity and an increase in the amount of interest costs of working capital and prices. The Latin American experience is illustrative in this respect.

When we turn to the devaluation case, the arguments we have mentioned raise doubts about the effectiveness of devaluation to restore the external balance and expand the level of economic activity. The supply and demand for exports may respond slowly to relative price changes; the demand for imports may be insensitive to real exchange realignments; intermediate imports and indexation of factor incomes may not allow the adjustment in the real exchange rate. This implies that devaluation will have severe inflationary consequences, as the Latin America experience illustrates. The empirical evidence is rather inconclusive with respect to the trade balance effect and affirmative with respect to the contractionary and inflationary effects of exchange-rate adjustment.

The absorption approach, which is usually used to complement the insights of the monetary approach, contains a number of unsatisfactory points. An external imbalance does not need to be caused by a government budget deficit, as is usually assumed. The trade imbalance may be caused by autonomous changes in the amount of imports or, exports, or the real terms of trade. Moreover, a deterioration of the trade balance may transform a fiscal balance into a fiscal deficit if a loss of earnings in the export sector reduces tax collection. The budget deficit can also be a direct consequence of the balance-of-payments constraint when exogenous changes in the flow and maturity pattern of government external debt shift, or when foreign interest rates increase. Doubts about the discretionary power that the government has to control a budget deficit arise if automatic stabilizers play a major role in the economy.

When we explore the issue of how fiscal restraint would improve the trade balance, we find that the most obvious mechanism is through the impact of private expenditure on the rate of capacity utilization and unemployment. Empirical studies also suggest that attempts at fiscal restraint carried out through public investment reductions may have a negative impact on private investment.

The Keynesian-monetary synthesis overcomes the critical assumption that real output is exogenously determined; however, neither the alternative of leaving the domestic price fixed (endogenizing the domestic interest rate) nor the option of assuming complete capital mobility (endogenizing the domestic price level) is satisfactory. This synthesis can be subject to the same criticism attributed to the monetary and absorption approach and to the expenditure switching mechanism. In addition, the synthesis does not offer a good basis for modeling investment. The level of investment is insensitive to the level of interest cost and to the availability of finance. Not only is absorption interest inelastic, but sterilization is also forbidden. The supply side is extremely simplified, and since intermediate imports do not exist, the exchange rate does not affect the aggregate supply function.

When looking at the integrated model, we notice that the conventional causal link between supply side-oriented measures and growth seems suspect. Both the monetary block and the balance-of-payments equation retain many of the limitations of the models employed to support stabilization that we have previously criticized. Similarly, the growth block is based on misleading accounting, and investment is assumed to be saving-constrained. Instead, we have argued that investment will determine savings through endogenous changes in income distribution (in a Keynesian–Kaldorian spirit). The causal link between supply-oriented policies and economic growth is not straight-forward either.

On the one hand, the proposals to eliminate price distortion and liberalize trade in order to overcome inefficiencies are often wildly overstated. Price liberalization may not work if capital and labor are not very mobile and if potential entrants are absent. Trade liberalization may not increase productivity and growth; instead, it may drive import propensities up. In empirical terms, the link between structural adjustment policies, economic efficiency and rapid growth cannot be strongly established. Most studies that restrict the attention to the growth effects of either IMF- or World Bank-supported programs seem to indicate that a positive relationship between structural adjustment and growth does not exist. Moreover, broad studies linking trade reform or "openness" to long-run growth are surprisingly fragile.

On the other hand, Latin American experiences with financial liberalization indicate that this will not lead to growth recovery but to financial collapse. Empirical studies confirm that there is no strong reliable interest-rate effect on savings. Additionally, the posited correlations between real interest rates and investment and between real deposit rate and saving and economic growth lack theoretical and empirical support.

Obviously, structural changes are needed if Latin American countries are to overcome the deficiencies of "maldevelopment" and to weather the shocks the future holds in store. But what should the characteristics of stabilization programs accompanying such changes be? This depends on the long-term objectives of the country's development policies and on the effectiveness of models and instruments used. We will turn our attention in the next section toward a tentative scheme of possible alternatives to orthodoxy. Such an alternative framework calls for far more selective economic measures, shaped according to the objectives of low inflation, a sustainable balance of payments, and growth. This framework takes into account the characteristics of modern capitalists economies and the particular socioeconomic internal structure of LDCs.

Notes

1. For a still-excellent analysis of the peculiarities of money and the inadequacies of the Walrasian general equilibrium approach see Davidson (1978).
2. It is a very well-known fact that money is an inessential addition to Walrasian models and as such its medium of exchange function is not necessary for the determination of an equilibrium solution. This is despite some neo-Walrasians' attempts to ensure that money has a medium-of-exchange function (see, for example, Clower 1967).
3. Above and to the left of LL the supply of money is greater than the demand, and below and to the right of LL the demand for money is greater than the supply. Points above and to the right of BB represent a deficit in the balance of payments, while points below and to the left of BB represent a surplus. Finally, note that points to the right of NN represent an excess supply of nontradeable goods, while points to left represent an excess demand for them.

4. A second type of counterexample, in which nontradeable goods appear, involves both inflation at home and a balance-of-payments surplus. Assuming that the market for nontraded goods always clears, that there is inflation in the outside world, and that the prices of traded and nontraded goods are rising together (imported inflation), it is conceivable for domestic inflation to become continually validated by a balance-of-payments surplus that increases the money supply. In that case money demand (which in the conventional case continually grows owing to the rise in prices of all goods) may continuously equal money supply (which increases owing to the balance-of-payments surplus). In other words, money supply and money demand may be rising together so that they are equal at the time that the balance of payments is in surplus.

5. Sau (1992) seems to make the assumption that foreign-controlled companies are import intensive.

6. Orthodox economists have tried to absorb this criticism in two different ways: One is recognizing that velocity, instead of being constant, increases at higher interest rates, but since these changes are not violent, it is reasonable to assume that the influence of interest-rate changes on the transactions demand for money will not nullify the higher demand for money as income increases. Another way is to assume that real income affects velocity, but since the income elasticity of the demand for money is close to one, then the demand for real balances would change in the same proportion as income, in which case changes in real income would not change velocity.

7. When variations of 1.25 to 5.25 percent are considered, there are significant "flaws" in the FED ability to control the money supply in the United States.

8. Copelman captures the effect of financial innovation by a set of dummy variables that account for transaction cost. She also uses an error correction model to estimate the short-run money demand.

9. Econometric estimations of finance motive in a demand-for-money function have been carried out by Meyer and Neary (1975) and Smith (1979). Their results confirm the existence of the finance motive.

10. This has become a common problem in Latin American countries, where exchange-rate fluctuations are persistent and chronic.

11. It is clear that from the monetarist viewpoint if we assume that the money supply is given from outside and willingly held by the public at the prevailing interest rate and real income configuration, and the central bank credit to the private sector either remains unaffected or decreases, then the reduction in the fiscal deficit implies an unambiguous improvement in the balance of payments.

12. The countries included are Argentina, Bolivia, Brazil, Chile, Colombia, Mexico, Peru, Uruguay, and Venezuela.

13. Leon and Oliva's (1992) study includes 12 Latin American countries: Argentina, Bolivia, Brazil, Chile, Colombia, Costa Rica, Ecuador, Mexico, Paraguay, Peru, Uruguay, and Venezuela.

14. Although this is not a central argument in this chapter, it is important to mention that the prices of industrial commodities produced domestically are influenced by a complex mix of economic variables. Technology, labor–capital relations, the price of inputs, barriers to entry, the degree of concentration, and the openness of national markets to foreign competition are among the main variables to be considered.

15. Sau (1988) estimates that working capital costs in Brazil come to as much as 10 percent of industrial sales.

16. This is a typical result of the type of models developed by Taylor (1983) and Buffie (1984).

17. This problem tends to differentiate primary-producing countries from industrial countries, which face fewer obstacles in adapting their existing manufacturing capacity to servicing additional export demand.

18. The assumptions on which the Marshall-Lerner condition applies are enumerated in the previous chapter in the description of expenditure switching models.

19. Very often IMF and World Bank scholars stress, in addition, that the key role of devaluation is that it increases relative prices of tradeable to nontradeable goods. However, we will argue here that the arguments against devaluation are particularly strong in this case. First, even accepting that devaluation is positively related to changes in relative prices of tradeables to nontradeables, this increase is far from being automatically linked to an increase in the level of activity of tradeables (i.e. export and import-competing goods). As we just mentioned, the pace and the extent to which exports respond to price changes in Latin American countries is limited by a variety of economic and social factors. But in addition to this, supply responses of tradeable goods are also severely restricted in LDCs, and particularly in Latin American countries through reliance on imported intermediate inputs (the demand for which is price inelastic). Insofar as firms in the tradeable-goods sector import their required intermediate goods, devaluation will raise production costs, and thereby reduce the incentive for increased tradeable goods production (Demery *et al.* 1987). Moreover, the extent to which tradeable sectors can absorb the resources liberated by other sectors is also limited if the resources of nontradeable industries are condemned to idleness (rather than sending them to the export- and import-competing industries). In the particular case of local import-competing industries (which are part of the tradeable sector) it is possible that devaluation will have little effect on output decisions since most of the firms involved are manufacturing monopolies and face downward sloping and kinked demand curves (Knight 1976). When indivisibilities exist, entry barriers are high, preventing the entry of new firms and restricting the expansion of manufacturing production in response to devaluation. In sum, given the circumstances we have described, it is very likely that trade balance adjustments will come not from an expansion in the production of tradeables, but from a fall in the demand for them. So, in the

absence of output response in the tradeable sector, devaluation will benefit the trade position in the short run, principally through the induced decline in imports. This is something that has been empirically confirmed in many Latin American countries during the 1980s.

20. The episode of hyperinflations in Central Europe in the 1920s stimulated a great deal of research and debate about the sources of inflation in the economics profession. Based on that experience some economists, such as Bresciani-Turroni and Joan Robinson, developed an approach that attributed the main cause of inflation to adverse shocks in the balance of payments. The basic elements of this approach were the result of a combination of (a) the existence of a wage indexation system, and (b) the need to change the real exchange rate in order to adjust the balance of payments against new external parameters. It is quite remarkable that within the context of monetarist and structuralist debate in Latin America, a group of Latin American economists (the structuralist side of this fierce polemic) was emphasizing similar explanations about the causes of inflation, i.e. sociopolitical tensions, sectoral imbalances, and the foreign exchange gap. With respect to the foreign exchange gap argument, structuralists have argued that the inelastic supply of exports, the deterioration of the commodity terms of trade, and the inflexibility of imports result in a foreign exchange gap whose fluctuations lead to periodic devaluations and increasing inflation (see Sunkel 1960 and Olivera 1964). The fact of the matter is that when the structure of the economy is such that (a) imports of capital and intermediate goods are required, (b) manufacturing industries are oligopolistic, and (c) social struggles are acute, there good reasons to believe that devaluation will lead to inflation.

21. Examples of devaluation-induced inflation are numerous in Latin America. In 1981, for example, the Mexican rate of inflation was 28 percent. A devaluation of the Mexican peso (under IMF pressure) in February 1982 set in motion a sequence of events much as had been predicted: inflation, wage demands, and further devaluation. As a consequence, the Mexican rate of inflation by the end of 1982 was about 100 percent per year. In Venezuela in 1989, as a precondition for an IMF agreement, the Venezuelan government devaluated the local currency by almost 100 percent. By the end of the year it had jumped from 20 percent to 81 percent per year.

22. Brazilian economists Simonsen (1984) and Modiano (1985) were among the first to illustrate the dynamics of real wages whose nominal values adjust to past inflation at fixed intervals.

23. This mechanism has been found to be important in the adjustment process in Latin America (Foxley 1983), and particularly in Chile (Ramos 1980). The latter is a dramatic illustration of how severe real-wage cuts contributed to the collapse of product markets in Chile in 1974–76.

24. There are several approaches suggested to measure the effects of IMF-supported programs. Among the most important we find the before–after approach, which

compares the macroeconomic performance under program and performance prior to the program; the with–without approach, which compares the macroeconomic performance in countries with programs and performance in a control group of nonprogram countries; and the generalized evaluation approach, which compares performance in program and nonprogram countries, adjusting for differences in initial conditions among countries and controlling for exogenous influences. A good evaluation of the pros and cons of the respective empirical methodologies can be found in Edwards (1990) and Haque and Khan (1998).

25. Albert Hirschman (1949) pioneered the structuralist position on the contractionary effects of devaluation.

26. This result will not occur if workers can defend their income level by forcing up money wages in the wake of devaluation. In that case, the real effects of devaluation will be largely nullified by inflation.

27. Diaz Alejandro also shows in his study that any improvement in the trade balance, following a devaluation, is due to a reduction in absorption (with respect to output) and not to substitutions effects.

28. Some orthodox authors, such as McKinnon (1981), believe that it will not even be necessary to change the exchange rate, for this rate is a price determined in the assets market.

29. Pastor (1989), for instance, using regression analysis, tests the relative importance of internal and external factors in causing current account deficits in Latin American countries for the period 1973–84. Various external variables, such as growth in the United States, the terms of trade, and the real interest rates, are generally significant in the expected directions. The budged deficit performs poorly, and the real exchange rate is significant in the expected direction.

30. Interest rates jumped from 8.4 percent in 1977–78 to 17.4 percent in 1981.

31. Steidl splits the private saving–investment gap into business and household sectors.

32. Of course, the trade liberalization episode in Chile occurred at the same time that the government undertook a major demand restraint stabilization program and an open policy of financial liberalization. So it is difficult to attribute the fall in output and employment to trade liberalization alone. The fact that output fell more than what had been registered during previous demand-management stabilization programs, however, indicates that trade liberalization contributed to the deteriorating performance of the economy.

33. This is consistent with the view that export intensities are high in the case of industries that are not capital intensive and are not intensive in the use of imported raw materials, but enjoy a high value added content. After all, in capital-scarce economies there is no reason to expect capital intensive industries to be major exporters.

34. The case of Mexico in the late 1980s and early 1990s seems to resemble this effect.

35. The World Bank's seminal *World Development Report: The Challenge of Development* (1991b), for instance, presents as a central analytical argument that economic growth is determined essentially by the growth of total factor productivity of capital and labor.

36. Estimates of total factor productivity for Taiwan and South Korea are found in Wang (1990) and Dollar and Sokollof (1990), respectively.

37. De Melo and Tybout (1986) is an early example of the simplest specification exercises that identify pre- and post-liberalization periods with a dummy variable.

38. The return in peso-denominated assets became very attractive, and Argentine citizens switched from foreign currency to peso assets. As a consequence of increasing inflation, the real exchange rate lost value and the country ended up with one of the most notorious capital flights in modern history.

39. In this case, liberalizing the rate of interest may have a perverse effect on the balance-sheet structure of the private productive sector and other financial units, causing bankruptcies, generating financial instability, and finally hindering the process of growth itself. These scenarios have been very common in several Latin American countries since the 1980s.

40. This should not be confused with Lewis's position about the role of savings on economic growth. Lewis still maintains the view that growth is saving constrained.

41. Guillen-Romo (1987) reports that in the two years of recession in Mexico, 1982 and 1983, high interest rates encouraged capitalists to shift their portfolios from real to financial assets. Diaz Alejandro (1981) mentions the case of Chile between 1975 and 1979 as an example of private sector caution in undertaking long-term commitments, particularly when the newly liberated financial system offers fairly liquid investment outlets with high yields. Morisset (1993) confirms this thesis in the case of Argentina.

42. This has been the case in several financial liberalization episodes in Latin America. In Venezuela, for instance, after the abolition of government controls on interest rates in 1989, the market-determined interest rate rose to almost 40 percent, and remained so for several months. The inflation rate, however, almost duplicated this value in the same year.

43. In particular, the sequence should start with inflation control, followed by interest rate liberalization, privatization, unification of foreign exchange rates, trade liberalization, and lastly opening up economies to capital flows.

CHAPTER 4

Toward an Alternative Approach to Stabilization and Growth

4.1 *Introduction*

Economists in Latin American countries find themselves today in a paradoxical position. On the one hand, the prolonged crisis has thoroughly discredited the dominant IMF/WB orthodoxy. Even though the overall external context has gradually improved, the instability of the economies of Latin America show only scant signs of receding, and even less of disappearing. The rather peculiar way in which successful economies in the region have managed to establish stability seems to indicate that the story of restructuring efforts in these countries has its own idiosyncratic side, for which a simple orthodox description of the facts does not account. On the other hand, the illusion that the economic problems of the region can be grasped using the basic notions of orthodox economic theory has been shattered by reality. The failure to resolve the basic problems was, and in part still is, a reflection of the erroneous conventional analysis. Conjectural models designed for the context of industrial countries, often applied in Latin America, have usually ended up provoking stagnation, inflation disorder, and greater income inequality. Nevertheless, devaluation, fiscal contraction, monetary restraint, financial liberalization, trade openness, and relative price realignment are still the ingredients of orthodox recipes, with little progress being made in serious discussions of structures, institutions, and history. On the theoretical side, several gaps in orthodox models for stabilization and adjustment have been exposed previously. It is astonishing that although even orthodox economists recognize some of the shortcomings of the conventional framework, the analytical models of the IMF and the

World Bank, and the way in which they are used, continue largely unaltered. Political officials and policymakers, however, are less persuaded than they once were of the virtues of orthodox packages to assure stabilization and sustainable growth, and they are now searching for alternatives.[1] At least with respect to structural reforms, more emphasis is put on institutional changes today. Nevertheless, it is unquestionable that there is a need for a theoretical framework that can provide us with a better understanding of macroeconomic issues and can stimulate the development of innovative economic policies to deal with stabilization and growth. This framework could be more useful and relevant than that provided by the orthodox analysis if its distinctive elements of analysis took into account the effective functioning of modern capitalist economies, and the particular historical, structural, and institutional features of Latin American economies. Our aim in this chapter, therefore, is to present a framework that it is just as comprehensive as that of the IMF's and the World Bank's, while at the same time far more close to the elements just mentioned (realism, history, structures, and institutions).

Neoclassical theory and its Keynesian variant may be the dominant orthodoxy within economic theory, but it is far from being universally accepted, either in industrialized or in less-developed countries. There has always been a significant number of economists who have rejected this orthodoxy as the appropriate starting point for understanding economic behavior. Among the most important heretics are post-Keynesian economists, although, of course, they are not the only ones. The core of the post-Keynesian paradigm derives from the efforts by several of Keynes's closest associates at Cambridge (in the years following his death in 1945) to go beyond the principle of effective demand in describing the dynamics of an "advanced" market economy. Given its anti-orthodox origins, post-Keynesian economics came to embrace a wide variety of approaches, broaching a wide range of issues. These models range from Sraffian theories of long-run equilibrium positions of price and output, to Keynesian theories where the long-run expectations induce short-run behavior. We find in the middle the Kalecki/Kaldor alternative, which contains a framework that allows the study of short-run phenomena in which there are also long-run factors in operation. Of course, this classification is used here only as a rough guide. Individual works often fall into two groups, or fall between groups. Moreover, the identification of the spectrum of post-Keynesian subschools is in some sense arbitrary.[2] These three post-Keynesian subschools are by no means the only ones, but just the most prominent among many. Each subschool has tended to highlight only a few aspects of its founding fathers to the exclusion of all others, but many could be considered to be complementary. For many this is the main advantage of the post-Keynesian approach, since it allows one to embrace different forms of abstraction to answer different questions. That is the essence of what Dow (1985) calls the "Babylonian method." Certainly the basic elements of the post-Keynesian paradigm were not initially brought out and fitted together in a unifying theoretical scheme. However, since the mid-1970s, exciting new work have been undertaken and attempts have been initiated to reconcile the short-period analysis with the long-period analysis.[3] In addition, we will stress here that many insights of the post-Keynesian school will help us reveal some of the complexities of LDCs.

It is precisely for these reasons that we must specify at the outset the theoretical framework we employ, which we identify as post-Keynesian. The post-Keynesian approach, as developed here, owes much to the writings of Michel Kalecki and Nicholas Kaldor. There are at least two basic reasons for adopting the Kalecki/Kaldor alternative. First, it is well known that Kalecki and Kaldor put a lot of time and effort into developing a macroeconomic framework for industrial countries in which institutions, class struggle, and industrial organization are of considerable importance in determining the distribution of income, the level and composition of output, the capacity for generating surplus, and the degree to which that surplus is expanded in such a way as to increase output and employment. Secondly, both Kalecki and Kaldor had a genuine interest in the problems of LDCs, a fact that is highlighted in their work on growth and income distribution.

Nevertheless, a typical LDC of the type we will delineate in this chapter cannot be adequately understood simply on the basis of a purely post-Keynesian frame of reference. Applying the post-Keynesian approach to LDCs requires moving beyond the set of presupposed notions of order. Complementary references have to be developed to deal with the particular aspects that define the operation and constraints of these economies. The old Latin American structuralist school has emphasized these aspects in a rather heuristic manner.

Although structuralist propositions have sometimes been insufficiently rigorous, over the years they have enriched our comprehension of certain economic processes in the region, and they suggest fruitful alternative routes for our own analysis. Some of these insights have recently been formalized by the new-structuralist revival.

What we suggest is that a synthesis of these traditions is not only possible but also desirable. On the one hand, post-Keynesian economics offers a very appropriate approach to the economic reality of market economies based on a money-production–distribution–class relationship. On the other hand, structuralist economics offers some minimal but essential sectoral distinctions, which help us to understand the principal internal features and constraints faced by LDCs. Furthermore, as we will argue in the first section, post-Keynesianism and structuralism not only use a similar methodology but also share important tenets.

The chapter is divided into two sections. The first section provides an introduction to the methodology employed by the post-Keynesian school and the structuralist tradition. We also discuss the essentials on the basis of which both paradigms construct their theories. It is not the purpose of the first section to provide an exhaustive account of these schools. Rather, we offer a summary that aims to illustrate the benefits of the proposed synthesis while presenting certain fundamental ideas and concepts, and essentially a way of approaching the analysis of capitalist economies of the Latin American region.

In the second section we outline a macroeconomic framework for the analysis of alternative policies in LDCs that could eventually lead to macrostability with growth. Here, we proceed in three stages. First, we outline the basic model, covering production, demand, income distribution, market-clearing conditions, external finance, the fiscal sector, and inflation dynamics. Second, we examine how equilibrium values of the endogenous variables are determined. The different equations taken jointly form an independent subsystem of the model, which suffices to determine the values of the endogenous variables. Third, the inflationary dynamics are described as the result of conflicting claims and changes in relative prices. Finally, we include the capital accumulation process in an analysis of steady state dynamics. In this way, we will be able to study the long-run interactions between investments, production capacities, and income distribution in a growth context.

Our basic model differs from the conventional macromodels for stabilization and adjustment in several respects. It is post-Keynesian in the sense that it takes as its central focus an approach to economic reality based on a money-production–distribution-class relationship. Oligopolistic product markets, collective bargaining in labor markets, and differentiated marginal propensities to save help us to determine not only output, employment, and prices, but also real profit and wage rate determination, which can then be used to investigate income distribution issues. Income distribution is important also because it determines the resources available for investment and growth. As an important distinctive feature, the model is not set up in real terms, but it includes prices and income flows in nominal (or money) terms.[4] We make some minimal, but essential sectoral distinctions so as to reflect the principal internal characteristics of LDCs. The primary (food or necessities) and industrial sectors are clearly distinguished, where production, pricing, and demand formation are established according to specific structural features. In this respect our study is inspired in several theoretical pieces. The chosen formulation owes a lot to the models of Cardoso (1981) and Taylor (1982, 1983) of a dual economy that captures the relationship between excess demand in the primary sector, inflation and wage formation. Rattso (1984), Modiano (1989), FitzGerald (1989, 1990), Parkin (1991), and Dutt (1991) have further contributed to this line of research.[5] Unlike Cardoso and Taylor and their associates, our model is very rich, as it includes not only primary- and secondary-sector supply and demand constraints, respectively, but a foreign exchange and a government budget constraint (introducing additional transmission mechanisms for policy variables). Moreover, we add a fully specified external sector with capital inflows rationing, in which, instead of deriving the conditions for improving the balance of payments at a given level of income, we study the conditions that can put a country on a higher growth path consistent with payments equilibrium. In two-sector models, some aspects, such as the treatment of the public sector, are simpler, and the battery of policy tools is restricted (see FitzGerald 1990 and Parkin 1991). We introduce a fiscal constraint in which the government cannot finance an increasing deficit, and the public sector borrowing requirement is constant, and, as a consequence, has to adjust public investment. Once we have formalized the links between the different constraints we will suggest in the next chapter some hypotheses regarding state policy toward stabilization and growth, a topic that remains unexplored in the literature.

4.2　Post-Keynesian Economics and Structuralism: Methodology and Main Tenets

Post-Keynesian economics has already established its foundations firmly as a forward-looking development with sound and distinct methodology and insights. At a methodological level, the main concern of post-Keynesian economists is to understand the important problems and constraints facing real-world economies. As such, the advantage of the post-Keynesian approach, in the words of Eichner (1979, p. 168), "is that it enables one to confront the problems directly and openly rather than to conceal them under simplifying assumptions." For Lavoie (1990, p. 6), in the post-Keynesian research program "a theory cannot be correct unless it incorporates realistic hypotheses." This explains, for instance, why Caldwell (1985, p. 55), in a recent contribution on post-Keynesian methodology, remarks that the major critique post-Keynesians make of orthodoxy is that the latter is unrealistic. There is nothing striking here. After all, the idea that economics should be realistic was an element that Kaldor, Kalecki, Robinson, and other post-Keynesian economists emphasized in a great part of their work. For them, assumptions should be sensible, the structure of the model should avoid unrealistic elements, and implausible or impossible behavior should never be assumed. Of course, realism by itself would not make a compelling case for introducing these considerations, since all economic theories leave out many aspects of reality. In fact, realists fully accept that any theoretical analysis requires abstraction (Donward and Reynolds 1996). But abstractions must be realistic rather than imaginary. The point is that abstractions should have a counterpart in reality, if the theory is to be a useful explanation of reality. The reason for emphasizing the role of realistic assumptions and plausible behavior is that they seem to allow a straightforward explanation of our theoretical and empirical puzzles.

This adoption of "realism" as an explicit or implicit methodological point of reference has several important consequences. First, the assumptions become subject to empirical scrutiny. Second, an explanatory power of current events becomes much more important than predictive accuracy. Finally, as Arestis (1990, p. 226) has correctly pointed out, "when realism is shown to be at the heart of post-Keynesian methodology, it becomes inevitable that history and institutions are an integral part of that methodology." We may infer, therefore, that history and institutions constitute the second essential element of post-Keynesian methodology. To understand how important history and institutions are, let us consider, for instance, the expenditure-switching model studied in chapter 2. The model attributes the impact that devaluation has on the trade balance to the relative price mechanism that makes home products relatively cheaper. It is clear that the orthodox position depends not only on the magnitude of certain elasticities but also on the "unrealistic" assumptions of homogeneous goods and competitive imports, the insensitivity of the domestic price level to exchange rate variations, etc. This position can only be maintained if the historical development of the productive structure in Latin America is ignored. The fact of the matter is that industrialization through import substitution in Latin America increased the import content of every unit of current output and investment, and helped to build a highly concentrated industrial sector behind protective barriers. How can we possibly assume competitive imports and the constancy of the price level after currency devaluation? If history and realism had been required at the level of the initial and essential hypothesis, the story would have been different.

The recognition of history and institutions lead us to the third essential element of post-Keynesian methodology, which is the need to develop context-specific frames of reference. This element is emphasized by Dow (1985, p. 15), who claims that "post-Keynesian theory is context-specific and, as such, requires continuous and repeated reappraisal of its uses in view of current changes." Hamouda and Harcourt (1989, p. 32) equally remark that "post-Keynesian analysis [is] much geared to concrete situations…of the economies concerned." Thus, the revision of theory in light of new empirical evidence is a necessary condition if we do not want to fall into the methodological trap of maintaining hypotheses that are no longer relevant.

At a methodological level, the compatibility between post-Keynesian economics and structuralism are remarkable. Structuralism is best thought of as denoting an approach or method of analysis of economic issues rather than a specific theory (or a set of theories). Unfortunately, a great deal of confusion remains in the academic literature, where structuralism is commonly associated with Prebish's thesis of the asymmetries in the dynamics of exchange relations between the "center" and the "periphery," or with the structuralist theory of inflation. It is misleading to reduce structuralism to these theories, though they were certainly present at its birth and have since played an important role in the evolution of structuralist thought. A careful scrutiny of the available work of structuralist authors indicates, however, that structuralism is more "a method of inquiry" than anything else (Palma 1987, p. 316). Structuralist economists, like post-Keynesians, advocate for and emphasize a "realist-historic-context-specific" approach to scientific knowledge. Jameson (1986, p. 226), for instance, identifies structuralism as "the discovery of scientifically correct representations of reality." In other words, structuralism is derived from a realist concept of science, in contrast with the approaches to scientific knowledge used in social sciences, such as positivism or instrumentalism. Schydlowsky (1990, p. 33) states that for structuralism "history matters…and institutions and the structure of the capital stock must be taken into account." Finally, Ffrench-Davis (1988, p. 40) describes the structuralist paradigm as one in which "the answers may vary, according to the point in time concerned and the prevailing institutional structure." These substantial similarities between the post-Keynesian and the structuralist methodologies come down to being a matter of qualitative importance with regard to the way in which the main hypotheses and features of the economy are established. Here, it is not difficult again to identify the common ground between these two alternative approaches.

As we have just mentioned, post-Keynesian economics is not a homogeneous body of thought; nevertheless, we may summarize, from a

Kaleckian/Kaldorian perspective, some of the essential tenets on which we believe all post-Keynesians may agree, and that we will incorporate into the economy modeled in the section that follows. These tenets are based upon what Kaldor (1961) called "stylized facts," or empirical generalizations drawn hierarchically at the macro, sectoral, and micro levels about the economy in question. Naturally, these empirical generalizations are the result of the realist-historical and context-specific methodological approach employed by post-Keyensian scholars.

Among the main features of the post-Keynesian (or Kaleckian/Kaldorian) approach, we mention the following.

First, the employment decisions of firms are portrayed as depending directly on the output decision. Given the level of output, the required level of employment is determined simply by the technical conditions of production. It follows, therefore, that the aggregate level of employment depends on the level of effective demand. This is, of course, an inherited element of Keynes's economic analysis that plays a central role in all the variants of post-Keynesian approaches (Dutt 1992).

A second tenet is the importance of class distinctions. Following the "classical" writers and the contributions of Kalecki (1971), Kaldor (1955–56), and Pasinetti (1962), post-Keyensians have emphasized the importance of distinguishing between classes and their income level.[6] Class analysis and income distribution are central to the analysis for at least four reasons:

(a) Class struggle will determine the distribution of income.
(b) Different classes have different saving propensities.
(c) Income distribution changes have an effect on the pattern of spending and saving, and on the rate of accumulation.
(d) Class struggle over the distribution of income affects the rate of inflation.

A third important feature is the way production is carried out in a capitalist economy. Production is central in post-Keynesian analysis. As Eichner (1985) has emphasized, the post-Keynesian theory of production is based, in the simplest case, on an "open Leontief model" in which a particular set of technical coefficients (labor and material inputs required to produce a given unit of output) exist independently of any particular set of prices. As a result, the production coefficients represent a given state of technology that has a logically prior existence.[7]

A fourth important feature is the presence of rules of thumb and conventions in the behavior of individuals and groups in their decision-making process. Individuals with limited capacities for acquiring information and processing it must rely on group behavior. As a result of these real-life deficiencies in the logistics of decision making, procedures and rules of thumb have to be followed. The following are some specific rules of thumb that post-Keynesians emphasize in their models.

(a) In a modern industrial economy markup pricing is the norm. Prices are set as a markup over average direct costs (wages and intermediate inputs), so that short-run variations in the level of demand will result in output-adjustments. This is very much the Kaleckian approach to pricing, though this is not the only rule of behavior employed by post-Keynesians in their price equations.

(b) The working sector negotiates money wages based on a target real wage and on expectations of the price level of the economy, as emphasized long ago by Sargan (1964). Hence money wage claims react to deviations of the current conditions with respect to the targets (see Sawyer 1982 and Arestis 1986).

(c) Investment behavior is governed by variations in current profitability (Kalecki 1971), which is supposed to be the best proxy for expected profitability, and by the rate of capacity utilization (Steindl 1952). Joan Robinson provided an illuminating exposition of the Kaleckian theory of investment and the so-called two-sided relationship between accumulation and profitability. Expected profitability (which is dominated by current profitability) induces accumulation, while realized accumulation itself creates the profitability that makes accumulation possible, partly through the supply of internal funds. Steindl, continuing in the direction taken by Kalecki, believed that the utilization of productive capacity was fundamental to the investment planning of oligopolistic firms. Confronted, for instance, with a decline in demand, firms would cut back output (as in Kalecki) rather than prices, but the resultant fall in output would reduce capacity utilization, and therefore reduce investment.

Fifth, post-Keynesians have a particular view of how the money stock comes into being. The stock of money in a capitalist economy is seen as being essentially demand driven or endogenous. Money is created alongside spending decisions, and as such its creation is essentially a disequilibrium phenomenon (Moore 1988) in the sense that some economic agents in the system must be anxious to expand their expenditure, in order for money to be created.

Sixth, post-Keynesians distinguished "cost-determined" prices, such as the prices of manufactured goods, from "demand-determined prices," such as those of raw materials and agricultural products. The supply of manufactured goods tends to be elastic, the firms being quite happy to supply more output at a constant price, while the supply of agricultural products tends to be inelastic, at least in the short period. This distinction is based on Kalecki's work (1943), but was also used by Kaldor (1976) to discuss a wide range of long-term phenomena observable from recent international experience.

Finally, even though post-Keynesian theory of growth is still in the formative stage, there are, certain discernible features of its central core that can be outlined. Drawing on a particular tradition in growth theory that dates back to the works of Kalecki and Steindl, the prominent features of these models are the presence of an investment function that depends on entrepreneurial expectations of future profitability, and the endogenous determination of the rate of capacity utilization. Given the expectations of future profit opportunities, it is the propensity to save out of current money income of the various savings groups, and the distribution of income among savers that are the "independent" forces upon which the accumulation of capital is dependent in a modern capitalist economy. For simplicity of the analysis, post-Keynesians in this case assume that steady-state growth is the result of the convergence of a dynamic income distribution process to equilibrium.

The particular stylized facts of modern capitalist economies outlined here are obviously the result of the particular methodology that underlies the post-Keynesian approach. It is not surprising, then, with this methodology as its starting point, that structuralism has emphasized very close stylized representations of the less-developed economies of Latin America. Curiously enough, leading post-Keynesian figures such as Kaldor and Kalecki interacted closely with a number of important figures of the structuralist school during the 1950s and 1960s, and even though it cannot be said that they brought structuralism to Latin America—because it was already in the air—there can be little doubt that they provided an important intellectual stimulus to its formulation.[8] Many structuralist authors actually acknowledge their proximity to post-Keynesian theories.[9]

A complete account of the main tenets of the structuralist approach is not an easy task; however, the best list of these elements can be found in Malan and Wells (1984), Ffrench-Davis (1988), Taylor (1983, 1991), and Lustig (1991). Summarizing the description made by these authors we can say that in a typical less-developed economy of Latin America we find:

(a) An economic structure that is insufficiently elastic to adapt continuously to match changing patterns of demand to supply produces great disparities between the growth of demand and supply in different markets.

(b) The supply of "key" goods may be very inflexible, and the factors of production may be unable to move quickly, if at all (production bottlenecks).

(c) Primary and secondary sectors adjust differently.

(d) The most relevant social actors are not price takers. It is, rather, the presence of economically powerful actors that influences price and/or quantity adjustment in certain markets.

(e) Macroeconomic causality flows from investment, exports, and fiscal demand to income, import, and output. Thus, predetermined variables generate savings (or leakages).

(f) For technological reasons, imported intermediate and capital goods are required to support local production and capital formation.

(g) Foreign exchange to buy imports can be a binding constraint (the economy suffers from "external strangulation").

(h) Changes in relevant relative prices can have output and distributional implications.

(i) Macroeconomic equilibrium does not involve full employment of either labor or installed capacity economywide.

(l) The roots of inflation lie in unresolved distributional conflicts and propagation mechanisms (such as the indexation of contracts).

(k) Money is "passive" or endogenously determined.

(l) The development process is neither balanced nor harmonious, and it arises from the incorporation and dissemination of technical progress. New investment is the principal instrument of this process.

(m) The public sector is severely constrained by a very rigid public expenditure, and by revenue and the existence of the outstanding external debt.

(n) Public investment can be complementary and encourages private investment (the crowding-in hypothesis).

As mentioned earlier, many of the stylized representations of institutions and structures of production built into the structuralist analysis very much resemble those proposed by post-Keynesians. There are, however, within the structuralist approach, some particular stylized representations that go some way toward overcoming a number of limitations—and filling some of the possible gaps—that could be associated with the post-Keynesian position. Sectoral distinctions, production and foreign-exchange bottlenecks, dependence on imported intermediate and capital goods, and the fiscal constraint caused by a highly indebted public sector become essential elements in any attempt to build an alternative merging framework. Similarly, a merging framework such as ours benefits not only from the existence of the structuralist alternative that deals with the peculiarities of the less-developed countries of Latin America, but also from the existence of a reasonably large post-Keynesian literature based on a money-production–distribution-class relationship.

4.3 The Basic Model: Outline and Justification

We next present the building blocks of our model. Although facts and empirical scrutiny scarcely ever carry the case in economic models, where necessary we present some relevant justification for the assumptions, structure, and behavioral equations of the model. Our basic model starts with a fully specified open economy in which two productive sectors exist: a primary sector producing a pure-consumption good (food, raw materials, and basic needs), and an industrial sector producing a consumption-cum-investment good. A government budget equation is included, as well as a fully specified monetary and external sector. The inflation dynamic directly follows the conflicting behavior of economic agents. The equation structure of the model is laid out in a compact form in table 4.1.

The basic model consists of the following relationships:

Table 4.1

Primary Sector		
$Q_1 = \psi u_1 k_1$	(4.1)	Output of basics
$Q_{1e} = (1 - \psi)u_{1e}k_{1e}$	(4.2)	Output of exports
$L_1 = Q_1/b_1$	(4.3)	Short-run employment (basics)
$L_{1e} = Q_{1e}/b_{1e}$	(4.4)	Short-run employment (exports)
$p_1 Q_1 = WL_1 + r_1 p_2 k_1$	(4.5)	Income distribution of basics
$p_{1e}Q_{1e} = WL_{1e} + r_{1e}p_2 k_{1e}$	(4.6)	Income distribution of exports
$p_1 Q_1 = \varepsilon WL$	(4.7)	Supply and demand balance of basics

Table 4.1   *(continued)*

$p_{1e}Q_{1e} = ep_{1e}^{*}x_1$	(4.8)	Supply and demand balance of exports
$p_{1e} = ep_{1e}^{*}$	(4.9)	Law of one price

Secondary Sector

$Q_{2f} = u_{2f}k_2$	(4.10)	Full capacity output
$Q_2/k_2 < Q_{2f}/k_{2f}$ or $u_2 < u_{2f}$	(4.11)	Excess capacity
$L_2 = Q_2/b_2$	(4.12)	Employment
$(p_2 - ep_m a)Q_2 = WL_2 + r_2p_2k_2$	(4.13)	Net income flows
$p_2 = (1 + \tau)[W/b_2 + ep_m a]$	(4.14)	Pricing
$p_2Q_2 = (1 - \varepsilon)WL + (1 - s_c) \times$ $[r_1p_2k_1r_{1e}p_2k_{1e} + r_2p_2k_2] + \zeta p_2I_2 + p_2x_2$	(4.15)	Supply and demand balance

Public Sector

$I_1p_2 + p_2G + J - t_c(r_2p_2k_2 +$ $r_{1e}p_2k_{1e} + r_1p_2k_1) - PSBR = 0$	(4.16)	Government fiscal account
$J = i^*D$	(4.17)	Net factor services to countries abroad
$PSBR = PSBR^*$	(4.18)	Public sector borrowing requirement

Balance of Payments

$X^{nom} - IM^{nom} + CF - J = \Delta R$	(4.19)	Balance-of-payments surplus
$X^{nom} = p_{1e}x_1 + p_2x_2$	(4.20)	Nominal exports
$IM^{nom} = ep_m aQ_2 + ep_m(1 - \zeta)I_2$	(4.21)	Nominal imports

Monetary Block

$LD = LD(p_{1e}Q_{1e} + p_1Q_1 + p_2Q_2, PSBR)$	(4.22)	Loan demand
$i_L = (1 + m)i_F$	(4.23)	Loan pricing equation
$LS + c_1DEP = DEP + TD$	(4.24)	Bank balance sheet constraint
$TD = c_2DEP$	(4.25)	Demand for time deposits
$CIR = c_3DEP$	(4.26)	Demand for currency
$HD = CIR + c_1DEP$	(4.27)	Total demand for base
$LS = LD$	(4.28)	Loan market clearing condition
$M = CIR + DEP$	(4.29)	Money supply M1

Inflation Dynamics

$p = p_1^{\varepsilon}p_2^{(1-\varepsilon)}$	(4.30)	Consumer price index
$\rho = p_1/p_2$	(4.31)	Relative prices
$w = W/p$	(4.32)	Real wage
$W = Tp$	(4.33)	Desired nominal wage

Table 4.1   *(continued)*

$(dp_1/dt)/p_1 = \Psi[\varepsilon WL/p_1 - Q_1]$	(4.34)	Movement of primary sector prices
$(dp_2/dt)/p_2 = \omega(dW/dt)/W$	(4.35)	Movement of secondary sector prices
$(dW/dt)/W = \varphi[T - w]$	(4.36)	Movement of nominal wages
$\pi = (p - p_{t-1})/p_{t-1}$	(4.37)	Inflation rate

Variables and Parameters of the Model are now listed

Sectors

1	=	Basic goods
1e	=	Primary Sector Exports
2	=	Industrial goods

Exogenous Variables

k_i	=	Capital stock in sector i
W	=	Nominal wage rate
p_{1e}^*	=	World price of primary exports in foreign currency
e	=	Nominal exchange rate
x_i	=	Volume of exports in sector i
p_m	=	Foreign currency price of intermediate imports
G	=	Real government expenditure
I_2	=	Real private investment
$PSBR$	=	Public sector borrowing requirement
D	=	Nominal stock of external debt in domestic currency
i^*	=	World interest rate
i_F	=	Central bank interest rate
CF	=	Nominal net capital flows

Intermediate Endogenous Variables

Q_1	=	Output of basic goods
Q_{1e}	=	Output of primary exports
Q_{2f}	=	Full employment manufacturing output
L_1	=	Employment level (basics)
L_{1e}	=	Employment level (exports)
r_i	=	Rate of profit in sector i
p_2	=	Price of industrial goods
p_{1e}	=	World price of primary exports in domestic currency
X^{nom}	=	Nominal exports
IM^{nom}	=	Nominal imports
i_L	=	Bank loan interest rate
LD	=	Loan demand
DEP	=	Demand deposits

Table 4.1 *(continued)*

CIR	$=$ Currency
HD	$=$ Total demand for base

Final Endogenous Variables

p_1	$=$ Price of basic goods
Q_2	$=$ Manufacturing output
u_2	$=$ Capacity utilization in the manufacturing sector
L_2	$=$ Employment level in the industrial sector
ΔR	$=$ Change in international reserves
I_1	$=$ Real public investment in infrastructure
M	$=$ Money supply $M1$
π	$=$ Inflation Rate
p	$=$ Consumer price index
ρ	$=$ Relative prices or domestic terms of trade
w	$=$ effective real wage
$[(dX/dt)/X]$	$=$ Rate of change of the respective variable

Parameters

ψ	$=$ Basics-to-primary exports composition
u_i	$=$ Output–capital ratio of sector i
b_i	$=$ Productivity of labor in sector i
ε	$=$ Proportion of wages spent on basics
τ	$=$ markup on unit cost
a	$=$ input–output coefficient for intermediates
s_c	$=$ Capitalists marginal propensity to save
ζ	$=$ Fraction of total investment satisfied by domestic producers
T	$=$ Target real wage
Ψ	$=$ Speed of adjustment of the price of basics to excess demand in the primary sector
ω	$=$ Degree of adjustment of industrial prices to changes in nominal wages
φ	$=$ Speed of adjustment of nominal wages to the gap between the target and actual real wage
m	$=$ Bank markup
c_1	$=$ Required reserve ratio for demand and time deposits
c_2	$=$ Time deposit/demand deposit ratio
c_3	$=$ Currency/demand deposit ratio

Specifically, the primary sector in this economy produces two outputs: "basics" (or necessities), Q_1, and exports, Q_{1e}, where the subscripts 1 and 1e refer to basics and exportables, respectively.[10] In this typical less-developed economy, basics consist almost wholly of agricultural products—especially foodgrains.[11] The output level of this type of goods is assumed to be fixed in the short run. Storm (1997) argues that most empirical studies show that price responsiveness of aggregate agricultural output is relatively weak, and Mamingi (1996), in an extensive review of the empirical literature for LDCs, finds that agricultural supply response is inelastic in the short run.[12] Taylor (1993), for instance, reports that supply elasticities in the 0.1–0.3 range are statistically typical in many LDCs, and Parkin (1991) estimates an average elasticity of food production with respect to lagged price of 0.26 for Brazil. These figures fit with the traditional structuralist view of food supply response. Structuralism sees "productive bottlenecks" as being the result of the traditional and unequal factor tenure structure that characterized the incipient mode of production of the agricultural sector of LDCs. The fact of the matter is that an economy that suffers from this kind of productive bottleneck cannot be perceived as a conventional economy with some temporary and not-too-significant deviations from equilibrium that can be overcome in the short term by merely submitting it to the actions of market laws. Instead, it has to be visualized as a peculiar configuration subject to different laws and priorities. Later on, we will argue that the productive bottleneck in the primary sector can only be overcome by the injection of some amount of infrastructure (or "primary capital").

As Diamond (1978, p. 20) points out, "a bottleneck . . . presupposes a production function of (approximately) fixed coefficients, at least in the short run." Hence, production of two outputs in the primary sector is determined by the output capital ratios u_1 and u_{1e} as shown by equations (4.1) and (4.2). The stock of capitals k_1 and k_{1e} are assumed to be non-shiftable. The coefficient ψ denotes the basics to exports composition, which is assumed to be fixed. There is an unlimited supply of labor in the sector in the sense that the amount of labor does not affect the level of primary sector output. In post-Keynesian fashion, equations (4.3) and (4.4) define short-run employment L_1 and L_{1e} as functions that depend on aggregate demand only (where b_1 and b_{1e} represent labor productivities). The demand for basics is determined solely by consumption expenditure of primary sector and industrial workers L, at an exogenous (for the moment) wage rate W (as shown in equation (4.7)). We assume for simplicity that a proportion ε of salaries is spent on basics. The good is sold in a competitive market, which implies that the basics price p_1 varies to clear the market. The primary sector exports market balance (equation (4.8)) is made of, first, supply determined by output at an exogenous world price p_{1e}^* (see equation (4.9)) and policy-determined exchange rate e; and second, demand made up of exports x_1 (exogenously given), again at world prices.[13] Equations (4.5) and (4.6) determine the distribution of income between wages and profits in both basics and primary exports, and will allow us to determine the profit rates r_1 and r_{1e}.

The industrial sector produces a single good, Q_2 (with the dual character mentioned above), and operates under oligopolistic conditions at a price p_2. Production requires capital k_2, intermediate goods, and labor L_2 in fixed coefficients. As in the primary sector the capital stock is fixed once it is installed. We will assume that excess capacity exists so that the economy does not reach full capacity output Q_{2f}. It is important to mention that excess capacity resembles modern industry and services in many LDCs. Evidence of this stylized fact is cited in Schydlowsky (1979) and Hughes (1976). In Latin American economies, where import-substituting industrialization policies generated oligopolistic market structures and a run against the limits of the size of the internal market, excess capacity must either exist in the economy or be created as a result of the recessive adjustments being adopted. Employment L_2 in industry is related in a fixed proportion b_2 to the level of industrial activity Q_2, as in equation (4.12). Since production here takes place under an oligopolistic environment, markup pricing along the lines urged by Kalecki is a plausible behavior. The markup τ is defined over "direct" cost of labor W/b_2 and imported intermediates $ep_m a$, as represented by equation (4.14). p_m and a represent the foreign price of intermediate imports and the imported physical component of the industrial product, respectively. As Ramos (1989) has emphasized, the assumption that the corporate sector has a certain margin to set prices clearly relates to the tradition of the south. The determination of manufacturing prices has been the subject of a number of empirical studies in Latin America. In general these studies suggest that the markup pricing hypothesis is capable of explaining the determination of manufacturing prices.[14] In Kalecki (1943) the margin is a positive function of the "degree of monopoly." The latter, he argued, depended upon the level of concentration in an industry, the development of sales promotion, overhead costs and the influence of trade unions. Equation (4.13) reflects the distribution of income $p_2 Q_2 - ep_m a Q_2$ that is made up of two categories: wage recipients WL_2 and profit recipients $r_2 p_2 k_2$. Industrial output demand is reflected by equation (4.15). Demand is made up of four elements: the nonbasic component of wage expenditure; that part of total profits that is not saved under the given capitalist propensity to save (s_c);

the investment requirement I_2, which is partly met by domestic production in ζ proportion; and export demand x_2, which is exogenously given.

Now let us describe the demand and supply balances for necessities and the industrial good. Notice that for simplicity we have assumed that capitalists do not consume basics or necessities, and that workers do not save and spend a high proportion of wages on necessities.[15] This composition of private consumption by income groups is consistent with the data reported by Flores and Espinasa (1979) for Latin American countries.[16] Recent empirical data collected by Mena (1996) for the Chilean economy suggests that for modeling purposes two different representative groups can be conceived: a group (called household owners) that owns the firms and can be described as individuals with perfect access to financial markets; and a group (that could be called household workers) whose income profile only allows them to be at a minimum subsistence level of consumption.[17]

Equation (4.16) introduces the fiscal sector into our analysis. As we claimed earlier, output in the primary sector is determined by the amount of infrastructure. The amount of infrastructure is determined by government investment I_1 (following the lines suggested by Rao 1993 and Dutt 1991). The level of primary output is therefore constrained by public "productive expenditure" $p_2 I_1$. The government has a fixed "unproductive" expenditure requirement $p_2 G_1$, which is assumed to be a fixed share of industrial capital stock,[18] and also pays interest i^* on the foreign stock of debt D (equation (4.17)), a fact that does no great violence to reality in Latin America, where governments hold nearly all external obligations, even those of the private sector (Taylor 1993). The government also obtains tax revenue from direct taxation of profit income rpk coming from all productive activities (we assume that the same tax t_c rate is applied to all sectors). Note from expression (4.18) that $PSBR$ is preset at a given level. Thus, for a given level of public sector borrowing requirement, a given level of unproductive expenditure, an exogenous interest payment, and a limited tax capacity, public investment becomes the only alternative to force the balance, an assumption that is real in highly indebted countries, and that we employ as a novelty in the model. In fact, by analyzing the impact of the external debt crisis on the Latin America region, Eyzaguirre (1989) speaks of a dominant fiscal constraint as a situation in which $PSBR$ is fixed and the variable that adjusts is government investment. The United Nations Commission for Trade and Development (1989, pp. 90–91) reports that fiscal adjustment during the 1980s involved mainly spending cuts rather than revenue increases, and "the burden fell primarily on capital spending, which was more than halved in a number of countries." Bresser-Pereira (1990, p. 507) remarks that the public sector adjustment of the early 1980s in Brazil "was achieved perversely through the reduction of public sector investment." But this idea that governments in LDCs often cut capital spending in order to achieve fiscal adjustment is not just anecdotal. Hicks (1991) reports this behavior in a sample that covers 15 LDCs and 11 Latin American countries, using data from the IMF's government finance statistics databank for the period 1979–85. The study shows that for highly indebted countries the sector that appears to have suffered the most is the infrastructure sector. Harris and Kusi (1992) reach similar conclusions for a selected group of African countries (see Hicks 1991, and Harris and Kusi 1992).

We open the economy by introducing commercial transactions and financial transfers. A well-documented amount of work indicates that any increase in the level of income or any growth strategy in a less-developed economy has to face the limitations imposed by the balance of payments. In nominal terms the balance-of-payments surplus is described by expression (4.19). There, the trade surplus $X^{nom} - M^{nom}$ plus the net financial transfers $CF - J$ should equal the change in international reserves ΔR. On the left-hand side of (4.19), CF represents the sum of nominal autonomous net capital inflows measured in domestic currency, and J denotes net factor services abroad. Net capital inflows may be aggregated and composed by direct foreign investment, portfolio flows, bank credits, and official development assistance. In general, we consider these flows to be driven by factors outside the control of governments, and few would now dare to prognosticate on this score. Direct foreign investment and portfolio flows may be expected to respond to disparities in expected profitability and interest rate differentials, but there are considerable international constraints that greatly reduce their international mobility.[19] In fact, they have more to do with events in the countries of origin and may, therefore, be taken to be exogenous in the present study. Nominal exports can come from the primary and the industrial sector, as set up in expression (4.20), and their respective volumes, x_1 and x_2, are determined exogenously, at least in the short run.[20] The price of primary exports is geographically arbitraged so that the law of one price applies, but since the country specializes also in the production of the manufacturing good, domestic and foreign manufacturing goods are less than fully homogeneous or substitutable, so prices will be given also. Dornbusch (1987, p. 95) refers to these as the "two extreme models of price relationships in the open economy literature" and writes that the first "will be a useful model of international price relations for materials—say sisal, cooper, tea—whereas [the second] more nearly describes what happen to manufactures." We should point out, however, that in most countries of

Latin America, the capacity to generate foreign exchange still rests much more upon traditional primary sector goods than upon nontraditional manufacturing exports. Data collected by Ibarra (1988) shows that although exports of manufactured goods increased almost tenfold between 1970 and 1981, they represented scarcely more than 8 percent of the total goods sold, and in 1985 their share of the world industrial goods trade was still less than 2 percent. Expression (4.21) presents nominal imports, which are considered non-competitive and broken down into two types of goods (entirely used by the industrial sector): intermediate and capital goods.[21] For 1990 the Inter-American Development Bank reports that 83.1 percent of imports in the region consist of intermediate and capital goods. Since the third world debt crisis began, most Latin American economies have become credit constrained in the sense that the amount of capital inflows and the net factor payments abroad are determined by decisions beyond the control of local governments. Vos (1993), for instance, argues that the central hypothesis that the global capital market is segmented, and that developing countries face credit-rationing rules set by official and private creditors in the industrialized counties, incorporates theories of international lending under sovereign risk and oligopolisitic behavior of the international bank firms. Given the con-figuration of the external sector, adjustment has to come from reserves accommodation (Arida and Bacha 1987).

In our model money is introduced into the economy through the pro-ductive activities as these activities generate nominal income. Contemporary work in the post-Keynesian tradition (such as Kaldor 1970, Moore 1979 and 1988, Lavoie 1984, Arestis and Eichner 1988, and Palley 1994) suggests that changes in output and in the direct cost of production lead to changes in the demand for credit finance. The banks create deposits as needed to meet this demand and then find the reserves later. The role of the central bank is to set the level of official short-term interest rates. There is no denial of a statistical association between changes in the money supply and changes in nominal income, but causation runs from nominal income to the money supply and not vice versa. This thesis of "endogenous money" and its validating char-acter has been also pointed out by some structuralist economists, such as Rangel (1963), Olivera (1970), and Bresser-Pereira and Nakano (1987).[22] It is clear, however, that the public sector borrowing requirement (*PSBR*) is one of the crucial factors that will influence money supply in LDCs (Ghatak 1981). Therefore, besides bank lending to the private sector, bank lending to the government will also determine the loan demand function. Our mone-tary block put together the ideas just expounded in a pure loan demand context based on Palley (1994). Equation (4.22) is a loan demand schedule,

LD, which is a positive function of the overall nominal income of the economy and the public sector borrowing requirement, $PSBR$. Equation (4.23) is the loan pricing equation, according to which the loan rate, i_L, is a fixed markup, m, over the central bank interest rate, i_F, which is set by the monetary authority. Equations (4.25) and (4.26) describe the demands for time deposits, TD, and currency, CIR, as fixed proportions of the demand for checkable deposits, DEP. The banks balance sheet constraint is represented by equation (4.24), where banks' total liabilities consist of demand and time deposits. Equation (4.27) defines the total demand for base, HD, as composed of reserves, $c_1 DEP$, and currency, CIR. Equation (4.28) is the loan market clearing condition, while equation (4.29) is the definition of the money supply, M_1. We should point out that although little attention is paid to either the asset and liability management decisions of banks, or the portfolio decisions of nonbanks, the monetary block captures the important post-Keynesian insight regarding the significance of bank lending for the determination of the money supply.

To us, the basic cause of inflation is not money. It is likely that monetary authorities are not causing an expansion *motu proprio*; rather, they are simply accommodating monetary pressures originating outside the money market. More specifically, inflation is the outcome of structural disequilibrium and conflicting claims among economic agents or sectors. Our model fully describes the dynamics of this kind of inflationary scenario. We define the consumer price index of general price level p as a linear homogeneous function of basics and industrial prices as represented by equation (4.30). We know that ε represents the portion of wages spent on basics. Equations (4.31) and (4.32) are trivial expressions for the primary sector manufacturing price ratio p_1/p_2 and the effective real wage w. Equation (4.33) can be interpreted as a simple version of the target real wage hypothesis, now very popular among post-Keynesian economists (see, for instance, Sawyer 1982 and Arestis 1986). Instances of the application of the target real wage model to LDCs are still very limited, but the real wage resistance hypotheses has been widely justified and used by structuralists to explain variations in nominal wages (see Diamand 1978, Cardoso 1981, and Taylor 1983).[23] Frenkel (1986) provides an up-to-date survey of the arguments and the outcomes of several empirical studies on wage formation in Latin American countries. An important common element he found in most studies is the significant impact that institutional factors play in the determination of nominal wages in the private sector. There are, in particular, organizational forms, rules, and social norms that indicate that some form of wage resistance prevails in these countries. According to the target real wage hypothesis, aimed at reaching a target real wage T, organized workers have to translate their basic objectives into a money wage objective, for bargaining takes place in money terms. Thus, money wages are not modeled as exogenous or predetermined anymore. In dynamic form we may see the movement in nominal wages $(dW/dt)/W$ as a gradual adjustment to the gap between the target and effective real wage, as represented by equation (4.36). Industrial price inflation adjusts instantaneously, however, to changes in cost. Therefore, assuming that the markup, the labor unit requirement, and the unit cost of intermediate inputs remain constant, the movement in industrial prices will be a fraction ω of the movement in nominal wages (equation (4.35)). Finally, equation (4.34) states that primary goods prices respond to excess demand for basics $(\varepsilon WL/p_1 - Q_1)$ at the adjustment rate Ψ. A dynamic process is implicit in this set of equations. An output increase in the industrial sector or any shock that causes excess demand for basics leads through equation (4.30) to a fall in the effective real wage (equation (4.32)). Moving down through equations (4.35) and (4.36) industrial prices will increase, generating an inflationary process. The dynamics of adjustment of this process will be explored in the next section.

4.4 Short-run Equilibrium

4.4.1 Market Clearing Conditions

It is clear from expressions (4.7) and (4.8) that primary products are either consumed by the working class (as food, for instance) or exported. However, the assumptions of a fixed basics-to-exports composition ψ, a nonshiftable capital, and an unlimited supply of labor make matters simpler, since primary exports become virtually an "enclave."[24] Primary exports do not compete for resources with any other sector of the economy.

Since primary exports production does not depend on prices, and the market price is determined by the world market, the supply curve will be perfectly inelastic and the demand faced by primary exports perfectly elastic, as shown in figure 4.1.

Basic goods are sold in a competitive market, which implies that the price varies to clear the market. Taking expression (4.7) and knowing that total employment L in the economy is given by the sum of employment in both primary and manufacturing sectors, we may define the excess demand function for the primary sector, ED_1, as:

$$p_1 Q_1 = \varepsilon W[(Q_1/b_1) + (Q_{1e}/b_{1e}) + (Q_2/b_2)] \qquad (4.38)$$

Figure 4.1

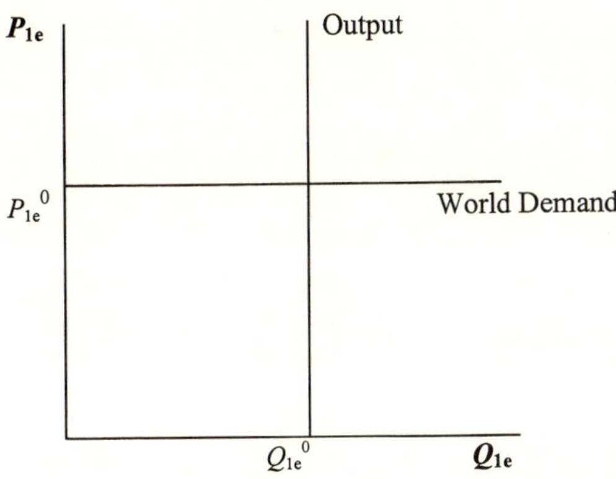

so that

$$p_1 = \varepsilon W(1/b_1 + Q_{1e}/b_{1e}Q_1) + (\varepsilon W/Q_1 b_2)Q_2 \tag{4.39}$$

with

$$\frac{dp_1}{dQ_{2|ED_1=0}} = \frac{\varepsilon W}{Q_1 b_2} > 0 \tag{4.40}$$

An increase in industrial output Q_2 increases the demand for basics and thus its market clearing price.

In order to obtain a similar expression for the manufacturing sector we first introduce profit rates in all sectors. After substitution of (4.1) and (4.3) for Q_1 and L_1 in (4.5), and (4.2) and (4.4) for Q_{1e} and L_{1e} in (4.6), the following expressions for profit rates of basics and primary exports yields

$$r_1 = [p_1 - W/b_1]u_1/p_2 \tag{4.41}$$

$$r_{1e} = [p_{1e} - W/b_{1e}]u_{1e}/p_2 \tag{4.42}$$

and substitution of (4.12) and (4.14) into (4.13) yields

$$(1 + \tau)[W/b_2 + ep_m a] = W/b_2 Q_2 + r_2[(1 + \tau)(W/b_2 + ep_m a)]k_2$$

Solving for r_2 and simplifying we get

$$r_2 = \frac{\tau}{(\tau + 1)} \frac{Q_2}{k_2} \tag{4.43}$$

Substitution of r_1, r_{1e}, and r_2, into (4.15) allows us to express the supply and demand balance for the manufacturing sector, ED_2, as

$$p_2 Q_2 = (1 - \varepsilon)WL + (1 - s_c)[(p_1 - W/b_1)u_1 k_1$$
$$+ (p_{1e} - W/b_{1e})u_{1e}k_{1e} + (\tau/(1 + \tau))p_2 Q_2]$$
$$+ \zeta p_2 I_2 + p_2 I_1 + p_2 x_2 \tag{4.44}$$

We already now that $L = (Q_1/b_1) + (Q_{1e}/b_{1e}) + (Q_2/b_2)$. Substituting L above and solving for p_1 we have

$$p_1 = \frac{-(1 - \varepsilon)\frac{W}{p_2}(L_1 + L_{1e}) - (1 - s_c)\left(r_{1e}k_{1e} - \frac{Wu_1 k_1}{b_1 p_2}\right) - \zeta I_2 - I_1 - x_2 + \left[1 - (1 - \varepsilon)\frac{W}{b_2 p_2} - (1 - s_c)\frac{\tau}{1 + \tau}\right]Q_2}{(1 - s_c)\frac{u_1 k_1}{p_2}}$$

$$\tag{4.45}$$

with

$$\frac{dp_1}{dQ_2}\bigg|_{ED_2 = 0} = \frac{\left[1 - (1 - \varepsilon)\frac{W}{b_2 p_2} - (1 - s_c)\frac{\tau}{1 + \tau}\right]}{(1 - s_c)\frac{u_1 k_1}{p_2}} > 0 \tag{4.46}$$

An increase in the price of basics raises the demand for manufactures, and industrial output grows in response to this excess demand.

Macroeconomic equilibrium will exist when supply equals demand simultaneously in both basics and industry, and savings equals investment. These three equilibrium conditions are not independent. It can easily be shown that if any two of the conditions hold, the third equation is necessarily satisfied.

This partial solution to the model is illustrated in figure 4.2.

The slope of the curve NN, which represents equilibrium in the market for basics, is positive. Points to the right of NN represent excess demand for basics and rising equilibrium prices in this market. Along it, the market for industrial products is in equilibrium. Points to the right of II indicate excess supply of manufactures and falling industrial output.

Stability of equilibrium will depend upon adjustment dynamics. Plausible dynamics are as follows. Assume, for instance, that the economy is at point

Figure 4.2

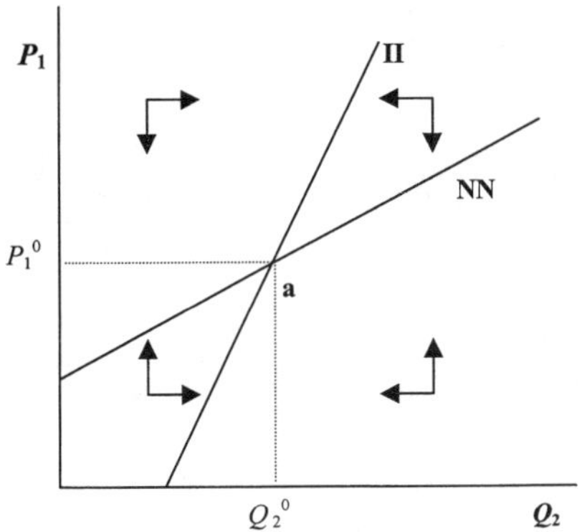

'b' in figure 4.2. There is excess demand for both basics and industrial goods. The excess demand for the basic good raises its price, and the excess demand for manufactures results in higher industrial output. Income growth leads the economy to point 'a', where NN and II intersect. Intuition will tell us that the system is stable if the slope of II is greater than the slope of NN, i.e. if

$$\frac{\left[1 - (1 - \varepsilon)\dfrac{W}{b_2 p_2} - (1 - s_c)\dfrac{\tau}{1 + \tau}\right]}{(1 - s_c)\dfrac{u_1 k_1}{p_2}} > \frac{\varepsilon W}{Q_1 b_2}$$

Formally, the (local) stability of this short-run equilibrium requires the Jacobian of the system formed by the excess demand functions has a negative trace and a positive determinant.

From (4.38) and (4.44) the excess demand functions for the industrial and primary sector are

$$ED_2 = (1 - \varepsilon) W \left(\frac{Q_1}{b_1} + \frac{Q_{1e}}{b_{1e}} + \frac{Q_2}{b_2}\right)$$

$$+ (1 - s_c)\left[\left(p_1 - \frac{W}{b_1}\right) u_1 k_1 + \left(p_{1e} - \frac{W}{b_{1e}}\right) u_{1e} k_{1e} + \frac{\tau p_2 Q_2}{(1 + \tau)}\right]$$

$$+ p_2 I_2 + p_2 I_1 + p_2 x_2 - p_2 Q_2 \tag{4.47}$$

$$ED_1 = \varepsilon W \left[\frac{Q_1}{b_1} + \frac{Q_{1e}}{b_{1e}} + \frac{Q_2}{b_2}\right] - p_1 Q_1 \tag{4.48}$$

and the specific adjustment rules are

$$\frac{dQ_2}{dt} = f[ED_2(Q_2, p_1)] \tag{4.49}$$

$$\frac{dp_1}{dt} = g[ED_1(Q_2, p_1)] \tag{4.50}$$

where the functions f and g satisfy $f(0) = 0$ and $g(0) = 0$.

The Jacobian of the system given by (4.47) and (4.48) is

$$\begin{bmatrix} \left[(1-\varepsilon)\dfrac{W}{b_2 p_2} + (1-s_c)\dfrac{\tau}{1+\tau} - 1\right] & (1-s_c)\dfrac{u_1 k_1}{p_2} \\[2em] \dfrac{\varepsilon W}{b_2} & -Q_1 \end{bmatrix}$$

The determinant of the Jacobian is

$$\det = \left[1 - (1-\varepsilon)\frac{W}{b_2 p_2} - (1-s_c)\frac{t}{(1+\tau)}\right]Q_1 - \frac{\varepsilon W}{b_2}(1-s_c)\frac{u_1 k_1}{p_2}$$

It is clear from this that for the determinant to be greater than zero, the conditions for the slope of II and NN have to be satisfied, i.e.

$$\left[1 - (1-\varepsilon)\frac{W}{b_2 p_2} - (1-s_c)\frac{\tau}{(1+\tau)}\right]Q_1 > \frac{\varepsilon W u_1 k_1}{b_2 p_2}(1-s_c)$$

but since $[(\varepsilon W u_1 k_1)/b_2 p_2](1-s_c) > 0$, then $[1 - (1-\varepsilon)W/b_2 p_2 - (1-s_c)(\tau/1+\tau)]$ will also be positive and the Trace of the system will be less than zero, i.e.

$$Tr = \left[(1-\varepsilon)\frac{W}{b_2 p_2} + (1-s_c)\frac{\tau}{(1+\tau)} - 1\right] - Q_1 < 0$$

Now, let us assume that the primary sector output can shift between export commodities and domestic basics at the margin with relative facility. In this case, prices are no longer set according to domestic supply and demand, but are set according to world prices, mediated by the exchange rate. A typical structuralist assumption is that increased domestic demand for the primary good will shift resources (or products) away from exports.[25]

Expression (4.7) applies with some modifications:

$$ep^*_{1e}x_1 = p_{1e}Q_1 - \varepsilon WL_1 - (\varepsilon W/b_2)Q_2 \qquad (4.51)$$

Exports represent a residual after domestic demand is met by domestic production. Increased domestic output in the manufacturing sector (increased demand for basics) will shift resources away from exports. An alternative closing rule will leave domestic demand as a residual after foreign demand for basics is satisfied. In either case it is obvious, that the productive bottleneck in the primary sector in a foreign exchange-constrained economy will bring about a trade-off between the domestic satisfaction of basics needs and the relaxation of the foreign exchange constraint.

The whole issue can be better illustrated diagrammatically. The horizontal axis in figure 4.3 represents the share of the domestic consumption of necessities in total primary output, ϑ, while the vertical axis measures $(1 - \vartheta)$, or the export share of basics in total primary output. The line RR reflects the supply restriction, which is given by

$$\frac{ep^*_{1e}x_1}{p_{1e}Q_1} = 1 - \left(\frac{\varepsilon WL}{p_{1e}Q_1}\right) \qquad (4.52)$$

The ray drawn from the origin HH indicates different bundles in which the shares of domestic consumption and exports of basics remain constant. At point "a," the value of ϑ is well below the "acceptable minimum consumption of basics," ϑ_m, and the excess demand in the domestic market can

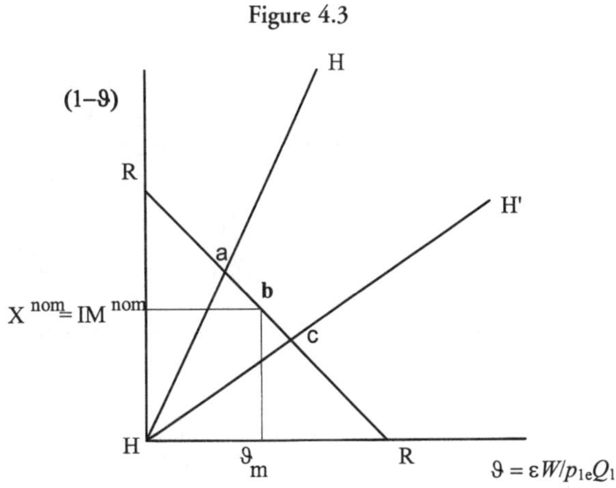

Figure 4.3

eventually activate an inflationary situation. At point "c" the value of ϑ is above ϑ_m, and exports of basics goods do not cover the amount of imports of the economy.

4.4.2 The Foreign Exchange Constraint

Macroeconomic equilibrium as we have defined it is consistent in the model with the balance between foreign exchange receipts and payments. The impact of external constraints on internal adjustment now becomes clear. From expression (4.19) we can see that imports of intermediate products for industry and complementary capital goods are supported by foreign exchange receipts from exports (from basics and manufacturing) and capital inflows. Since the economy is credit constrained (or capital constrained), the value of CF is determined by decisions beyond the control of the economy. Thus, the output limit in the manufacturing sector will be defined by the availability of foreign exchange. However, short-run adjustments to trade imbalances can be accomplished through changes in the level of international reserves accumulation. Using (4.19), (4.20), and (4.21) we can drive (4.53) as

$$\Delta R = ep_{1e}^{*}x_1 + p_2x_2 + CF - ep_m aQ_2 - ep_m(1 - \zeta)I_2 - J \qquad (4.53)$$

Of course, once reserves are exhausted, the foreign exchange constraint can be expressed as

$$ep_m aQ_2 + ep_m(1 - \zeta)I_2 + J \leq ep_{1e}^{*}x_1 + p_2x_2 + CF \qquad (4.54)$$

While the functioning of the economy and government policies do not exhaust the amount of international reserves, the level of industrial production Q_2 that maintains the external balance is determined as

$$Q_2 = \frac{1}{a}\left[\frac{1}{ep_m}(p_2x_2 + CF - J - \Delta R) + \frac{p_{1e}^{*}}{p_m}x_1 - (1 - \zeta)I_2\right] \qquad (4.55)$$

Industrial output is constrained by industry dependence on imports (ζ and a), the external terms of trade (p_{1e}^{*}/p_m), and the purchasing power of capital inflows and interest payments.

Figure 4.4, which is adapted from Modiano (1989), displays the balance-of-payments condition ($-\Delta R$). The positive-sloped line $-\Delta R$ will intercept the vertical axis on the negative range, where international reserves accumulate. Notice that the higher the level of industrial activity the more imports of intermediate products are required, and hence, the larger the balance-of-payments deficit that must be covered through declining reserves. The equilibrium price p_1^0 and output Q_2^0, determined by the intersection of II and NN in figure 4.4a, determines the corresponding equilibrium variation in reserves $-\Delta R^0$. The vertical line labeled $\Delta R = 0$ stands at the level of industrial activity for which the external sector is balanced. Positions to the left of $\Delta R = 0$ represent a balance-of-payments deficit.

Figure 4.4

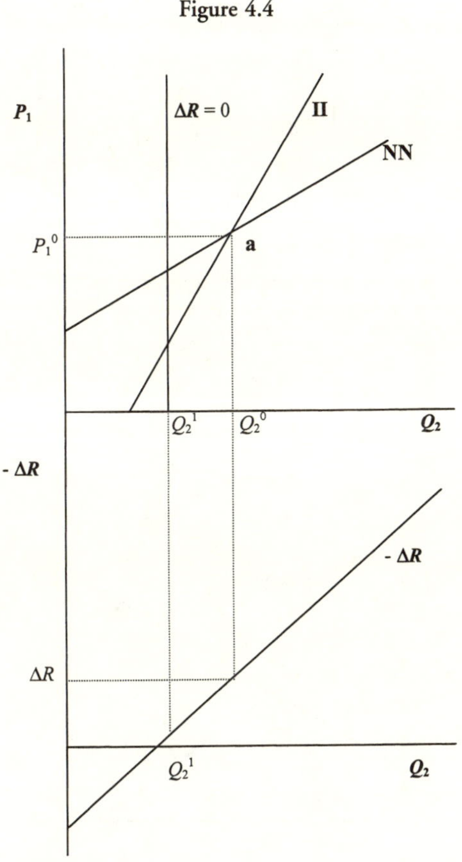

Adapted from Modiano (1989)

4.4.3 The Public Sector and the Fiscal Constraint

Taking the government fiscal account we will speak of a fiscal constraint if the government cannot increase *PSBR* beyond certain limit. This can be expressed as

$$I_1 p_2 + p_2 G + J \le t_c (r_2 p_2 k_2 + r_{1e} p_2 k_{1e} + r_1 p_2 k_1) \qquad (4.56)$$

Substitution of (4.41), (4.42), and (4.43) into expression (4.16) yields,

$$I_1 p_2 + p_2 G + i^* D - t_c [\tau/(1+\tau) Q_2 p_2 + r_{1e} p_2 k_{1e} + r_1 p_2 k_1] = PSBR \qquad (4.57)$$

Government activity affects the equilibrium values of Q_2 and p_1.

$$Q_2 = \frac{1}{t_c \dfrac{\tau}{(1+\tau)}} \left[I_1 + G + \frac{i^* D}{p_2} - \frac{PSBR}{p_2} \right.$$

$$\left. - \frac{t_c}{p_2} \left[r_{1e} p_2 k_{1e} + \left(p_1 - \frac{W}{b_1} \right) u_1 k_1 \right] \right] \qquad (4.58)$$

The fiscal balance ($PSBR = PSBR^*$) is drawn as GG in figure 4.5 and derives from the expression

$$p_1 = \frac{I_1 + G + \dfrac{i^* D}{p_2} - t_c r_{1e} k_{1e} + \dfrac{t_c W u_1 k_1}{p_2 b_1} - \dfrac{PSBR}{p_2} - \dfrac{t_c \tau}{(1+\tau)} Q_2}{\dfrac{t_c u_1 k_1}{p_2}} \qquad (4.59)$$

Figure 4.5

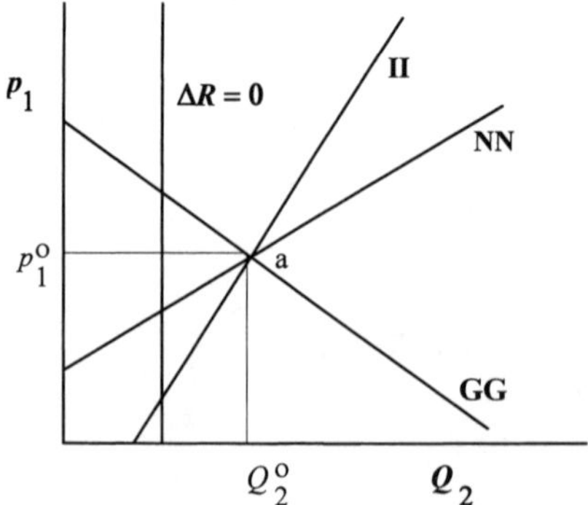

where

$$\frac{dp_1}{dQ_2}\bigg|_{PSBR=PSBR^*} = \frac{-\tau p_2}{(1+\tau)u_1 k_1} < 0 \qquad (4.60)$$

The GG curve is shown with a negative slope, indicating that the more favorable the industrial output becomes (higher tax collection), the lower the price in the primary sector must be to maintain fiscal balance (lower tax collection). Positions to right and above the curve represent fiscal surplus.

If it is inadmissible or impossible to cover an increasing level of *PSBR* to finance a fiscal imbalance, an adjustment will probably be required in the amount of public investment since other variables usually present little flexibility. This yields

$$I_1 = \frac{PSBR}{p_2} - G - \frac{i^* D}{p_2}$$
$$+ \frac{t_c}{p_2}\left[\frac{(1+\tau)}{\tau}Q_2 + p_2 r_{1e} k_{1e} + \left(p_1 - \frac{W}{b_1}\right)u_1 k_1\right] \qquad (4.61)$$

The presence of the public sector introduces some minor but important changes in expressions (4.5), (4.6), and (4.13). Expressions (4.5) and (4.6) for the income distribution in the primary sector become

$$P_1 Q_1 = WL_1 + (1 - t_c)r_1 p_2 k_1 \qquad (4.62)$$

$$P_{1e} Q_{1e} = WL_{1e} + (1 - t_c)r_{1e} p_2 k_{1e} \qquad (4.63)$$

Similarly, the distribution of income in the industrial sector will be

$$(p_2 - ep_m a)Q_2 = WL_2 + (1 - t_c)r_2 p_2 k_2 \qquad (4.64)$$

Public sector activity will also affect domestic demand in the secondary market, so that (4.15) can in fact be rewritten as

$$p_2 Q_2 = (1 - \varepsilon)WL + (1 - s_c)(1 - t_c)p_2[r_1 k_1 + r_{1e} k_{1e} + r_2 k_2]$$
$$+ p_2(\zeta I_2 + x_2 + I_1 + G) \qquad (4.15a)$$

which can be solved for p_1.

$$p_1 = \frac{-(1-\varepsilon)\frac{W}{p_2}(L_1 + L_{1e}) - [1 - s_c(1 - t_c)]\left(r_{1e}k_{1e} - \frac{Wu_1k_1}{b_1p_2}\right) - \zeta I_2 - I_1 - x_2 + \left[1 - (1-\varepsilon)\frac{W}{b_2p_2} - (1 - s_c(1 - t_c))\frac{\tau}{1+\tau}\right]Q_2}{[1 - s_c(1 - t_c)]\frac{u_1k_1}{p_2}} \tag{4.65}$$

These minor changes do not affect drastically the shape of the II schedule.

Though the instruments of taxation considered so far are rather simple, it would not be difficult to consider among other instruments the incidence of indirect taxation, such as a tax on the consumption of "nonbasics."

4.4.4 Endogenous Money

Following the post-Keynesian theory of money and credit our model focuses on the availability of and demand for credit rather than on the supply of what is usually defined as the money stock. In particular, it is the demand for credit that is viewed as the critical link between the real and monetary sectors. The availability of credit is perfectly elastic at the lending rate, and the demand for credit depends on private sector nominal income and the public sector borrowing requirement. Using (4.28) and (4.22) we get the loan market clearing condition

$$LD(p_{1e}Q_{1e} + p_1Q_1 + p_2Q_2, PSBR) = LS \tag{4.66}$$

Substituting (4.25) and (4.66) into (4.24) we may determine the level of demand deposits associated with any given level of bank lending, i.e.,

$$DEP = \frac{LD(p_{1e}Q_{1e} + p_1Q_1 + p_2Q_2, PSBR)}{(1 + c_2 - c_1)} \tag{4.67}$$

This expression captures the fundamental post-Keynesian claim that loans create deposits. Substituting (4.26) and (4.67) into (4.27) yields

$$HD = \frac{(c_3 + c_1)LD(p_{1e}Q_{1e} + p_1Q_1 + p_2Q_2, PSBR)}{(1 + c_2 - c_1)} \tag{4.68}$$

which determines the demand for base associated with the level of demand deposits. Similarly, substituting (4.26) and (4.67) into (4.29) we get the full expression for the narrow money supply, i.e.

$$M1 = \frac{(c_3 + 1)LD(p_{1e}Q_{1e} + p_1Q_1 + p_2Q_2, PSBR)}{(1 + c_2 - c_1)} \tag{4.69}$$

Expansionary shifts of loan demand increase the level of bank lending, and thereby increase the level of demand deposits ("loans create deposits") and the narrow money supply. The reverse holds for contractionary shifts of loan demand.

4.5 Inflation Dynamics

In this section we show how inflation develops as a symptom of structural disequilibrium and conflict distribution among economic agents. First, it will be useful to express the relative price between basics and manufacturing goods ρ in terms of the effective real wage w. To do so, we use equations (4.32) and (4.30) to obtain

$$w = W p_1^{-\varepsilon} p_2^{(\varepsilon-1)} \tag{4.70}$$

Dividing (4.70) by p_2 and rearranging, we get[26]

$$w = \left[\rho^{\varepsilon} \left[\frac{(1+\tau)(W b_2 + a e p_{\mathrm{m}})}{W} \right] \right]^{-1} \tag{4.71}$$

which can also be expressed as

$$\rho = \left[\left[\frac{(1+\tau)(W b + e a p)}{W} \right] w \right]^{-1/\varepsilon} \tag{4.72}$$

Equation (4.72) is similar to that presented by Cardoso (1981) and Taylor (1983) but includes the effect of unit costs of intermediate imports. By making the assumption that workers push up money wages to maintain a target real wage T (4.72) may be rewritten as

$$\rho^0 = \left[\left[\frac{(1+\tau)(W b + e a p)}{W} \right] T \right]^{-1/\varepsilon} \tag{4.73}$$

Equation (4.73) represents the non-inflationary relative price, ρ^0, i.e. a relative price that requires exact consistency between the fixed markup and the target real wage. No conflict occurs since both these aspirations are satisfied. Higher markups, higher unit costs, or higher desired real wage will cause a decline in ρ^0.

Again (4.73) can be rearranged and expressed in terms of p_1, so we have

$$p_1^0 = \left[\frac{W}{T} [(1+\tau)(W b_2 + a e p_{\mathrm{m}})]^{\varepsilon-1} \right]^{1/\varepsilon} \tag{4.74}$$

Figure 4.6

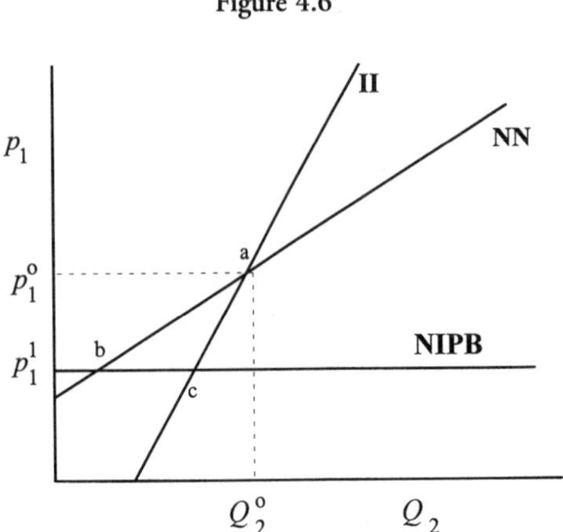

The non-inflationary basics price (NIBP), p_1^0, is plotted as the line NIBP in figure 4.6.

In figure 4.6, the line NIBP is shown together with equilibrium in the markets for basic goods and industrial products, represented by NN and II, respectively. It is obvious that barring the coincidental case in which the three curves meet at a point, there is no equilibrium, that is, it is not possible for markets to clear and for the aspirations of different classes to be satisfied. We have, then, two prices for basic goods (p_1^1) and (p_1^0). If they coincide, a non-inflationary equilibrium in basics and industrial goods prevails. If, however, as in figure 4.6, the economy is at point 'a' where goods markets clear but the prevailing real wage is too low to satisfy workers' aspiration $(p_1^0$ is too high), a price inflation will be sparked off.

Hence, the behavior of this economy depends crucially on our assumptions about the responses of the variables and agents to disequilibrium. We have assumed that primary goods suffer from rigidities so that output in that sector is fixed in the short run and movements in p_1 clear the market. In sector 2, if demand exceeds supply, Q_2 increases. But this increase in output in the industrial sector will raise demand for basics. To restore primary sector equilibrium, then, p_1 moves up. If p_1 rises, then workers push up W. To this the entrepreneur in sector 2 responds by pushing up p_2. The net effect is that if p_1 is too high, i.e. p_1 is above the non-inflationary price of basics, then p_2 rises.

From the definition of ρ in (4.31) we obtain

$$\frac{(d\rho/dt)}{\rho} = \frac{(dp_1/dt)}{p_1} - \frac{(dp_2/dt)}{p_2} \tag{4.75}$$

In the primary sector the price p_1 adjusts as per excess demand for basics (as represented by equation (4.34)).

$$\frac{dp_1/dt}{p_1} = \Psi\left[\frac{\varepsilon WL}{p_1} + Q_1\right] \tag{4.34}$$

Worker's indexation rule has been formalized by equation (4.36) as follows:

$$\frac{(dW/dt)}{W} = \varphi(T - w) \tag{4.36}$$

When the effective real wage w is below the target T, workers will react, pushing up nominal wages. The coefficient φ describes the speed of adjustment.

In the market for industrial goods, we will continue assuming that the markup remains constant, and that capitalists do not have an anticipatory behavior with respect to possible losses in real income caused by an increase in the price of basics.[27] The negative impact of an increase in the price of basics will make workers to react. Firms pass on the increase in production cost by raising industrial prices. This dynamic can lead to conflict inflation since price changes in the industrial sector become a function of the gap between the effective price of basics and that compatible with the aspirations of workers and capitalists, i.e.

$$\frac{(dp_2/dt)}{p_2} = \omega\left(\frac{dW/dt}{W}\right) = \omega\varphi(T - w) = \omega\varphi(p_1 - p_1^0) \tag{4.76}$$

Notice that the impact of a change in nominal wages upon industrial prices is less than complete since wages represent only a portion of unit cost.

4.6 A Growth Extension

The basic model can be extended to a model of growth that permits a role for both the primary sector supply constraint and the aggregate demand constraint. The aim is to formalize the links between the two constraints and suggest some hypotheses regarding state policy toward growth. In the framework of two-sector growth models this line has been explored by Dutt (1991) and Rao (1993). We extend the analysis to an open economy with a fiscal restraint, and later in the text we will evaluate some novel policy implications.

Growth in our model means that in the long run the stocks of capital in each sector can change. In a model of the type set up here, intersectoral linkages can complicate economic analysis. Thus, for simplicity, we may assume, under certain stability conditions, that the system will settle down to a steady state, with all sectors' capital stock expanding at the same rate. We may start, then, by introducing the following relations in our system.

$$g_1 = I_1/k_1 \tag{4.77}$$

$$g_2 = I_2/k_2 \tag{4.78}$$

$$\lambda = k_1/k_2 \tag{4.79}$$

These expressions describe the growth rates of the stocks of capital in both sectors 1 and 2 (assuming away depreciation) and the ratio between the stocks of capital, respectively.

The next step is to transform (4.39) and (4.44) into equivalent expressions in growth terms. In order to do that, we first rearrange (4.41) and (4.43) to obtain

$$P_1 = (r_1 p_2/u_1 - W/b_1) \tag{4.80}$$

$$Q_2 = k_2(1 + \tau)r_2/\tau \tag{4.81}$$

Substituting into (4.39) and solving for r_2 we get

$$r_2 = \left[r_1 \psi \lambda p_2 - \frac{1}{b_{1e}k_2} - \frac{(1 + \varepsilon)WQ_1}{b_1 k_2} \right] \frac{b_2 \tau}{\varepsilon W(1 + \tau)} \tag{4.82}$$

Now substituting (4.80) and (4.81) into (4.15a) and recalling that $L = (Q_1/b_1 + Q_{1e}/b_{1e} + Q_2 + b_2)$ we may solve also for r_2

$$r_2 = \frac{(1 - \varepsilon)\dfrac{W}{p_2 k_2}(L_1 + L_{1e}) + (1 - s_c)(1 - t_c)\left(r_1 \lambda + r_{1e}\dfrac{k_{1e}}{k_2}\right) + \zeta g_2 + \dfrac{I_1}{k_2} + \dfrac{x_2}{k_2} + \dfrac{G}{k_2}}{\dfrac{(1 + \tau)}{\tau}\left[1 - \dfrac{(1 - \varepsilon)W}{p_2 b_2}\right] - (1 - s_c)(1 - t_c)}$$

$$\tag{4.83}$$

As before, these equations describe equilibrium conditions in the primary sector and the manufacturing sector, respectively. Now using these equations we can solve the system for the equilibrium expressions r_1 and r_2:

$$r_1^e = \frac{\dfrac{(1-\varepsilon)\dfrac{W}{p_2 k_2}(L_1 + L_{1e}) + (1-s_c)(1-t_c)\left(r_{1e}\dfrac{k_{1e}}{k_2}\right) + \zeta g_2 + \dfrac{I_1}{k_2} + \dfrac{x_2}{k_2} + \dfrac{G}{k_2}}{\dfrac{(1+\tau)}{\tau} - (1-s_c)(1-t_c) - (1-\varepsilon)\dfrac{Wb_2}{p_2}\dfrac{(1+\tau)}{\tau}} - \left(\dfrac{-Wu_1(1-\varepsilon)\psi\lambda}{b_1} - \dfrac{\varepsilon WQ_{1e}}{k_2 b_1}\right)\dfrac{b_2\tau}{\varepsilon W(1+\tau)}}{\dfrac{b_2\tau\psi\lambda p_2}{\varepsilon W(1+\tau)} - \dfrac{(1+\tau)}{\tau}\left[1 - \dfrac{(1-\varepsilon)W}{p_2 b_2}\right]\dfrac{(1-s_c)(1-t_c)\lambda}{\,} - (1-s_c)(1-t_c)}$$

$$(4.84)$$

$$r_2^e = \frac{b_2\tau}{\varepsilon W(1+\tau)}\left[\left[p_2 r_1^e - Wu_1/b_1(1-\varepsilon)\right]\psi\lambda - \frac{\varepsilon WQ_{1e}}{k_2 b_1}\right] \qquad (4.85)$$

From (4.84) and (4.85) it can be seen that the profit rate in the primary sector and the profit rate in the manufacturing sector are functions of the capital stock ratio λ. Assuming that a steady state is actually attained so that $r_1 = r_2$ and $g_1 = g_2$, we may equalize (4.84) and (4.85) and get an equilibrium solution value for λ. Note that under these conditions a long-run equilibrium solution for λ^e, r_1^e, and r_2^e can be attained.

Now the discussion about inflation and income distribution conflict can be extended in this model. If there is only one value of p_1^0 that is consistent with workers' and capitalists aspirations, then by equation (4.41) there will be only one value r_1^0 where both groups will reach such aspirations, i.e.

$$r_1^0 = [p_1^0 - W/b_1]u_1/p_2 \qquad (4.86)$$

If for some reason r_1^0 is lower than r_1^e, the equilibrium growth situation will be characterized by persistent inflation. As in our short-run analysis, the general conclusion of this section is that a trade-off between inflation and growth will exist due to the primary sector supply constraint. Therefore, in order to achieve growth without inflation, changes in the structural parameters and policy options have to occur, so that $r_1^0 = r_1^e$.

Given the importance of public investment in the primary sector we will see how the primary sector constraint in contexts such as the one in Latin American countries is ultimately located in the dynamics of the industrial sector.

In short-run equilibrium we assume that the excess demand for basics and industrial goods are driven to zero, so that the short-run equilibrium conditions lead to the saving–investment identity

$$I_1 p_1 + \zeta I_2 p_2 = S_c + S_e \qquad (4.87)$$

The first term on the right side of (4.87), S_c, represents nominal domestic savings (out of profits) from all activities. The second term, S_e, is the amount of foreign savings generated by the trade deficit minus the net financial transfers.

Nominal savings can be expressed as

$$S_c = s_c(1 - t_c)p_2(r_1k_1 + r_{1e}k_{1e} + r_2k_2) \qquad (4.88)$$

$$S_e = ep_m aQ_2 + ep_m(1 - \zeta)I_2 + J - ep^*_{1e}x_1 - p_2x_2 - CF \qquad (4.89)$$

When the assumption previously stated that public investment is financed by public savings holds, we have[28]

$$I_1 = PSBR^*/p_2 - G + t_c(r_1k_1 + r_{1e}k_{1e} + r_2k_2) \qquad (4.90)$$

Substitute for S_c, S_e, and I_1 into (4.87), assume additionally for simplicity that $ep_m = p_2$, and solve for I_2p_2 to get

$$I_2p_2 = [s_c(1 - t_c) - t_c]p_2(r_1k_1 + r_{1e}k_{1e} + r_2k_2) - PSBR^* + Gp_2$$

$$+ p_2aQ_2 + J - ep^*_{1e}x_1 - p_2x_2 - CF \qquad (4.91)$$

With the help of equation (4.43), Q_2 can be replaced by $Q_2 = [(\tau + 1)/\tau] \times k_2r_2$ in (4.91). Then dividing through by p_2k_2 and solving for I_2/k_2 we get

$$g_2^s = \left[[s_c(1 - t_c) - t_c](r\lambda_1 + r_{1e}k_{1e}/k_2) - \frac{PSBR^*}{p_2k_2} + \frac{G}{k_2} + \frac{J}{p_2k_2} \right.$$

$$\left. - \frac{ep^*_{1e}x_1}{p_2k_2} - \frac{x_2}{k_2} - \frac{CF}{p_2k_2} \right] + \left[s_c(1 - t_c) - t_c + \frac{a(1 + \tau)}{\tau} \right] r_2 \qquad (4.92)$$

or

$$g_2^s = \gamma_1 + \gamma_2 r_2$$

where

$$\gamma_1 = \left[[s_c(1 - t_c) - t_c](r_1\lambda_1 + r_{1e}k_{1e}/k_2) - \frac{PSBR^*}{p_2k_2} + \frac{G}{k_2} \right.$$

$$\left. + \frac{J}{p_2k_2} - \frac{ep^*_{1e}x_1}{p_2k_2} - \frac{x_2}{k_2} - \frac{CF}{p_2k_2} \right]$$

and

$$\gamma_2 = \left[s_c(1 - t_c) - t_c + \frac{a(1 + \tau)}{\tau} \right]$$

Expression (4.92) give us the rate of growth of the industrial sector from the saving side. It implicitly states that when the market for basic goods is in equilibrium and investment and saving are equal, the industrial sector will also be in equilibrium. Therefore, expression (4.92) must hold along any equilibrium growth path.

Now equilibrium growth in steady state requires that the rate of change of the capital stock ratio λ is zero, which means that the growth rates in both sectors (basic goods and nonessentials) should be equal:

$$\frac{d\lambda/dt}{\lambda} = g_1 - g_2 = 0 \quad \text{or} \quad g_1 = g_2 = g^0 \qquad (4.93)$$

Desired industrial investment is a key variable in this analysis. Albeit in a different time frame, the lines of causality in post-Keynesian growth models are clear and similar to those established for the equilibrium level of output: investment demand is the volatile variable that drives the system, determining equilibrium output growth. Thus, to the rate of growth of the two sectors, we add an investment demand function for the industrial sector.

Empirical studies of investment demand in Latin America are not abundant. There are, however, four recent studies that seem to shed light on the variables that determine the desire to invest in some countries of the region. Agosin (1996) envisions an econometric model for the ratio of private investment to GDP in Latin America (over the period 1970–90). The results and causal examination of the data suggest that slower growth of aggregate demand, more stringent domestic credit restraints, the adverse impact of the debt crisis, and relative price instability explain the poor performance of private investment. Ocampo, Londoño, and Villar (1985) survey the literature on the determinants of investment in Colombia. The evidence suggests that domestic demand is the major determinant of investment demand. Warman and Thirwall (1993) use regression analysis to test an investment function for Mexico over the period 1960–90. They conclude that demand-side determinants, specifically the lagged accelerator, explain very well variations on investment demand. Cardoso (1993) explores the determinants of investment in six Latin American countries (Argentina, Brazil, Colombia, Chile, Mexico, and Venezuela). The regressions use quadrennial panel data for the period

1970–85. The results show that the decline in growth explains much of the decline in private investment share. Here, we use a demand for investment function of the type advanced by Rowthorn (1981), Dutt (1984), and Taylor (1987b), where the first term γ_0 stands for "animal spirits" and can have either positive or negative signs, while γ_4 and γ_5 are positive constants. $R_2 = r_2 p_2 k_2$ stands for money income profits and is justified as representing an incentive for investment spending (actual profits serving as the best proxy for expected profits). The last term posits a positive relation between investment and short-run economic activity. This is a contemporaneous version of the accelerator introduced by Steindl (1952).

$$p_2 I_2 = \gamma_0 + \gamma_4 + \gamma_5 (Q_2 p_2) \tag{4.94}$$

Dividing (4.94) by the value of the stock of capital $p_2 k_2$ we get the rate of increase of k_2

$$I_2 / k_2 = \gamma_3 + \gamma_4 r_2 + \gamma_5 u_2 \tag{4.95}$$

where $\gamma_3 = \gamma_0 / p_2 k_2$

Substituting equation (4.43) for utilization capacity, u_2, into (4.95) we get

$$g_2^{\mathrm{d}} = \gamma_3 + \gamma_6 r_2 \tag{4.96}$$

where $\gamma_6 = \gamma_4 + \gamma_5 ((1 + \tau)/\tau)$.

Equations (4.86), (4.92), and (4.96) describe the steady state configuration of the rate of growth, the industrial profit rate, and the capital stock ratio. We chart the investment demand and savings relationships in figure 4.7.

The graph is drawn holding λ and r_1 (or equivalently p_1) constant. The line labeled $g^{\mathrm{d}} = g^{\mathrm{d}}(r_2)$ shows the investment demand function. From (4.96) it has a positive intercept equal to γ_3 and its slope is γ_6. From (4.92), the supply of savings $g^{s} = g^{s}(r_2)$ has either a positive or negative intercept, and its slope is positive. The point of interception, $g^{\mathrm{d}}(r_2) = g^{s}(r_2)$, gives the equilibrium profit and growth rates for given λ and r_1. The conditions for stability implies, as usual, that the slope of $g^{s} = g^{s}(r_2)$ exceeds the slope of $g^{\mathrm{d}} = g^{\mathrm{d}}(r_2)$, which is to say that investment in the industrial sector must be less responsive than saving to changes in the rate of profit. Figure 4.7 also shows the inflation line as a function of r_2. As we have argued, there is only one value $r_1^0 = r_2^0$ (at steady state) where workers' and capitalists income aspirations will coincide.

Somehow the model assumes that supply constraints on the primary basic goods sector depend on industrial conditions. The industrial profit rate not only regulates the pace of industrial investment, but also

Figure 4.7

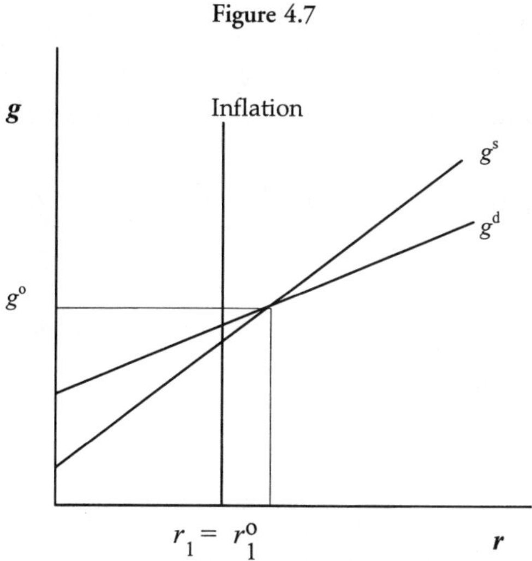

determines government's ability to finance infrastructure investment. Hence, improved industrial performance has a favorable impact on basic goods performance.[29]

4.7 Conclusions

Our aim in this chapter has been to develop a framework as comprehensive as the IMF/WB approach, while at the same time being far more close to the elements of modern capitalist economies and the particular structural and institutional features of Latin American countries. Under the post-Keynesian rubric we have constructed a model that offers what we think is a very appropriate approach to the reality of market economies in LDCs. This model is able to deal with both stabilization and growth issues. It also makes some minimal but essential distinctions so as to reflect the principal internal features and constraints faced by the countries in the Latin American region. Structuralist economists have pointed out most of these peculiarities over the years. We have argued that a synthesis of certain aspects of the post-Keynesian approach with structuralism is rewarding in view of their complementarities. In that sense we have offered a brief but important discussion of the methodology and main tenets of both approaches.

The basic model has several antecedents, most notably Kalecki's (1976) and Taylor's (1982, 1983) flex-price/fix-price models, which capture the sectoral distinctions between agriculture and industry. Among the novelties, however, we find the introduction of both a balance-of-payments and a fiscal constraint, as well as the interaction between the monetary and real sectors. Both the external and fiscal closures resemble very much the contemporary experience of Latin American countries. Within the public sector, public investment is the adjustment variable, while foreign reserves variation adjusts the external balance. The modeling of the money supply simply assumes that the level of expenditure and the borrowing requirements of the public sector call forth an increase in the amount of bank money. The model also contributes to understanding the way in which inflationary tensions developed in this type of less-developed economy. We have described and incorporated into the model the non-inflationary relative price, i.e. the relative price that is compatible with the fixed markup set by capitalists and the target real wage of workers.

Our strategy for deriving an equilibrium representation of the basic model was to construct five schedules in the $P_1 - Q_2$ space. In this way we have combined a rich economic structure where the primary sector supply constraint, the low capacity utilization in industrial units, the fiscal and external constraints, and the inflationary aspiration gap threw light on some of the most important issues relating to macroeconomic stabilization. In general, we may perceive that any shock to the system will reveal conflicting objectives. Output solutions in the manufacturing sector are consistent with the balance between foreign receipts and payments. Equilibrium values for the price of necessities and industrial output also affect the fiscal balance through income flows (and taxation) coming from both productive sectors. The public sector may affect the supply constraint in the primary sector, depending on the way the fiscal balance is closed. This, in turn, can raise inflationary tensions.

The model has been extended to allow for changes in the stock of capital in each productive sector. When assuming that the system settles down to a steady state, supply-and-demand balances in the basic goods and industrial sectors can be transformed into equivalent expressions in growth terms. The industrial investment function is shown to be the variable that drives the system, determining equilibrium output growth. It is interesting to note that in this growth extension of the model there is only one value of the profit rate where income aspirations by capitalists and workers will be satisfied. Among other things, the growth extension put us in a position to examine the implications of changes in the distribution of income and the impact that policy variables and exogenous shocks—either in primary sector production relations or in the way government raises and spends revenues—can have on growth and inflation.

The model becomes, then, a serious alternative to the neoclassical-oriented growth model of the type recently outlined by the IMF/WB (the integrated model), since it enables us to study the impact of policy instruments on standard adjustment targets, incorporating existing development constraints.

In the long run the stocks of capital in each sector can change. For simplicity, we assume, under certain stability conditions, that the system will settle down to a steady state, with all sectors' capital stock expanding at the same rate. An investment function of the type advanced by Rowthorn (1981), Dutt (1984), and Taylor (1985, 1987) is used, so investment demand or desired accumulation in the industrial sector depends on the conditions of profitability and capacity utilization.[30] We shall assume, in post-Keynesian fashion, that savings adapt to industrial investment demand out of long-run equilibrium, i.e. that investment intentions are completely realized. Primary sector investment is proportional (or equivalent) to public investment (see Rao 1993). Once we divide public investment by the primary sector capital stock we get the rate of growth in that sector. Finally, equilibrium growth in steady state requires that the rate of change of the capital stock ratio is zero.

Notes

1. The search for alternative and less socially costly forms of short-term adjustment gave rise to the heterodox programs of 1980s: The "Austral Plan" in Argentina (April 1985), the "Cruzado Plan" in Brazil (February 1986), and the "heterodox shock" in Peru. The feature most generally put in practice was the prices-and-incomes policy, ranging from outright freeze (by agreement or by decree) to controlled slide. In all these experiences the results, though successful in the short term, were highly disappointing in the long run. Looking at the recent experiences of the 1990s, the only conclusion we can draw is that successful countries in Latin America are very far from using traditional IMF/WB recipes. For instance, between 1987 and 1992, Mexico undertook a process of macroeconomic adjustment based on a social pact. In Argentina a convertibility reform launched by the Menem's administration reduced inflation from 30 percent a month in March 1991 to an average 0.4 percent a month during 1994. Peru's broad success against inflation has been based on institutional reform and a massive program of privatization. Brazil's successful "Real Plan" was based on the structuralist proposal of indexed money.

2. Carvalho (1984–85), for instance, identifies five traditions among post-Keynesians: the Garegnani/Eatwell, Kaldor/Pasinetti, Kaleckian, Davidson/Kregel/Minsky, and Shackle approaches. But Arestis (1996) identifies just three: the Marshallian, Kaleckian, and institutional traditions.

3. Eichner (1987) is a good example of what is meant here. Arestis (1989) is another significant attempt that encapsulates in the analysis a macromodel in which short-term influences affect deviations from trends, along with long-term influences on trends.

4. This emphasis on money (or nominal) income goes back to Kalecki and was practically dropped from view until the seminal Weintraub writings opened up the subject. As Weintraub (1973, p. 140) points out, [in mainstream analysis] "pricing has generally been suppressed while the argument has been conducted in real terms."

5. Rattso (1984) discusses the economic adjustment mechanism in a dual economy when government controls the domestic terms of trade. Modiano (1989) opens the economy by introducing commercial transactions and financial transfers and analyzes some policy impacts. FitzGerald (1989, 1990) shows how the monetary and financial analysis can be linked directly to the major real side variables. Dutt (1991) uses the two-sector setting to analyze the impact of income redistribution and government investment in infrastructure upon the long-period equilibrium rate of growth.

6. This emphasis on classes is an important departure from the methodological individualism of the neoclassical analysis in which everybody is the same.

7. This view has been recently emphasized by Morroni (1992, p. 1), who claims that "input combinations are for the most part technically determined, by their indivisibility characteristics and by their complementary relations."

8. The close contact that many early structuralist economists had with Kaldor and Kalecki is, however, another important element that could partially explain the reasonably close perspective between the structuralist and post-Keynesian schools. We should recall, for instance, that the first formulators of the structuralist theory of inflation, Noyola (1956) and Sunkel (1960), cited an article by Kalecki published in Mexico in 1955 as being the definitive resource on structural factors. The article was based on lectures that Kalecki gave in Mexico in 1953, and the main point of that piece was the stress on the potential inflationary consequences of aggregate demand increases in the primary sector due to the inelastic supply of food. Additionally, Kalecki was the intellectual leader of group of economists working at the Oxford Institute of Statistics during and after the war (Dudley Seers and Thomas Balogh are among the most well-known) whose work had an important impact on the development of the structuralist literature. Kaldor, on the other hand, worked as a consultant for the United Nations Commission for Latin America (ECLA) in Chile (for three months in 1956) as a result of an invitation made by Raul Prebisch. In ECLA, Kaldor gave about 20 lectures to a special training program for Latin American economists and started to develop a deep analysis of the distributional and growth problems faced by the Chilean economy, whose structuralist flavor was quite innovative and influential at that time. Later in the year, Kaldor traveled to Brazil, where he attended a meeting of the International Economic

Association and gave several lectures that contained his first systematic formulation of the link between the primary and the industrial sector in LDCs (Palma and Marcel 1989). It is for this reason that Kay (1989, p. 229), for instance, mentions Kaldor as one of the pioneers (among some others) who most "influenced the Latin American structuralist school."

Over the years both Kaldor and Kalecki remained interested in the economics of LDCs. During the 1960s, Kaldor traveled with some regularity to Latin America as a consultant to the government of Mexico, and developed his ideas further in a previous and polemic paper published in 1959 on the Chilean economy. In 1976, he went to Venezuela as advisor in the process of fiscal reform. From this point on, Kaldor reduced his visits abroad but continued writing on Latin America. Kalecki's interests in the fundamental issues faced by LDCs continued in the 1960s. His findings are best summarized in his *Essays on Developing Countries*.

9. See, for instance, Frenkel (1979), Bresser-Pereira and Nakamo (1987), and Ffrench-Davis (1988).

10. We should not confuse the Sraffian definition of "basics" with the definition that we employ here. Although the terms "basics" or "necessities" are still a novelty in macroeconomic analysis, we follow Kalecki (1976) and the "basic needs" approach, in which some inescapable irreversibilities in the process of consumption lead consumers to meet certain goods before the consumption of nonbasics or supplementaries can begin.

11. Borpujari (1985), for instance, reports the marginal budget share in basic supplies for rural and urban areas in India. He found that 72 percent of the marginal budget shares of basics of the lower-income groups in urban areas were for food. In rural areas the figures were not significantly different: 73 percent of the marginal budget share of basics of the lower-income groups were for food.

12. Mamingi (1996) also reports that aggregate output elasticities are higher than individual crop elasticities; however, he points out the weak understanding that most studies have of the quantitative dimensions of supply response and the failure that the literature presents regarding the issue of simultaneity of variables, data pooling, asymmetry in supply responses to price changes, omitted variables, and the comparability of variables across countries.

13. Through the model we have assumed a fixed exchange rate regime. In support of this assumption Agenor and Montiel (1996, p. 19) indicate that "in contrast to the major industrial countries, the vast majority of developing countries have not adopted flexible exchange rates."

14. See, for instance, Ros (1980) and Aceituno (1984) for Mexico; Calabi (1982), Considera (1981 and 1983), Modiano (1983), and Parkin (1991) for Brazil; Chica (1983) for Colombia; Frenkel (1984) and Villanueva and Echeverry (1991) for Argentina; and Corbo (1982) and Jadresic (1985) for Chile.

15. With respect to workers we have implicitly assumed a utility function of the type $U = \varepsilon \mathrm{Log}\, C_{1w} + (1 - \varepsilon)\mathrm{Log}\, C_{2w}$, where C_{1w} and C_{2w} represent workers'

real consumption of basics and industrial goods, respectively. The result is workers' constant expenditure shares on the two goods.

16. The data provided by Flores and Espinasa (1979) shows that upper-income groups consume 74 percent of durables in Latin America. The consumption of durables by lower-income groups only reaches a marginal 9 percent of the total consumption.

17. Mena (1996) estimates the number of individual stockholders per firm, the value of the shares held by each stockholder, and the financing sources for the Chilean private nonfinancial business sector. The evidence collected indicates that the economy is comprised of family-held business that are actually owned and run by a small subset of households within the economy, and that consumers are irrelevant as suppliers of credit. Therefore, it is not (in principle) legitimate to analyze the aggregate economic behavior of all private economic agents and decisions by focusing on a single representative individual.

18. Alternatively, we may consider government unproductive expenditure a variable determined by the wage bill of workers in the public sector.

19. One problem that has drawn our attention is that capital movements have been cast exclusively in terms of flows that respond to interest rate changes, and that no balance sheet constraints are imposed either on the public sector or on the monetary authorities of the country under examination. The fact is that, in the presence of uncertainty, an interest rate change will lead to a once-and-for-all adjustment of portfolios, rather than a perpetual flow of the type suggested by orthodox models. It is more appropriate, then, to depict capital movements as changes in portfolio positions held by residents or non-residents; and capital movements cease when portfolio equilibrium is restored. Criticism of the orthodox approach can be also raised when we compare the way in which balance-of-payments adjustment is achieved in most orthodox models with the external adjustment experience of Latin American economies in the 1970s and 1980s. In orthodox models (with fixed exchange rates and less-than-perfect capital mobility), the IS curve determines domestic income and a trade balance not necessarily zero. Any trade disequilibrium causes changes in the money supply, which in turn changes the domestic interest rate. Thus, current account imbalances are immediately neutralized by capital flows (or by what happen in the capital account), and the interest rate emerges explicitly as the mechanism for achieving the external adjustment. However, the Latin American experience seems to contradict this logic. First, Latin American capital flows have traditionally come from official organizations, direct investments, or commercial loans; therefore, the behavior of capital flows do not respond necessarily to the situation of financial markets. Moreover, the strong supply restrictions in the international financial markets that Latin American countries have faced after the debt crises have made capital flows very insensitive to interest rate differentials. Second, when the current account is in poor condition, the capital

account suffers an even greater deterioration, so the variations in the capital account reinforce what happens in the current account. For example, if there is a current account deficit, the possibility of devaluation prompts a flight of capital. In other words, the mobility of capital is proportional to what happens in the current account; what is more, the proportionality factor could be greater than one. There is no doubt that something of this kind occurred in Latin America in the 1970s and 1980s.

20. In a long-run context we will allow later industrial exports to be determined by an index of competitiveness and the price elasticity of foreign demand.

21. Truncated import substitution industrialization has meant than most of these economies have become dependent on import of intermediate goods, and that the process itself rarely extends to capital goods.

22. It is interesting to observe the pioneering character of Rangel's contribution, made several years before Kaldor's well-known paper (1970).

23. The target real wage hypothesis was originally developed by Sargan (1964) and played an important role in the inflation explanation advocated by British Keynesianism in the 1970s (see Crips and Godley 1976, and Henry *et al.* 1976) and post-Keynesians in the 1980s and, '90s (see Arestis 1992, Marglin 1984, and Sawyer 1982). Diamand (1976) was among the first structuralists who stated it clearly: "Psychologically, the level once achieved by real wages becomes a 'normal' standard of reference and its reduction is felt as an attempt against acquired rights. Therefore, while [conventional] economic thought treats real wages as an equilibrating variable to be adjusted according to the forces of the market, to modern society their preservation is a fundamental objective" (p. 22).

24. In the economic development literature an "enclave" refers to a sector of the economy that, lying inside the boundaries of the country, is tied to rest of the world.

25. Braun and Joy (1968) see it as a food/export trade-off.

26. Dividing (4.70) by p_2 we get

$$\frac{w}{p_2} = \frac{W}{p_2} p_1^{-\varepsilon} p_2^{(\varepsilon-1)}$$

Rearranging this expression we have

$$w = \frac{W}{p_2} p_1^{-\varepsilon} p_2^{(\varepsilon-1)} p_2 = \frac{w}{p_2} \left(\frac{p_1}{p_2}\right)^{-\varepsilon}$$

Now, we know that $\rho = p_1/p_2$; therefore, $w = (\rho)^{-\varepsilon}(W/p_2)$, but using (4.14) for p_2 we get

$$w = \left(\frac{p_1}{p_2}\right)^{-\varepsilon} W[(1+\tau)(wb_2 + aep_{\mathrm{m}})]^{-1}$$

which is equal to

$$w = \left[\rho^{\varepsilon} \frac{(1+\tau)(Wb_2 + aep_{\mathrm{m}})}{W} \right]^{-1}$$

27. In other words, capitalists in the industrial sector are only interested in maintaining a constant purchasing power of profits in terms of industrial goods.
28. In order to avoid double counting we have subtracted the term J from the public sector equation.
29. This configuration contrasts with Taylor's (1982) pioneering work on the two-sector fix-price/flex-price growth model, in which the growth rate of the primary sector (agriculture) is exogenously given by institutional factors.
30. Investment functions of this type fit very well into the empirical generalizations in Latin America. See Ocampo (1985), Warman and Thirlwall (1993), and Cardoso (1993).

CHAPTER 5

An Economic Policy Perspective

5.1 *Introduction*

In this chapter we consider some of the economic policy implications of the formal analysis of the previous chapter. Before analyzing the short-run impact of policy-induced and parametric changes in the model, we summarize the four equations expressing the relationships between four basic endogenous variables, namely, industrial output, the price of basic goods, public investment in the basic goods sector, and reserves variation. In this way, in what follows we extend the analytical model in several important ways.

First, in order to address the issue of stabilization we make use of what may be called Marshallian–Keynesian short-run analysis, which has the following characteristics: (a) the period is short enough for it to be reasonable to assume no significant change to capital stock, and (b) there are no appreciable time lags in the adjustment of the endogenous variables. Short-term variations of the basic endogenous variables to exogenous shocks and changes in policy-induced variables are investigated. From the demand side we confine ourselves to evaluating the impact of changes in direct taxation, *PSBR*, government expenditure in nonessential goods, and private investment. The short-run impact of debt relief and income distribution policies is also analyzed. The essential point we want to make is that instruments with a broad aggregative impact are incomplete (and sometimes inappropriate) for meeting the stabilization targets of a non-inflationary increase in output and employment without balance-of-payments difficulties. Indeed, some instruments need to be combined with measures aimed at correcting specific sectoral imbalances and constraints. The reader will note, in particular, the dominant role played by the price of basics. The model can potentially explain an inflationary situation in an endogenous manner, since the price of basics is determined by output considerations (though of course we do not discard exogenous shocks). Though static in nature, our analysis extends here to a fundamental dynamic problem: conflicting claims and the inflationary process.

Second, a meaningful relation between policy and targets tells us that the logical policy for controlling the price level by keeping consumption in line with supply, has to address the lack of "capital" in the basic goods sector. Moreover, to overcome the balance-of-payments constraint resorting to manufacturing exports is essential. But here the analysis has to proceed with care. As Harris (1967) and, more recently, Thirwall (1988) have claimed, the balance of payments needs to be modeled in a growth context. Explaining a balance-of-payments equilibrium or desequilibrium ideally requires, for analytical completeness, dynamic analysis of the adjustment process and the mechanisms, that sustain the condition over time. The balance-of-payments expression of the basic model is used and extended to a growth context. We try to show that inducing through government strategic intervention a cumulative causation between the growth of industrial exports and a more rapid growth of productivity can activate an industrial export–led growth process.

Third, besides the short-run stabilization issues, the type of model we employ can address factors that affect prospects for economic growth and equitable distribution. In our model, growth can be financed in various ways. In particular, we explore the impacts generated by changes in government and foreign saving and external shocks. Autonomous investment decisions in the manufacturing sector will be important also. The inescapable and quite important link between changes in the distribution of income and processes of accumulation and growth is also analyzed. We exploit the longer-term dynamics arising from capital accumulation and the evolution of the markup to determine the impact effects obtained in both the transition and the steady state.

5.2 *The Basic Four Equations*

Equations (4.39) and (4.15a) are the two fundamental equations of the model we have just presented. They can be solved simultaneously for the equilibrium output in the manufacturing sector, Q_2, and the equilibrium price of primary goods, p_1. With this we can further solve for the level of reserve variations, ΔR, and the equilibrium level of public investment, I_1.

Summarizing, we have a four-equations system:

$$p_1 = \varepsilon W \left(\frac{1}{b_1} + \frac{1}{b_{1e}Q_1} \right) + \left(\frac{\varepsilon W}{Q_1 b_1} \right) Q_2 \tag{4.39}$$

$$Q_2 = (1 - \varepsilon) \frac{WL}{p_2} + \frac{(1 - s_c)(1 - t_c)}{p_2} y_c + \zeta I_2 + x_2 + I_1 + G \tag{4.15a}$$

$$I_1 = \frac{PSBR}{p_2} - G - \frac{i^*D}{p_2} + \frac{t_c}{p_2} \left[\frac{\tau}{(1 + \tau)} Q_2 p_2 + p_2 r_{1e} k_{1e} + \left(p_1 - \frac{W}{b_1} \right) u_1 k_1 \right] \tag{4.53}$$

$$\Delta R = e p_{1e}^* + p_2 x_2 + CF - e p_m a Q_2 - e p_m (1 - \zeta) I_2 - J \tag{4.61}$$

where

$$y_c = \left[\left(p_1 - \frac{W}{b_1} \right) u_1 k_1 + \left(p_{1e} - \frac{W}{b_{1e}} \right) u_{1e} k_{1e} + \frac{\tau}{(1 + \tau)} p_2 Q_2 \right]$$

To simplify the analysis we discuss short-run equilibrium under the assumption that both the primary sector and the manufacturing sector markets clear immediately. Substituting (4.16) and (4.39) into (4.15a) and simplifying we get

$$Q_2^0 = \frac{(1 - \varepsilon) \frac{W(L_1 + L_{1e})}{p_2} \left[\frac{1 - s_c(t_c + 1)}{p_2} \right] \left[p_2 r_{1e} k_{1e} + \varepsilon W \left(\frac{1}{b_1} + \frac{1}{b_{1e}Q_1} \right) u_1 k_1 - \frac{W u_1 k_1}{b_1} \right] + \zeta I_2 + x_2 + \frac{PSBR}{p_2} - \frac{J}{p_2}}{1 - [1 - s_c(t_c + 1)] \left[\frac{\tau}{\tau + 1} + \frac{\varepsilon W u_1 k_1}{Q_1 b_2 p_2} \right] - (1 - \varepsilon) \frac{W}{b_2 p_2}} \tag{5.1}$$

which is a reduced form equation for the manufacturing sector equilibrium output level. The sign of the denominator in equation (5.1) will be important in the forthcoming analysis. Reasonable assumptions will set the capitalist saving and tax rates to values less than one, with the term $(\varepsilon W u_1 k_1 / Q_1 b_2 p_2)$ being between zero and one.[1] The last term $(1 - \varepsilon)(W/b_2)(1/p_2)$ is clearly less than one. With these plausible values the overall result will be unambiguously positive.

Substituting (5.1) into (4.39) we get a reduced form equation for p_1:

$$p_1^0 = \varepsilon W \left(\frac{1}{b_1} + \frac{1}{b_{1e}Q_1} \right) + \left(\frac{\varepsilon W}{Q_1 b_2} \right) Q_2^0 \tag{5.2}$$

Figure 5.1

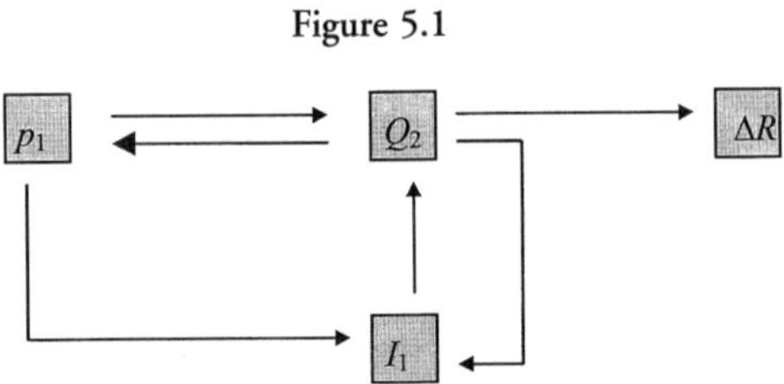

Hence, the equilibrium level of reserves variations and the equilibrium level of public investment occur when

$$\Delta R^0 = ep^*_{1e}x_1 + p_2 x_2 + CF - ep_m a Q_2^0 - ep_m(1 - \zeta)I_2 - J \qquad (5.3)$$

$$I_1^0 = \frac{PSBR}{p_2} - G - \frac{i^*D}{p_2} + \frac{t_c}{p_2}\left[\frac{\tau}{(1+\tau)}p_2 Q_2^0 + p_2 r_{1e}k_{1e}\right.$$

$$\left. + \left(p_1^0 - \frac{W}{b_1}\right)u_1 k_1\right] \qquad (5.4)$$

In figure 5.1, endogenous variable relations are shown schematically in the simplest terms.

5.3 Demand-Side Policies

Given the inelastic nature of the supply of primary products in our model, demand policy in the short run can aim only to vary the level of output (and capacity utilization) in industry. With oligopolistic price formation, industrial expansion and contraction may be achieved, respectively, through an effective positive and negative stimulus to demand.

5.3.1 A Higher *PSBR*

Finding sources of domestic borrowing to meet the public sector requirements becomes a major issue in Latin American economies. A particular method chosen to finance a high level of government spending is, however, the bond market. A market for government bonds can only be sustained through programs oriented to the institutional development of financial markets. Bonds issued by the government and sold to the general public can pay the fixed nominal interest rate, i. Given the closing rule of the fiscal sector; the funds collected through the sale of bonds are immediately channeled to investment in the basic goods sector.[2] Another formulation, however, may assume that public enterprises do issue their own debt securities in order to finance their investment projects in the primary sector. In any case, an increase in *PSBR* improves the fiscal position as we can see by differentiating (5.4) with respect to *PSBR*.

$$\frac{\partial I^0}{\partial PSBR} = \frac{1}{p_2} > 0 \tag{5.5}$$

But the effects on manufacturing output, reserve variations, and primary goods prices should be evaluated. Differentiating Q_2^0, ΔR^0 and p_1^0 partially with respect to *PSBR* in (5.1), (5.3), and (5.2) yields

$$\frac{\partial Q_2^0}{\partial PSBR} = \frac{p_2}{1 - [1 - s_c(t_c + 1)]\left[\dfrac{\tau}{1+\tau} + \dfrac{\varepsilon W u_1 k_1}{Q_1 b_2 p_2}\right] - (1-\varepsilon)\dfrac{W}{b_2 p_2}} > 0 \tag{5.6}$$

$$\frac{\partial \Delta R^0}{\partial PSBR} = \frac{-ep_m a p_2}{1 - [1 - s_c(t_c + 1)]\left[\dfrac{\tau}{1+\tau} + \dfrac{\varepsilon W u_1 k_1}{Q_1 b_2 p_2}\right] - (1-\varepsilon)\dfrac{W}{b_2 p_2}} < 0 \tag{5.7}$$

$$\frac{\partial p_1^0}{\partial PSBR} = \frac{\dfrac{\varepsilon W p_2}{Q_1 b_2}}{1 - [1 - s_c(t_c + 1)]\left[\dfrac{\tau}{1+\tau} + \dfrac{\varepsilon W u_1 k_1}{Q_1 b_2 p_2}\right] - (1-\varepsilon)\dfrac{W}{b_2 p_2}} > 0 \tag{5.8}$$

The increase in *PSBR* leads in the short run to higher output and employment in the manufacturing sector; to a lower level of reserves, since the trade deficit increases with the expansion of intermediate imports for industry; and to higher prices.

Graphically these results are depicted in figure 5.2. The II curve shifts to the right while the GG curve shifts to the left. Macroeconomic equilibrium is achieved at 'b', with higher output Q_2, a higher p_1, and a lower level of reserves. An increase in *PSBR* eases the fiscal constraint and results in a sort of expansionary fiscal policy that increases output and employment in industry. The adjustment mechanism, however, implies a rising general price level and a worse balance-of-payments position. We have, therefore, a case in which the economy cannot jointly attain multiple policy objectives by using just a single policy variable. The following economic policy discussion is cast in terms of these conflicting objectives.

Figure 5.2

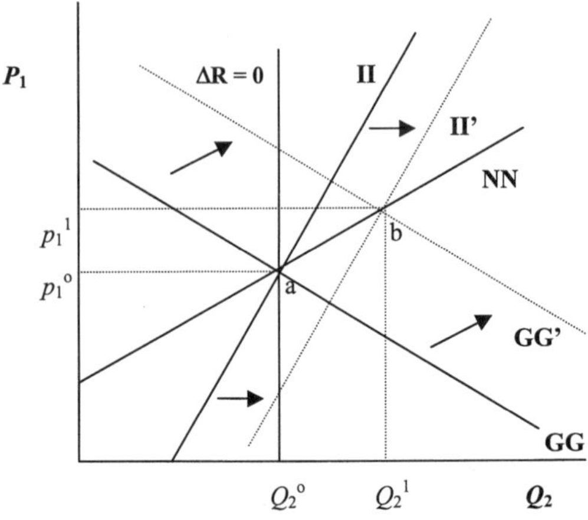

The increase in the price level of the primary sector lowers workers' effective real wages (see equation 4.71), and price inflation is sparked off through equation (4.76). We may highlight this inflationary dynamics briefly.

From (4.76) and the analysis we developed in the previous section we know that price changes in the industrial sector become a function of the gap between the effective price of basics and the price compatible with the aspirations of workers and capitalists, i.e.

$$\frac{(dp_2/dt)}{p_2} = \omega\left(\frac{dW/dt}{W}\right) = \omega\varphi(T - w) = \omega\varphi(p_1 - p_1^0) \qquad (4.76)$$

which can be written as

$$\frac{dp_2}{dt} = \omega\varphi(p_1 - p_1^0)p_2 \qquad (5.9)$$

Expression (5.8) represents a variable coefficient case of a homogeneous linear differential equation.[3] We have, by integrating both sides with respect to t,

$$\int \frac{1}{p_2}\frac{dp_2}{dt}\,dt = \int \omega\varphi(p_1 - p_1^0)(t)\,dt$$

$$\ln p_2 = -c + \int \omega\varphi(p_1 - p_1^0)(t)\,dt$$

The time path $p_2(t)$ can then be obtained by taking the antilog of $\ln p_2$:

$$p_2(t) = e^{\ln p_2} = e^{-c} e^{\int \omega\varphi(p_1 - p_1^0)(t)\,dt} \tag{5.10}$$

We may expect that the sign of $\omega\varphi(p_1 - p_1^0)$ will give the key to the convergence of the time path. The assumption is that $0 < \omega < 1$ and $0 < \varphi < 1$ lead directly to the result $\omega\varphi(p_1 - p_1^0) > 0$ if excess demand occurs in the primary goods sector (i.e. if $p_1 > p_1^0$). We have, then, that $p_2(t)$ cannot converge and that inflation is dynamically unstable since $e^{\int \omega\varphi(p_1 - p_1^0)} \to \infty$ as $t \to \infty$.

5.3.2   Expanding Public Expenditure in Nonessentials

A government attempt to increase its consumption level of nonessentials (an increase in G) will have the very unusual result of having no impact on output. This is due to the particular fiscal sector macroclosure that we use. Initially, the increase in G will have an expansionary effect on manufacturing output, but the dominant fiscal constraint implies a drop in public investment I_1 even greater than the additional government revenue generated by the expansion in output.[4] We may check the response of I_1 to changes in G to get

$$\frac{\partial I_1^0}{\partial G} = -1 \tag{5.11}$$

which confirms that in a fiscal-constrained economy, government spending for consumption purposes crowds out government spending for investment purposes.

With no impact on industrial output, equilibrium price of basics and variations of reserves will remain the same.

5.3.3   An Increase in Capitalist Income Taxes

An economy that presents a chronic fiscal constraint may rely on direct taxation to close the gap. In our model direct taxes are levied on profits. To calculate the impact of an increase in capitalists' income on industrial output, we need to simplify (5.1). If we replace both the numerator and the denominator of (5.1) by d_1 and d_2 (where both magnitudes are positive), then differentiating with respect to t_c we get

$$\frac{\partial Q_2}{\partial t_c} = \frac{-s_c(1-\varepsilon)W\dfrac{L_1 + L_{1e}}{p_2}\left[k_{1e}r_{1e} + \varepsilon W\left(\dfrac{1}{b_1} + \dfrac{1}{b_{1e}Q_1}\right)\dfrac{u_1 k_1}{p_2} - \dfrac{Wu_1 k_1}{b_1 p_2}\right]d_2 + s_c\left[\dfrac{\tau}{\tau + 1} + \dfrac{\varepsilon W k_1 u_1}{Q_1 b_2 p_2}\right]d_1}{\{d_2\}^2}$$

$$\tag{5.12}$$

The impact appears to be ambiguous. On the one hand, a higher tax rate, t_c, implies a lower capitalist consumption and a lower demand for nonessentials. On the other hand, the tax rate increase means extra revenues for the public sector, which in turn expands public sector demand for industrial goods. This latter case is not straightforward in any sense since there is a direct effect of a change in the tax rate upon government revenues, and an indirect effect that depends on how capitalist profitability in sectors 1 and 2 react to changes in Q_2 and p_1. Once again, we may have a case (the expansionary case) in which public investment increases so strongly that it offsets the negative consumption response of capitalists. This is due to the reinforcing effect that capitalist expansion induces in capitalist profit income and to the higher basic goods sector profitability level induced via price. Of course, through (4.39) the output and employment expansion in industry adds to basic goods demand and exerts an upward pressure on the price of basics. The trade deficit increases with the expansion of intermediate imports for industry. The contractionary case will reverse these results, leaving the economy with the paradoxical result of a larger budget deficit (which is adjusted via public investment decline) and a lower level of employment and industrial output.

Figures 5.3a and 5.3b show the expansionary and contractionary cases of a direct tax increase on capitalist income. The tax increase only affects (in a direct way) the II and the GG schedules. Equation (4.65) tell us that an increase in t_c will reduce both the slope and the intercept of the II schedule.

Figure 5.3a   An Expansionary Increase in Capitalist Income Tax

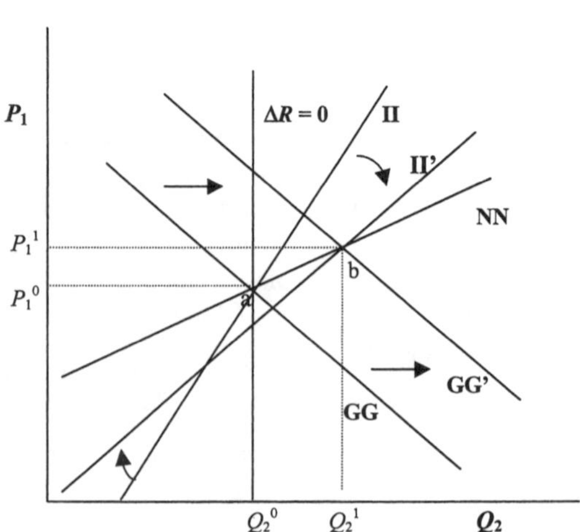

Figure 5.3b   A Contractionary Increase in
Capitalist Income Tax

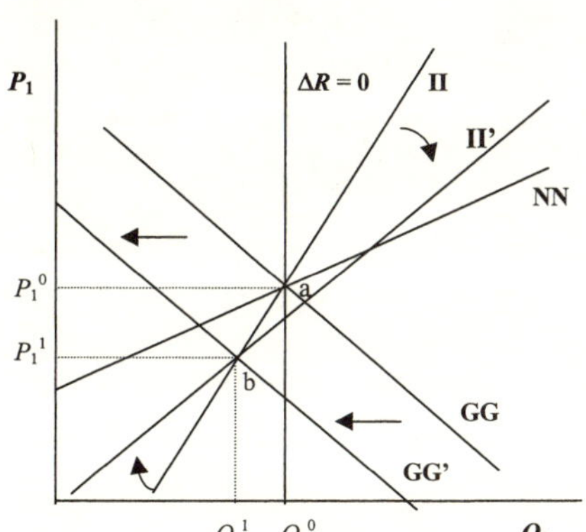

The II schedule rotates clockwise and shifts to the left. Expression (4.59) indicates that the same increase in t_c will affect only the intercept of the GG schedule, but in fact it may increase or decrease, depending on whether the difference between government total expenditure and the public sector borrowing requirement $(I_1 + G + i^*D/p_2 - PSBR/p_2)$ is positive or negative. Figure 5.3a shows the case in which $PSBR/p_2 > I_1 + G + i^*D/p_2$. The new short-run equilibrium at point 'b' shows a rise in output, a rise in the price of basic goods, and a trade deficit. The case in which $PSBR/p_2 < I_1 + G + i^*D/p_2$ is analyzed in figure 5.3b. Industrial output falls, and as a result the price of basic goods decreases and the trade deficit improves.

5.4   A Private Investment Shock

A rise in the rate of new-capital formation in the private sector of the economy (which we have assumed to be exogenous in the short run) expands industrial output, raises the price of basic goods, increases the public investment level, and deteriorates the level of reserves.

The differentials for manufacturing output, the price of basics, public investment, and reserves variations are

$$\frac{\partial Q_2^0}{\partial I_2} = \frac{\zeta}{1 - [1 - s_c(t_c + 1)]\left[\dfrac{\tau}{1 + \tau} + \dfrac{\varepsilon W u_1 k_1}{Q_1 b_2 p_2}\right] - (1 - \varepsilon)\dfrac{W}{b_2 p_2}} > 0$$

$$(5.13)$$

$$\frac{\partial p_1^0}{\partial I_2} = \frac{\dfrac{\varepsilon W}{Q_1 b_2}\zeta}{1 - [1 - s_c(t_c + 1)]\left[\dfrac{\tau}{1 + \tau} + \dfrac{\varepsilon W u_1 k_1}{Q_1 b_2 p_2}\right] - (1 - \varepsilon)\dfrac{W}{b_2 p_2}} > 0 \quad (5.14)$$

$$\frac{\partial I_1^0}{\partial I_2} = \frac{\dfrac{t_c}{p_2}\left(\dfrac{\tau p_2}{\tau + 1} + \dfrac{\varepsilon W}{b_2}\right)\zeta}{1 - [1 - s_c(t_c + 1)]\left[\dfrac{\tau}{1 + \tau} + \dfrac{\varepsilon W u_1 k_1}{Q_1 b_2 p_2}\right] - (1 - \varepsilon)\dfrac{W}{b_2 p_2}} > 0 \quad (5.15)$$

$$\frac{\partial \Delta R^0}{\partial I_2} = - \frac{e p_m a p_2}{1 - [1 - s_c(t_c + 1)]\left[\dfrac{\tau}{1 + \tau} + \dfrac{\varepsilon W u_1 k_1}{Q_1 b_2 p_2}\right] - (1 - \varepsilon)\dfrac{W}{b_2 p_2}}$$

$$- e p_m(1 - \zeta) < 0 \quad (5.16)$$

Industrial output expands via the multiplier process, as indicated by (5.13). The effect is traced in figure 5.4, where the II line shifts to the right. Increased employment in the industrial sector adds to basics demand and, with supply fixed in the short run, the domestic primary sector price level

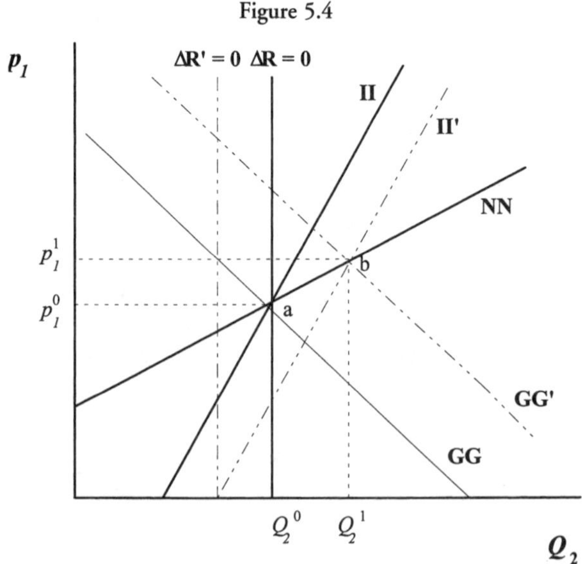

Figure 5.4

rises. Public investment rises as a consequence of higher tax revenues that come from higher profits in manufacturing and the basic goods sector, and the GG schedule starts shifting outwards to GG′. The trade deficit increases and the level of reserves declines for two reasons: directly, due to the increase in the demand for imported capital goods (this shifts the $\Delta R = 0$ schedule to the right), and indirectly, due to the increase in demand for intermediate imports required for industrial expansion.

5.5 Debt Relief

Since the debt crisis, external disequilibrium has become structural in Latin America. It is not generated by differences between flows of income and spending but from stock-flow disequilibrium between foreign obligations and current incomes, as reflected by high debt/GDP ratios. Moreover, the external crisis assumed a fiscal form since in most highly indebted econo-mies of the region, governments hold nearly all the external obligations; therefore, solvency problems fall into the hands of the public sector. The strong linkage between fiscal weakness and external solvency leads us to the conclusion that the problems have to be addressed simultaneously. The assumption of relief of the external debt is obviously unrealistic or at least merely indicative of the extent of international goodwill that Latin America (and other regions of the world) needs in order to ease the foreign exchange and fiscal crunch; however, it will be important to illustrate the effects of such attempts, since for the international economic system debt relief is costless, although the short-run gains to Latin American countries could be substantial.[5]

Consider the consequences on industrial output of a change in J, a term that in our model represents the external debt service

$$\frac{\partial Q_2^0}{\partial J} = \frac{-(1/p_2)}{1 - [1 - s_c(t_c + 1)]\left[\dfrac{\tau}{1+\tau} + \dfrac{\varepsilon W u_1 k_1}{Q_1 b_2 p_2}\right] - (1-\varepsilon)\dfrac{W}{b_2 p_2}} < 0 \qquad (5.17)$$

Debt relief is expansionary since it eases the fiscal constraint and helps increase public investment. We may see this transmission channel by dif-ferentiating public investment I_1 with respect to J in equation (4.53)

$$\frac{\partial I_1}{\partial J} = -\frac{1}{p_2} < 0 \qquad (5.18)$$

A fall in J will also increase the price of basic goods, as it can be observed from its respective differential

$$\frac{\partial p_1^0}{\partial J} = \frac{-\dfrac{\varepsilon W}{Q_1 b_2 p_2}}{1-[1-s_c(t_c+1)]\left[\dfrac{\tau}{1+\tau}+\dfrac{\varepsilon W u_1 k_1}{Q_1 b_2 p_2}\right]-(1-\varepsilon)\dfrac{W}{b_2 p_2}} < 0 \qquad (5.19)$$

The reserves variation response remains ambiguous, however, since $\partial \Delta R^0 / \partial J$ is greater or less than zero, i.e.

$$\frac{\partial \Delta R^0}{\partial J} = \frac{\dfrac{e p_{\mathrm{m}} a}{p_2}}{1-[1-s_c(t_c+1)]\left[\dfrac{\tau}{1+\tau}+\dfrac{\varepsilon W u_1 k_1}{Q_1 b_2 p_2}\right]-(1-\varepsilon)\dfrac{W}{b_2 p_2}} - 1$$

$$(5.20)$$

The term in the numerator ($e p_{\mathrm{m}} a / p_2$), the ratio of intermediate imports unit cost to unitarian price in industry, and the term in the denominator are between 0 and 1. Thus, to sign the expression we need to evaluate whether or not the whole fraction exceeds unity. Note that a high enough import content in unit cost with respect to prices tends to make $\partial \Delta R^0 / \partial J$ positive and greater than 1. Under these circumstances, therefore, it is readily seen that debt relief deteriorates the balance of payments and decreases the level of reserves. Hence, debt relief works better (in terms of the external position) in economies that are not greatly dependent on intermediate imports.

Figure 5.5 gives a graphical representation of short-run impacts of debt relief in the case in which the external transfer effect is larger than the intermediate inputs effect.

The rightward shift in the II curve occurs because increased demand for industrial goods coming from the public sector drives manufacturing output and basic goods prices up; this, in turn, raises capitalist income and consumption of nonessentials, generating a further expansion in output through the multiplier. The conditions in the public sector improve notoriously (the fiscal constraint is eased), and more resources are available for public investment. The GG curve does not shift anywhere since the fall in J is offset by the increase in I_1. Finally, the $\Delta R = 0$ curve shifts to the right, leaving at point 'b' the level of reserves in a better position.

Figure 5.5

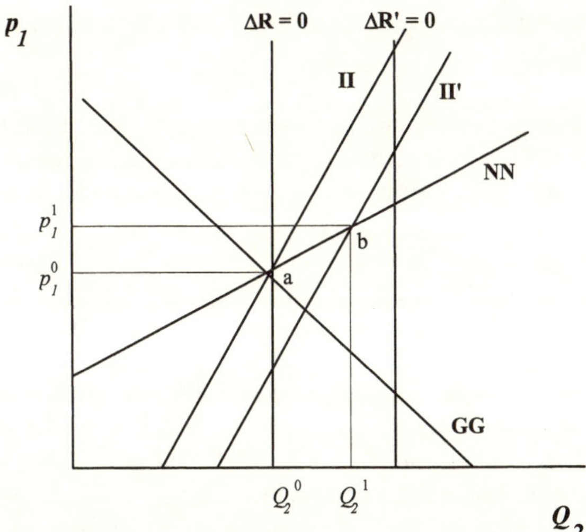

5.6 *Income Distribution Policies in the Short Run*

For the post-Keynesian and structuralist traditions distributional shifts have usually been associated with growth paths and inflationary targets. Dutt (1984), Marglin and Bhaduri (1988), and Blecker (1989), just to mention some recent efforts, have developed models aimed at examining the growth consequences of income distribution changes. Dutt, for instance, shows that a shift in the distribution of income in favor of wage earners will raise the rate of growth if investment increases with higher capacity utilization, though Marglin and Bhaduri point out that the result depends on specific circumstances. As Blecker indicates, the issue is complicated further in the presence of an economy open to foreign competition. Taylor (1982, 1983, 1985, and 1991), Dutt (1990, 1991), and Rao (1993) extend the analysis to two-sector models. In general this literature is inconclusive in the sense that higher rates of growth may be associated with either more or less equal distribution of income.

The interaction between income distribution and inflation has also been widely analyzed in the framework of the conflicting claims theories of inflation. In practice, price freezes and deindexation seem to be the income-policy responses to chronic inflation in most heterodox programs of the 1980s, although a social pact variant that moderates the interest groups' aspirations has worked better.[6]

The model we present here allows us to evaluate the ignored short-run impacts of income polices. Attention is restricted to changes in the industrial markup, τ, and the economy's nominal wage rate, the traditional incomes-policy variables.

Although direct action on the industrial markup may be carried out via specific guidelines or price controls, government action can affect the industrial markup indirectly through instruments that either stimulate or retard advances in this variable. Incentives to externally generate funds to finance investment can lower the markup. These incentives can be the response to artificially low interest rates, greater access to international financial markets, or less restriction upon debt/equity ratios.[7] In a long-run perspective, the government attitude towards how the credit system functions could affect the degree of concentration and the markup. Competition policy and the conditions of entry as governed by industrial licensing would also affect markup rates.[8]

We have to resort to rather messy algebra to determine the overall impact of markup changes on the endogenous variables. Nevertheless, some intuitive observation of the reduced form equations will help this task. A fall in τ decreases p_2 and raises industrial demand by wage recipients in (4.15a). An enhanced purchasing power of wages follows the fall in industrial prices. In an analogous fashion, the demand that comes from primary sector capitalists increases as profits on capital from basic goods and primary exports $[(p_1 - w/b_1)u_1 k_1]/p_2$ and $[(p_{1e} - w/b_{1e})u_{1e}k_{1e}]/p_2$ increase. A lower markup, however, reduces industrial capitalists' income and their consumption expenditure (in real terms) of industrial goods.[9] The question is, then, whether the fall in industrial capitalists' consumption expenditure may exceed the expansionary forces. The importance of the propensity to save, s_c, and the tax rate, t_c, is now clearly pictured. If industrial capitalists save a fraction of the decremental income lost through the lower markup rate, then excess demand appears in the industrial sector, and the net result will be output expansion in the manufacturing sector.

The price of basics changes with industrial output and employment variations according to (4.39); however, the overall balance in the external sector is ambiguous. Export earnings of industrial goods will decrease with the lower markup (under the extreme assumption that relative prices have no impact on the demand for exports), but this partial effect can be offset by a stronger contractionary effect of intermediate imports, $ep_m a Q_2$. The behavior of public investment is inconclusive. It depends on how capitalists' income flows and tax revenues vary with manufacturing output, and also on the comparison between the external debt service and the public sector borrowing requirement, as set by expression $(PSBR - J)/p_2$.

We now turn to the wage policy side. Wage policy has been an important source of controversy in LDCs. There are those who believe that adjustment in money wages will promote output and employment and improve the distribution of income (this line of thought has a Kaleckian background), whereas others argue that to avoid inflationary pressures and indeed to reduce the rate of inflation, a policy of restraining money wage expenditures should be adopted (the IMF could adhere to this approach). Thus, the choice between restriction of money wages to fight inflation and expansion of demand to fight unemployment is an important ingredient in the present polarization between extremists on the right and on the left. Let us analyze the consequences of a fall in money wages so as to evaluate its impact on output, prices, reserves variations, and the fiscal sector.

A fall in nominal wage rate generates an immediate decrease in the industrial price level. Due to the intermediate imports component, however, industrial prices fall by less than the wage decrease. The wage fall also increases profits for primary exports and basic goods production by decreasing the labor costs.

According to (4.15), industrial output contracts if the fall in demand by wage recipients overshadows industrial and primary sector capitalists' consumption demand and public sector demand for manufactured goods, and expands otherwise. The overall result will be determined by the saving propensity, s_c; workers' propensity to consume basic goods, ε; the structure of the fiscal accounts as given by the tax rate, t_c; and the *PSBR* and debt service components of the fiscal balance.

The short-run effects upon the price of basics deserve some comments. This is given by

$$\frac{\partial p_1^0}{\partial W} = \varepsilon\left(\frac{1}{b_1} + \frac{1}{b_{1e}Q_1}\right) + \frac{\varepsilon}{Q_1 b_2}\left(\frac{\partial Q_2^0}{\partial W}\right) \qquad (5.21)$$

According to (5.21), the price of basics increases if wage reduction is expansionary, and decreases otherwise. In the former case, the consumer price index of the economy will increase if the proportion of wages spent on basics, ε, is very high (see equation 4.30). This suggests that the fall in industrial prices caused by a fall in W is not sufficient to circumvent, in the short run, the higher price of basic goods, and in this case the orthodox argument is severely undermined. In the latter case (a reduction of wages that contracts industrial output), the overall price level of the economy falls in the orthodox fashion, but the "stagnationist" case for an income shift from high to low income groups is still valid. The point is that we have an assignment problem in which every target (employment and price stability) needs an independent policy.

The short-run effect upon reserves variation is also ambiguous, and the impact is given by

$$\frac{\partial \Delta R^0}{\partial W} = \frac{1}{b_2}(1 + \tau)x_2 - ep_{\mathrm{m}}a\frac{\partial Q_2^0}{\partial W} \qquad (5.22)$$

Export earnings from the manufacturing sector fall with the decline in p_2, and intermediate imports will increase or decrease depending on the wage change effect on industrial product.

The effect on public investment of a change in the money wage is also rather inconclusive. Capitalists' income flows and tax revenues do not vary in a predictable manner, and neither do the real $PSBR$ and the real external debt service.

5.7 Short-run Objectives in Conflict

Until now, attention has been restricted to changes in the macroeconomic demand instruments, debt relief and income policies. Observation of demand policies, for instance, suggests that these may have varied but incomplete results upon the macroeconomic objectives. Income policies may also have undefined impacts upon the relevant target variables. In general, we have seen that by altering the setting of any of the instrumental variables, we should not expect to improve all macroeconomic imbalances.

The relevant trade-offs among industrial output, the price of basic goods, the balance of payments, and public investment are summarized in table 5.1.

Table 5.1 Macroeconomic Impact

	Q_2	p_1	ΔR	I_1
Government Spending	=	=	=	−
Tax on Profit Incomes	−/+	−/+	−/+	−/+
Debt Relief	−	−	−/+	−
PSBR	+	+	−/+	−
Private Investment	+	+	−	+
Nominal Wage Rate	−/+	−/+	−/+	−/+
Markup	−/+	−/+	−/+	−/+

An increase in government spending on nonessentials will deteriorate the fiscal balance and will not have any significant effect on manufacturing output, the external balance, and the price level of basic goods. The shift toward changes in direct taxes does not help much, since the directions are unpredictable. A financing measure such as an increase in *PSBR*, in the manner outlined here, improves the fiscal balance and the level of economic activity, but it may also have the unwanted effect of raising the rate of inflation and the trade deficit.

An increase in private investment and debt relief, though beyond the entire government control will have an expansionary effect on industrial output, public investment, and prices. Furthermore, the former will deteriorate the reserve position while the latter will have an unknown effect.

There is, therefore, some mix of measures that ought to be able to reconcile the achievement of a high level of activity, low inflation, and an adequate level of a country's international reserves without putting too much pressure on the public budget. Attempts to force the level of economic activity without attending to the supply and external constraints will only cause inflation and balance-of-payments disequilibrium. We will pay attention to the former problem first and leave the external strangulation issue for the next section.

5.8 Expansion of the Basic Goods Frontier

An increase in the supply of basics is the strongest force against rising basic goods prices. Much of the emphasis of Kalecki's writings on development were on identifying and then planning to remove the relevant binding supply constraints. But he found that the expansion of productive capacity may be limited if private investment is not forthcoming at the desirable rate. This means that the government needs to step in to ensure that the total investment reaches the required level. Capital-augmenting investment is the leading input, and much of this takes place under government direction and financing. Usually infrastructure capital includes investment in research, favorable credit conditions, extension services, roads, storage, power, irrigation, etc. Since government investment in infrastructure is totally endogenous in our economy, any improvement in industrial or primary exports profitability will also determine government's ability to finance infrastructure. Thus, the expansion of the basic goods frontier results from past government investment.

We can now differentiate partially Q_2, p_1, ΔR, and I_1 with respect to k_1. First, an increase in capital for the production of basic goods may either expand or contract industrial output and employment. The direction of the macroeconomic adjustment is given by the partial derivative

$$\frac{\partial Q_2^0}{\partial k_1} = \frac{[1 - s_c(t_c + 1)](\varepsilon - 1)\dfrac{u_1 W}{b_1 p_2}}{1 - [1 - s_c(t_c + 1)]\left[\dfrac{\tau}{1 + \tau} + \dfrac{\varepsilon W u_1 k_1}{Q_1 b_2 p_2}\right] - (1 - \varepsilon)\dfrac{W}{b_2 p_2}} \qquad (5.23)$$

To sign this expression, note first that under plausible assumptions already discussed, the denominator is positive. Thus, with $0 < \varepsilon < 1$, the numerator will be positive if $s_c(t_c + 1) > 1$. In fact, if s_c and t_c are large enough, $s_c t_c \cong 1$, industrial output expands. Otherwise, a contraction in industrial output follows the capital expansion in the basic goods sector. On intuitive grounds the explanation for this inconclusive result is not difficult to follow. As employment in the basic goods sector is limited by capital, an increase in employment accompanies basic goods expansion. While the enlarged basic goods labor force tends to create excess demand in the industrial sector, the reduced profitability on capital for basics production may dampen demand. Industrial output and employment will either expand or contract depending upon the strength of the two forces.

The impact upon the fiscal balance in the short run is also ambiguous, being highly dependent upon the magnitude of same two effects: (a) the reduced profits on capital for basic goods production that reduces tax revenues, and (b) the excess demand effect in the industrial sector that can eventually increase demand (in the case of $s_c t_c \cong 1$) and increase profits in industry.

$$\frac{\partial I_1}{\partial k_1} = \frac{t_c \tau}{(1 + \tau)}\frac{\partial Q_2^0}{\partial k_1} - \frac{t_c W}{p_2}\left(\frac{\varepsilon}{b_{1e}\Psi k_1^2} + \frac{u_1}{b_1}\right) \qquad (5.24)$$

The impact on reserves variation is given by

$$\frac{\partial \Delta R^0}{\partial k_1} = \frac{-e p_m a[1 - s_c(t_c + 1)](\varepsilon - 1)\dfrac{u_1 W}{b_1 p_2}}{1 - [1 - s_c(t_c + 1)]\left[\dfrac{\tau}{1 + \tau} + \dfrac{\varepsilon W u_1 k_1}{Q_1 b_2 p_2}\right] - (1 - \varepsilon)\dfrac{W}{b_2 p_2}} \qquad (5.25)$$

If industrial output expands (contracts), the increase (decline) in intermediate imports further increases (reduces) the trade deficit, reducing (increasing) the level of reserves.

Lastly, the impact on the price of basic goods is unambiguous. At the new short-run equilibrium, an increase in k_1 lowers the price of basics.

$$\frac{\partial p_1^0}{\partial k_1} = -\frac{\varepsilon W}{b_{1e}\Psi u_1 k_1^2} < 0 \tag{5.26}$$

Figures 5.6a and 5.6b depict graphically the macroeconomic impact of an expansion of basic goods capital. Two possibilities are considered: one in which industrial output and the level of reserves contracts, and one in which

Figure 5.6a An Expansionary Increase in Basic Goods Capital

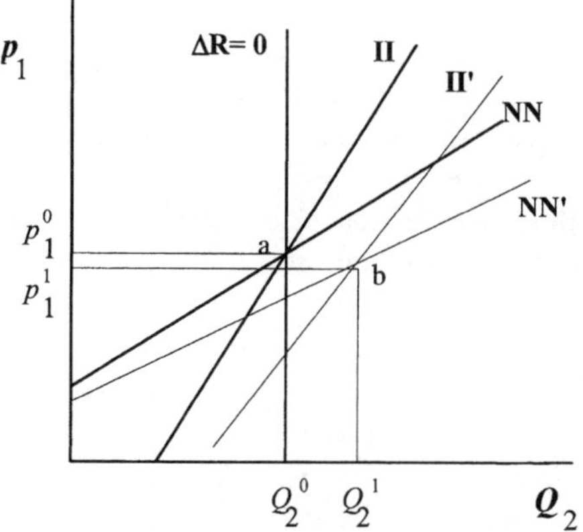

Figure 5.6b A Contractionary Increase in Basic Goods Capital

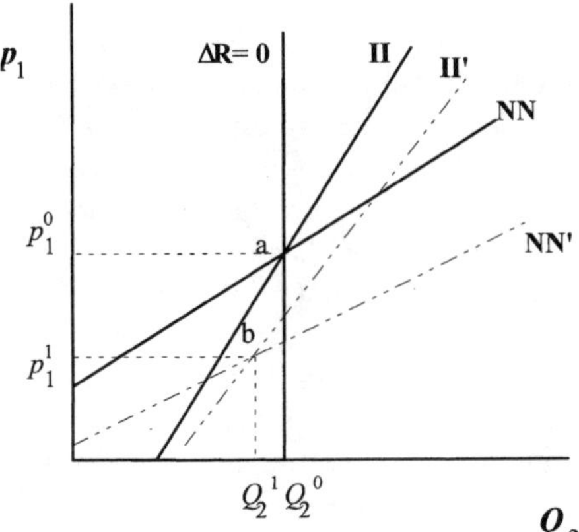

industrial output and international reserves increase. In both cases, however, the price of basics declines (for simplicity the GG schedule has been omitted). As we can verify from expression (4.39) in response to the rise in k_1 and Q_1, both the slope and the intercept of the NN schedule (the macroeconomic balance of the primary sector) fall. The slope of the II schedule also falls, but the effect of the increase of k_1 on the intercept of NN is ambiguous. The final solution to an increase in k_1 will depend on this latter effect.

5.9 *Relaxing the Balance-of-Payments Constraint*

In LDCs a major source of trade imbalances and inflation arises from the foreign exchange gap. On the one hand, it is not a secret that the level of primary exports are, with few exceptions, stagnant or slow growing, so that primary exports cannot play the role of an engine in the process of economic growth. On the other hand, imports are inflexible, because they are mainly raw materials, spare parts, and capital goods that are necessary for sustaining economic activity. The resultant foreign exchange gap leads to periodic devaluation, and thus rising internal prices. This is one of the tenets of most of the writings associated with Raul Prebish, the Economic Commission for Latin America and the Caribbean (ECLAC) school, and some others. This explains why Prebish and Kaldor, for instance, were longstanding advocates of the need for developing industrial exports in LDCs. In our context of a credit (or foreign capital) constraint economy, industrial export growth plays a key role for a simple reason: the more rapid it is, the less need to constrain output to avoid an adverse trade balance.

The essence of Kaldor's argument in favor of industrial exports has been recently interpreted using the so-called Verdoorn relation (see, for instance, Dixon and Thirlwall 1975, and Thirlwall 1983). In this case, exports of industrial goods whose price are to some extent controlled by domestic producers are considered to be the major component of autonomous demand to which other components adapt. Therefore, growth is fundamentally determined by the growth of demand for industrial exports. The process develops in a cumulative way in the tradition of circular and cumulative causation mechanisms that were brought to the fore in the postwar period by Myrdal (1957) and Hirschman (1958), and that have at their base the phenomenon of macro-increasing returns. Elsewhere Thirlwall (1979) and Thirlwall and Hussain (1982) introduce the balance-of-payments constraint growth rate under the assumption that balance-of-payments equilibrium (either in the current account or in the current and capital account) is preserved. However, in Dixon and Thirlwall (1975) and

Thirlwall (1983), models of export-led growth with a feedback relation through the Verdoorn effect, no attention is paid to the fact that the rate of growth of output may generate a level of imports in excess of exports. As they explicitly state: "we have neglected…the consideration of the balance of payments constrained growth in order to concentrate on the basic model" (Dixon and Thirlwall 1975, p. 213).

In the subsystem that we will develop here, the balance-of-payments constrained growth rate will be modeled, making allowance for the fact that industrial export prices are set up internally, and that labor productivity growth responds among other variables to the growth of output in the economy. In other words, we will try to match two parts of one whole process, which has been analyzed separately by Thirlwall and his coauthors.

The cumulative nature of the success originates with some initial improvement in a country's competitiveness, measured in terms of relative prices of industrial products among trading partners, which spurs export growth. This leads to a more rapid growth of demand and output through the export multiplier. Rapid output growth provides an additional link in this cumulative process, by permitting the realization of dynamic economies of scale, whereby the rate of growth of labor productivity is a positive function of the rate of growth of output. Thus, the initial increase in the growth of exports induces a more rapid growth of productivity, which provides a further improvement in competitiveness, completing the circle. In trying to match the Verdoorn relation with the notion of the balance-of-payments equilibrium growth rate, we will obtain quite interesting results that can be more diverse than those obtained by Thirwall. As it is clear from the external block of the model we start with a much more precise definition of the balance-of-payments expression in which exports are separated into those of primary and industrial source, and imports respond to variations in industrial output and investment.[10]

Remembering the balance-of-payments expression (4.54), we have

$$ep_m a Q_2 + ep_m(1 - \zeta)I_2 = ep_{1e}^* x_1 + p_2 x_2 + CF - J - \Delta R \qquad (4.54)$$

Overall balance-of-payments equilibrium means that $\Delta R = 0$. Calling $U = CF - J$ the net financial transfers and rearranging we get

$$P_{1e} x_1 + p_2 x_2 + U = ep_m a Q_2 + ep_m(1 - \zeta)I_2 \qquad (5.27)$$

In a growing economy, the condition for balance-of-payments equilibrium through time is that the rate of growth of the value of exports plus the rate of growth of the net financial transfers equals the rate of growth of the value of imports, i.e.

$$\phi_1(\hat{p}_{1e} + \hat{x}_1) + \phi_2(\hat{p}_2 + \hat{x}_2) + v\hat{U}$$
$$= \varsigma_1(\hat{e} + \hat{p}_m + \hat{a} + \hat{Q}_2) + \varsigma_2(\hat{e} + \hat{p}_m + (1 - \zeta) + \hat{I}_2) \tag{5.28}$$

where a circumflex $\wedge$ over the variable denotes the rate of growth of the variable. The parameters ϕ_1, ϕ_2, and v stand for the share of primary exports, industrial exports, and net financial transfers as a proportion of total receipts, respectively. ς_1 and ς_2 represent the share of imported intermediate and capital goods as a proportion of total imports.

An expression for the output growth rate in the industrial sector may be derived from this, i.e.:

$$\hat{Q}_2 = \frac{1}{\varsigma_1}[\phi_1(\hat{p}_{1e} + \hat{x}_1) + \phi_2(\hat{p}_2 + \hat{x}_2) + v\hat{U} - \varsigma_2(\hat{e} + \hat{p}_m + (1 - \zeta) + \hat{I}_2)$$
$$- \varsigma_1(\hat{e} + \hat{p}_m + \hat{a})] \tag{5.29}$$

In general, expression (5.29) can be regarded as analogous to what Thirlwall (1979) calls the balance-of-payments equilibrium growth rate (of course, with the specific differences I have included here).

Since we are particularly interested in the industrial export–led growth thesis, we will pay close inspection to the second term on the right hand of (5.29). In a dynamic setting, the rate of growth of industrial goods is governed by the rate of growth of exports. In such a case expression (5.29) reduces to

$$\hat{Q}_2 = \frac{1}{\varsigma_1}\phi_2(\hat{p}_2 + \hat{x}_2) \tag{5.30}$$

In particular, the growth rates of the quantity demanded and the price of industrial exports capture important relationships that are crucial to our analysis.[11] Here we will consider a subsidy for exports of industrial goods, a proposition that Kaldor, particularly, stresses: "The ideal way of promoting industrialization, as several economists pointed out, is not by tariff at all but by straightforward subsidies paid to industry by the government" (1978, p. 135).

We specify the industrial export demand function as

$$x_2 = x_0 A^{-n} \tag{5.31}$$

where

$$A = (p_2/ep_{2e}^*) \tag{5.32}$$

Notice that A measures the real terms of trade or the relative competitiveness of industrial exports domestically produced (where p_{2e}^* is the internationally set price of industrial exports), n measures the price elasticity of the foreign demand for the country's industrial exports, and x_0 is the autonomous component of exports demand.

A subsidy will be equivalent to an improvement in competitiveness. This transforms A into

$$A = \left[\frac{p_2(1-z)}{ep_{2e}^*} \right] \tag{5.33}$$

where z is the subsidy rate, whose value is between 0 and 1. For simplicity we can make the term $(1-z) = \delta$. Thus, (5.33) may be expressed in dynamic form as

$$\hat{A} = \hat{p}_2 + \hat{\delta} - \hat{e} - \hat{p}_{2e}^* \tag{5.34}$$

It is apparent from this that an increase in z will decreases δ, which in turn will raise the relative competitiveness of industrial exports.

Taking rates of change of the variables involved in (5.31) and replacing the rate of growth of competitiveness from (5.34) we have the following equation for the growth of demand for industrial exports:

$$\hat{x}_2 = \hat{x}_0 - n(\hat{p}_2 + \hat{\delta} - \hat{e} - \hat{p}_{2e}^*) \tag{5.35}$$

The rate of growth of domestic industrial prices p_2 can be derived from the markup pricing equation (4.14). Thus, we can write the approximation

$$\hat{p}_2 = (1+\tau) + h_1(\hat{W} + \hat{b}_2) + h_2(\hat{a} + \hat{e} + \hat{p}_m) \tag{5.36}$$

Here h_1 and h_2 represent the share of labor unit cost and raw material unit cost as a proportion of total unit cost, respectively.

If we now consider labor productivity growth to be partly a function of the growth of output, we have

$$\hat{b}_2 = \hat{b}_0 + \theta\hat{Q}_2 \tag{5.37}$$

where θ is usually called the "Verdoorn coefficient" and b_0 is the autonomous component of labor productivity. It is the relation between output growth and labor productivity growth that makes this extension of the model "circular and cumulative." In other words, the subsidy induces fast industrial export growth that leads to higher output growth, leading to fast productivity growth, which feeds back to fast export growth and output growth through the favorable impact of productivity growth on relative price and competitiveness. Industrial export promotion becomes, then, the route for escaping from external "strangulation", as set up in expression (4.39).

To consider the balance-of-payments equilibrium growth rate, it is useful first to substitute (5.37) into (5.36) and then into (5.35) to get the expression

$$\hat{x}_2 = \hat{x}_0 - n[(1 + \tau) + h_1(\hat{W} + \hat{b}_0 + \theta\hat{Q}_2)$$
$$+ h_2(\hat{a} + \hat{e} + \hat{p}_m) + \hat{\delta} - \hat{e} - \hat{p}_{2e}^*] \tag{5.38}$$

Substituting (5.38) and (5.36) into (5.29) gives, after some simplification,

$$\hat{Q}_2 = \frac{1}{\varsigma_1 + \phi_2 h_1 \theta(n-1)} \phi_2[(1-n)[(1+\tau) + h_1(\hat{W} + \hat{b}_0) + h_2(\hat{a} + \hat{e} + \hat{p}_m)]$$
$$+ \hat{x}_0 - n[\hat{\delta} - \hat{e} - \hat{p}_{2e}^*]] \tag{5.39}$$

Assuming that no changes in $(1 + \tau)$, W, b, a, e, p_m, and p_{2e}^* occur (5.39) reduces to

$$\hat{Q}_2 = \frac{-\phi_2 n\hat{\delta}}{\varsigma_1 + \phi_2 h_1 \theta(n - 1)} \tag{5.40}$$

Differentiating (5.40) with respect to δ gives

$$\frac{\partial \hat{Q}_2}{\partial \hat{\delta}} = \frac{-\phi_2 n}{\varsigma_1 + \phi_2 h_1 \theta(n - 1)} < 0 \tag{5.41}$$

which implies that a higher subsidy to industrial exports will result in a higher balance-of-payments constrained growth rate of manufacturing output.

5.10 Growth Considerations

The growth aspects of IMF/WB adjustment programs rely on a merged framework that, as we have shown before, cannot be accepted as a theoretically useful tool for analyzing adjustment with growth issues in LDCs. Accepting growth as an indispensable component of an adjustment strategy is indeed a positive step. Theoretical models, however, need to focus on trying to identify and incorporate non-neoclassical behavioral relations, macro-imbalances, and institutional rigidities that are thought to better reflect the features of LDCs.

In the previous chapter we showed how the basic model could be extended to a model of growth. We have used and extended Thirwall's notion of growth's being consistent with balance-of-payments equilibrium. In this section, we will use the growth extension of the two-sector model developed previously to analyze several policy aspects and to examine the conditions under which the economy can achieve growth with and without inflation. We further analyze the impact that changes in the distribution of income will have on the rate of growth.

Recall first the saving supply and the investment demand relationships (4.92) and (4.96)

$$g_2^s = \gamma_7 + \gamma_8 r_2 \tag{4.92}$$

$$g_2^s = \gamma_3 + \gamma_6 r_2 \tag{4.96}$$

where

$$\gamma_3 = \frac{\gamma_0}{p_2 k_2}, \qquad \gamma_6 = \gamma_4 + \gamma_5 \frac{(1 + \tau)}{\tau}$$

$$\gamma_1 = \left[[s_c(1 - t_c) - t_c](r\lambda_1 + r_{1e}k_{1e}/k_2) - \frac{PSBR^*}{p_2 k_2} \right.$$

$$\left. + \frac{G}{k_2} + \frac{J}{p_2 k_2} - \frac{ep_{1e}^* x_1}{p_2 k_2} - \frac{x_2}{k_2} - \frac{CF}{p_2 k_2} \right]$$

and

$$\gamma_2 = \left[s_c(1 - t_c) - t_c + a\frac{(\tau + 1)}{\tau} \right]$$

5.10.1 Parametric Shifts

We first examine the effects of some parametric shifts, using figure 4.7 when necessary. Changes in the term γ_3 in equation (4.96) are governed by "animal spirits." Any increase in γ_3, as in Taylor (1983), raises the rate of growth of the economy. In this two-sector version of the growth model, however, the adjustment process is a little bit more complex.[12] The higher the level of investment in the industrial sector, the higher the level of output and of the profit rate in industry. Higher profits mean higher government revenues,

Figure 5.7a

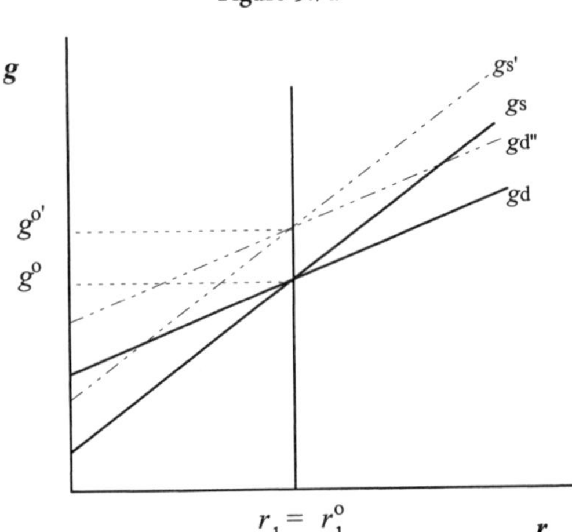

Figure 5.7b

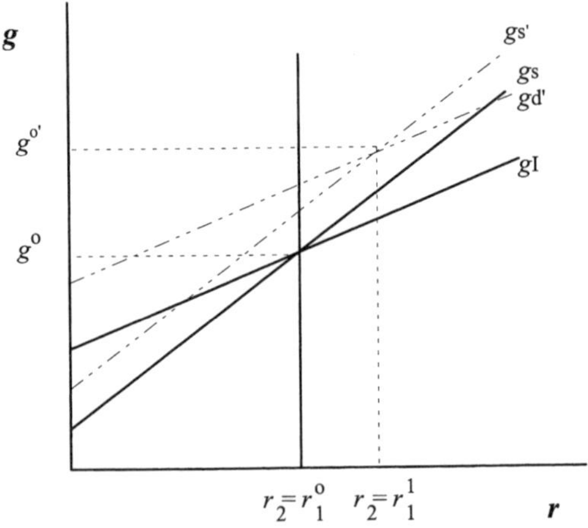

which in turn are saved and invested in the expansion of infrastructure for the basic goods sector. Graphically, the change in γ_3 is shown by a shift of the g^d line. But at the initial basic goods price, the rise in the primary sector capital stock will call forth a fall in basic goods price (and profitability), while the rise in industrial investment will have multiplier effects on output and employment, increasing basic goods demand. As the price of basic goods and r_1

change, the g^s will shift either to the left or to the right. If, for instance, the price of basic goods increases (as a result of the interactive character of the investment demand and primary sector supply constraints), the parameter γ_1 in (4.92) rises or falls (and the g^s schedule shifts upward or downward). The capitalist propensity to save and the income tax rate will be critical here. As long as $t_c < s_c(1 - t_c)$ the g^s schedule will shift upward. In steady state the profit rates will not change (from their initial values), and the growth rate of the economy may be higher as long as the shifts of the curves are of the same magnitude (see figure 5.7a). Weak γ_1 responsiveness to a change in r_1 makes the lower picture's configuration, 5.7b, more likely.

The point that we want to make is simple. In post-Keynesian two-sector growth models with an independent investment function but no essential role for the government (see, for instance, Taylor 1982 and 1983; and Dutt 1990), an expansionary force on investment increases the rate of growth, and conflict inflation will emerge since the steady state profit rate $r^e = r^1 = r^2$ will be higher than the non-inflationary profit rate r_1^0. The question here is: Does this relationship between inflation and growth hold in two-sector models with public investment in infrastructure as a macroclosure? The answer is, in general, ambiguous.

5.10.2 Government Saving, Foreign Saving, and Export Revenues

Faster growth requires a higher quantity of investment, and higher levels of "financing" should match higher investment. There is no question that the cessation of capital flows to the Latin American region and the rise in interest rates from the 1980s onward produced a turnaround in the net financial transfers of resources from abroad (net capital inflows CF minus interest payments J to abroad).[13] Recovering investment presupposes increasing domestic saving or decreasing the net flow of resources abroad. The last alternative, as we argued before, involves trying to renegotiate the external debt, increase creditworthiness, and bring about lower international interest rates.[14] With regard to domestic financing, we share the idea that raising public saving is the most direct, powerful, and immediate way that government policy can contribute to higher domestic saving (Shmidt-Hebbel and Webb 1992). To avoid government investment cuts, the public sector can increase its savings and finance its plans for investment through taxation or by selling domestic debt. An increase in $PSBR$ raises public saving (which is equal to public investment minus deficit, as shown in 4.57). Once $PSBR$ is increased, investment in basic goods production increases, jumping the steady state growth to a higher rate.

Formally, the equilibrium growth of the system, g^0, is obtained by the equality

$$g^0 = \frac{\gamma_3 - \dfrac{\gamma_6 \gamma_1}{\gamma_2}}{1 - \dfrac{\gamma_6}{\gamma_2}} = \frac{\gamma_2 \gamma_3 - \gamma_6 \gamma_7}{\gamma_2 - \gamma_6} \tag{5.42}$$

which results from substituting (4.92) into (4.96). The net effect of a change in *PSBR* is thus

$$\frac{\partial g^0}{\partial PSBR} = \frac{\left[\gamma_4 + \gamma_5 \dfrac{(1+\tau)}{\tau}\right] \dfrac{1}{p_2 k_2}}{\left[s_c(1-t_c) - t_c + a\dfrac{(1+\tau)}{\tau}\right] - \left[\gamma_4 + \gamma_5 \dfrac{(1+\tau)}{\tau}\right]} = \frac{\gamma_6 \dfrac{1}{p_2 k_2}}{\gamma_2 - \gamma_6} \tag{5.43}$$

which is positive provided that $[s_c(1-t_c) - t_c + a(1+\tau)/\tau] > [\gamma_4 + \gamma_5(1+\tau)/\tau]$. But this condition is precisely the stability condition that requires the assumption that the g^s line be steeper than the g^d line.

Graphically, the effect of higher *PSBR* reduces to a shift of the g^s to the right. The equilibrium growth rate changes from g^0 to a higher level at $g^{0'}$.

Figure 5.8

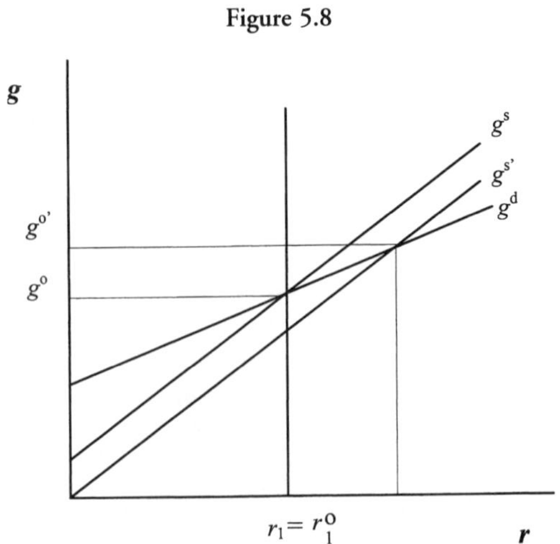

It is interesting to note that, granted the stability condition of equilibrium, the effect of a parametric change in foreign savings, primary exports revenues, and *PSBR* will have similar impacts.

$$\frac{\partial g^0}{\partial CF} = \frac{\partial g^0}{\partial (ep^*_{1e}x_1)} = \frac{\partial g^0}{\partial PSBR} > 0 \qquad (5.44)$$

Moreover, an exogenous change in the foreign demand for manufacturing exports will also increase the equilibrium growth rate of the economy, as shown by

$$\frac{\partial g^0}{\partial x_2} = \frac{\gamma_6 \dfrac{1}{k_2}}{\gamma_2 - \gamma_6} > 0 \qquad (5.45)$$

The differentials $\partial g^0/\partial(ep^*_{1e}x_1)$ and $\partial g^0/\partial x_2$ are meaningful in the sense that both the value of primary exports and the volume of manufacturing exports are determined exogenously. It is interesting to note that an increase in the value of primary exports acts as a positive external transfer, since it allows the financing of a higher level of imports (in the same fashion as in two-gap models).[15] An increase in the volume of manufacturing exports yields a higher equilibrium growth rate since it adds to the demand for industrial goods and generates foreign exchange receipts for imports. Unfortunately, the higher growth rate associated with the above parametric changes will raise the equilibrium profit rate, and we know that inflation increases when the profit rate in the basic goods sector is higher than r^0. Under those circumstances, the system shows a strong inflationary bias.

5.11   Income Distribution and Growth

It is reasonable to ask now whether or not income distribution policies will stimulate economic growth without inducing inflation. Regarding capitalists in the industrial sector, a fall in the markup seems initially to improve income distribution. Thus, differentiating (5.42) with respect to τ and rearranging we get

$$\frac{\partial g^0}{\partial \tau} = \frac{\left[-\left(\dfrac{a\gamma_3 + \gamma_5\gamma_6}{\tau^2}\right) - \dfrac{UCk_2\gamma_0\gamma_2}{(p_2k_2)^2} - \dfrac{\gamma_6 UC}{p_2k_2}(PSBR^* + ep^*_{1e}x_1 + CF - J)\right](\gamma_2 - \gamma_6) + \dfrac{(a + \gamma_5)}{\tau^2}(\gamma_2\gamma_3 - \gamma_6\gamma_1)}{(\gamma_2 - \gamma_6)^2}$$

$$(5.46)$$

where $UC = (W/b + eap_m)$, i.e. total unit cost.

To sign this expression, note first that $\gamma_1 - \gamma_3 < 0$ and $\gamma_2 - \gamma_6 > 0$ are the conditions for the existence and stability of equilibrium that are imposed to the system. This implies that the last term in the numerator of (5.46), $(a + \gamma_5)/\tau^2(\gamma_2\gamma_3 - \gamma_6\gamma_1)$, should be positive. Therefore, depending on the initial configuration of the model's parameters, the equilibrium growth rate may well fall or increase when the markup declines. If the first square-bracketed term on the right-hand side of (5.46) multiplied by $(\gamma_2 - \gamma_6)$ is negative and greater than the term $(a + \gamma_5)/\tau^2(\gamma_2\gamma_3 - \gamma_6\gamma_1)$, the whole expression will be negative. In this case, we are back to the under-consumptionist argument in which a higher real wage (lower markup) keeps effective demand and growth buoyant. However, counterpoised against this regime we may have the opposite situation. In such a case a decrease in the markup will lower the rate of growth of the economy.

To understand these possible results, it is analytically convenient to decompose the impact of a fall in the markup rate into (a) the effect of changing intersectoral savings flows and (b) the effect of capacity utilization on investment demand.[16] An income distribution shift favoring workers, who have a higher propensity to consume than capitalists, increases total consumption demand and will usually raise the rate of capacity utilization and hence the rate of industrial investment. Since this raises industrial income at a faster rate, tax proceeds also expand faster, and so does government investment in the basic goods sector. However, a higher level of consumption due to redistribution may raise the income of primary sector capitalists if excess demand for basic goods prevails. In that case, aggregate saving increases (at the initial equilibrium profit rate), reducing industrial output and growth rates. Of course, the two forces interact. Whether or not the economy will face stagnation depends on the relative strength of the two forces.

Figure 5.9 depicts a very pleasant situation, though this is one of many possible scenarios. The fall in τ increases $\gamma_5(1 + \tau)/\tau$, and as a consequence, γ_6. The slope of the g^d function rises (see equation 4.70). Graphically, it is shown by an anti-clockwise rotation of the g^d line to the position $g^{d'}$. But the fall in τ will also increase γ_3 as p_2 falls. Therefore the g^d line will also shift upward. Turning to the g^s schedule, the fall in the markup will increase the saving flows at the given rate of capacity utilization because it increases the term γ_2 in equation (4.74). This induces an anti-clockwise rotation of the g^s line. But the g^s also shifts downward, provided that $PSBR + ep^*_{1e}x_1 + CF > J$. When the magnitude of the shifts is such that in the new equilibrium the profit rate does not change, then the rate of growth of the economy rises without generating conflicting claims. Of course, this result should be viewed as a possibility and not as an iron law.

Figure 5.9

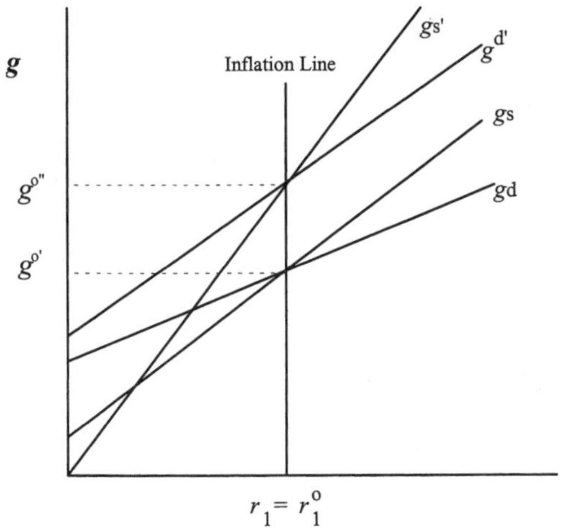

5.12 *Income Distribution and Growth: A Dynamic Analysis*

To examine how our economy moves through time, we rely on the analysis in Dutt (1984), in which the markup rate is endogenized. By contrast, our analysis allows for an extended saving–investment balance and for the existence of two different regimes.

Recall first that the relation between g^0 and τ, based on the saving–investment equality and showing equilibrium at a point in time for the economy, is given by

$$g^0 = \frac{\gamma_3 - \dfrac{\gamma_6\gamma_1}{\gamma_2}}{1 - \dfrac{\gamma_6}{\gamma_2}} = \frac{\gamma_2\gamma_3 - \gamma_6\gamma_1}{\gamma_2 - \gamma_6} \tag{5.42}$$

Equation (5.46) can be simplified to show that

$$\frac{\partial g^0}{\partial \tau} = \frac{\Gamma_1(\gamma_2 - \gamma_6) + \Gamma_2(\gamma_2\gamma_3 + \gamma_6\gamma_1)}{(\gamma_2 - \gamma_6)^2} \tag{5.46a}$$

where

$$\Gamma_1 = -\left(\frac{a\gamma_3 + \gamma_5\gamma_6}{\tau^2}\right) - \frac{UCk_2\gamma_0\gamma_2}{(p_2k_2)^2} - \frac{\gamma_6 UC}{p_2k_2}(PSBR^* + ep_{1e}^*x_1 + CF - J) < 0$$

and

$$\Gamma_2 = \frac{a + \gamma_5}{\tau^2} > 0$$

Note that we have identified two different regimes:

If $\Gamma_1 > \Gamma_2$ then $\partial g^0 / \partial \tau < 0$
If $\Gamma_1 < \Gamma_2$ then $\partial g^0 / \partial \tau > 0$

Moreover, $\partial g^0 / \partial \tau$ falls as τ rises, as we can verify by differentiating (5.46) with respect to τ. Hence, we may depict a saving–investment balance schedule in the g–τ plane showing a curve that is downward sloping and convex to the origin.

Next, consider the determinants of changes in τ. Denoting the time derivative of τ by $d\tau/dt$, we assume, following Dutt (1984, 1990), that it depends on τ, g, and ξ (a government policy variable), i.e.

$$\frac{d\tau}{dt} = F(\tau, g, \xi) \tag{5.47}$$

with $(d\tau/dt)/dg < 0$ and

$$\left(\frac{d\tau}{dt}\right)/d\tau > 0, \quad \forall\, 0 \leq \tau < \tau'$$

$$\left(\frac{d\tau}{dt}\right)/d\tau < 0, \quad \forall\, \tau > \tau'$$

Notice that we have assumed that a higher growth rate reduces $d\tau/dt$. Industrial organization literature gives support to this thesis by claiming that rapid growth may erode concentration and reduce entry barriers (for a review, see Shepherd 1985, pp. 196–197). Lower concentration reduces, then, the size of the markup.[17] The relation established between $d\tau/dt$ and τ is more complex. It seems that at least at low levels of τ, higher τ will imply greater market power, and hence greater ability on the part of firms to push up markup rates, implying a higher $d\tau/dt$. But beyond a certain level of τ, say τ', further increases in it will reduce $d\tau/dt$ for at least three reasons: (1) high markups will induce greater entry and faster falls in concentration (as suggested by limit pricing models of oligopoly); (2) existing firms may apprehend government action if they push up their markup rates excessively; and (3) firms cannot push up markups indefinitely, in any case. Finally, as we remarked previously, the function F can be assumed to depend on certain policy actions carried out by the government.

Figure 5.10a depicts both relationships g^0 and $d\tau/dt = 0$ in the case in which $\partial g^0/\partial \tau < 0$. The saving–investment balance is downward sloping, while the curve $d\tau/dt = 0$, which yields a relation between g and τ with τ stationary, has a bell shape.

Assuming that the goods market is always in equilibrium, the economy will always be on the g^0 curve. Also, as shown by the arrows, τ falls above the $d\tau/dt = 0$ and rises below it. While there are a variety of possible configurations of these two curves, the figure shows one interesting possibility. Since the economy is restricted to points on the g^0 schedule, it can admit two possible long equilibria 'A' and 'B'. Point 'A' is unstable, but point 'B' is stable. An economy starting from any $\tau > \tau_1$ will over time tend to move toward 'B'. With a low g and τ the economy can be described as being trapped in a difficult situation with low growth and very high income inequality.

If instead of $\partial g^0/\partial \tau < 0$, the economy presents a nonstagnationist regime, i.e. $\partial g^0/\partial \tau > 0$, the g^0 schedule will show a positive slope in the g–τ plane. Once again the multiple equilibrium situation emerges as a possibility. Figure 5.10b shows how 'B' will be again a stable state. But in contrast with the previous situation the economy can perform better in terms of growth and income distribution.

The central feature of this distinction among regimes can be better appreciated once we introduced government action. We mentioned before that the government can affect the markup via specific guidelines or price

Figure 5.10a

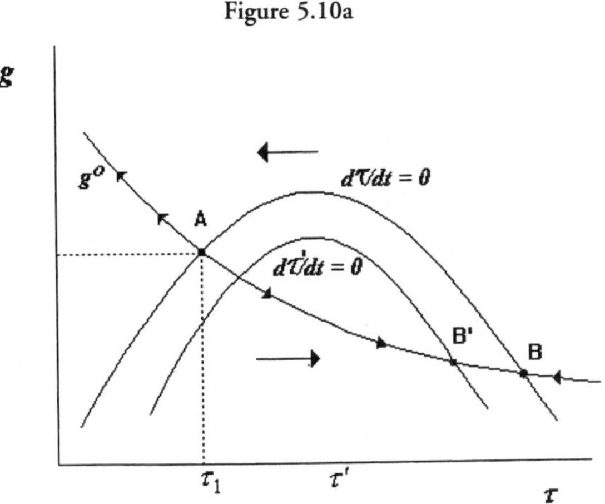

Figure 5.10b

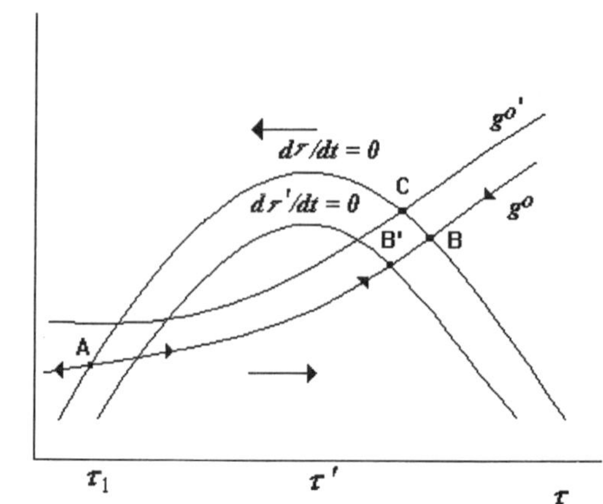

controls, and also indirectly through instruments of industrial or competition policy that either stimulate or retard advances in this variable. In any case, the position of the $d\tau/dt = 0$ curve is assumed to depend on changes in ξ (government policy variable); for example, government action promoting competition would shift the curve down to the position showed by the $d\tau'/dt = 0$ line in both figures. Let us assume then than the economy is initially located (or trapped) at point 'B'. In the first case (the stagnationist regime), when government tries to affect the markup and income distribution, the economy will converge to a long-run equilibrium (point 'B' in figure 5.10a), at which it will attain a higher growth rate and a better income distribution. But, if the $\partial g^0/\partial \tau < 0$ condition is violated (the nonstagnationist case), the g^0 will have a positive slope, and the adjustment process will lead the economy towards a long-run equilibrium with a better income distribution but a lower growth rate (point 'B' in figure 5.10b). Therefore, in this case we should not confine the discussion to policies promoting changes in the markup, but rather should consider shocks that change the relationship between τ and g. As an example, we choose to change *PSBR*, but changes in $ep_{1e}^* x_1, x_2$ and *CF* (all exogenous) will have the same impact. Such a change will lower γ_7 and increase g (in 5.42) at each τ so that they imply an upward shift in the g^0 curve, as shown in figure 5.10b, from a position like g^0 to one like $g^{0\prime}$. In the long run, the economy therefore moves from point 'B' to point 'C', implying increasing g and falling τ. On the basis of these observations we are led to believe that the underlying structure of the economy matters.

5.13 Conclusions

This chapter has examined the policy implications of the model developed in this book. We have devoted a great deal of space to this issue because it does relate directly to the discussion initially presented in this work. Moreover, it seems worth pointing out that policy issues are often ignored or simply underdeveloped by heterodox critics, though some efforts has been made recently on this front by post-Keynesians.[18]

We started summarizing the four equations (and four endogenous targets) to which the model collapses. Subsequently, we introduced additional extensions and attention to dynamics issues, including inflation and growth. We have investigated the short-term variations of the basic endogenous variables to exogenous shocks and changes in policy-induced variables.

From the demand side, we have evaluated the impact of changes in direct taxation, in government funding, and in government expenditure (government investment is an endogenous variable). Demand management policies have several complex effects on output, capitalist profitability, budget deficit, and public investment. But in general, we have shown that by changing the setting of government demand policies we would not expect an overall macroeconomic balance. Relevant trade-offs appear among industrial output, the price of necessities, and the change in net international reserves and public investment.

Events outside the complete control of the government, such as debt relief and a change in private investment impetus, reveal interesting results. Debt relief is expansionary in the short run since it eases the fiscal constraint and helps increase public investment. But it increases the price of necessities and may in some cases deteriorate the level of net international reserves (if the import content in unit cost is high enough). An increase in private investment leads us to similar results. A multiplier process expands industrial output, but a higher demand increases the price of necessities. The trade deficit is amplified due to the higher demand for imported capital goods and to the increase in intermediate inputs required for output expansion. Income policies do not allow us to be precise about the position the economy is going to achieve. In drawing these conclusions, however, we should remind ourselves of the restrictive nature of our formalization, since we have analyzed the effects of changes in the markup and the nominal wage rate in isolation.

One thing is clear: demand policies alone do not solve all macroeconomic balances. Kaldor (1986) is very clear in this respect when he says: "I believe that the four objectives listed there ([a] full and stable employment, [b] a satisfactory balance of payments, [c] the absence of inflation, [d] a high rate of economic growth) should severely and jointly, be regarded as the main objectives of governmental economic management ... the simultaneous pursuit of these objectives requires a multiplicity of instruments (ideally the same number as there are objectives) though a given policy measure might have a favourable effect on the attainment of several objectives simultaneously" (p. 39).

We need both demand management and supply-side policies. There is consequently a potential role for governments to pursue capital-augmenting investment in those sectors where the supply side is constrained. In fact, our framework clearly demonstrates that public sector investment in the primary sector minimizes the damage that demand and/or incomes policies are likely to do in the inflationary front. Again, Kaldor (1978), this time using the experience of Latin American countries, clearly remarked: "... the remedies to Latin America inflation will not be found in monetary and fiscal reforms—though this is not to say that these, particularly fiscal reform, may not be necessary, and important as accompanying measures. ... Two basic remedies are first stimulating domestic food production, which requires far-reaching land reform in most countries, as well as public investment and promotional policies, e.g., in irrigation schemes, etc., and second, appropriate policies for industrial rationalization and the promotion of exports of manufactures." (p. 134)

Kaldor's last idea, of the promotion of manufacturing exports, has also found support in our policy evaluation. We have shown how an initial improvement in competitiveness develops a circular and cumulative causation mechanism. We have modeled a balance-of-payments constrained growth rate, making allowances for the fact that industrial export prices are set up internally and that labor productivity growth responds among other variables to the growth of output in the economy. This major innovation, suggested by Thirlwall, allows us to evaluate the positive impact that a higher subsidy rate has on the balance-of-payments constrained growth rate of industrial exports.

We have presented an additional way of addressing output growth. We impose long-run equilibrium conditions on our sectoral model. This involves the usual assumption that sectoral rates of profits are equalized, and that the economy is on a steady state growth path, with stocks of productive capital in each sector growing at the same rate. It is interesting to note that the system shows a strong inflationary bias if growth is stimulated either by autonomous investment shocks or by higher levels of financing.

Income distribution policies show complex effects on growth and inflation. At least four cases can fit into the low inflation–high growth desirable scenario. To see how the economy moves through time, we have taken this relationship between income distribution and growth and examined in a purely dynamic context how both the markup and the steady state rate of growth move through time. The markup is endogenized, and the saving–investment balance allows the existence of two regimes (stagnationist and nonstagnationist). Both regimes may admit two possible equilibria. In the stagnationist case the economy may be trapped into a situation of low growth and very high income inequality. We have shown that incomes policy, as well as industrial and competition policies that try to affect the markup, may lead the economy to a better position in terms of the growth-distribution record. However, in a nonstagnationist regime we have found that the direct mechanism of financing government investment (in the basic goods sector) as an increase in *PSBR* does a better job.

Notes

1. In fact, the term $(\varepsilon W u_1 k_1 / Q_1 b_2 p_2)$ can be rearranged to yield the expression $\varepsilon(W/b_2)(1/p_2)$, which is the ratio of labor unit cost to prices (with values between zero and one) multiplied by ε (where $0 < \varepsilon < 1$).
2. Since our analysis here is limited to the short run, we are not concerned with the issue of debt-income ratio and fiscal sustainability. We also neglect the depressing effect that a bond sale to the public may bring about by diverting funds from private industry as a result of the offer of higher interest rates by the government.
3. Observe that the term $(p_1 - p_1^0)$ varies with time.
4. Output expansion increases government revenues in two ways: (a) by increasing profits in the industrial sector and (b) by increasing profitability in the basic goods sector through induced price increases.
5. The impact of debt relief on GDP growth has been analyzed in the framework of gap models by Bacha (1990 and 1992), Nicolini (1991), and Dias Carneiro and Werneck (1990). However, the short-run effects of such strategies have hardly been explored.
6. The success of the Economic Solidarity Pact in Mexico in curbing inflation (from December 1987 until the early 1990s) relied greatly on the way decisions were made. In this case decisions were made through "concertation" and price deindexation was progressive rather than decreed. For details see Guillen Romo (1990), Lasa (1992), and Ros and Lustig (1993).
7. Of course this applies in those cases in which the markup is chosen so as to balance the incremental benefits from new investment with the incremental cost associated with internally generating the funds needed to finance this investment.

8. Later in the analysis we will endogenize the markup rate by assuming an inverse relation between the rate of growth of the economy and industrial concentration.

9. A remaining effect will come from the ambiguous response of public investment to the change in the markup.

10. Thirlwall (1979) and Thirlwall *et al.* (1983), for instance, use multiplicative functions to express the quantities of exports and imports demanded. In these functions, the arguments are relative prices and foreign and domestic income, respectively.

11. Neither Dixon *et al.* (1975) nor Thirlwall (1983) analyze, for instance, the elements that could eventually induce a higher demand for industrial exports.

12. Our argument is based on the fact that solving the two simultaneous equations of this growth model yields the result that the two curves shift simultaneously.

13. Eyzaguirre (1989) reports the transfer in about -4 percent of GDP for the period 1982–87. Fernandez-Arias and Montiel (1996), however, report that on average the long-term capital net flows were about 2.5 percent of GDP for the period 1990–93. The World Bank (1994) confirms this significant increase in net flows to LDCs, and, especially to some Latin American countries for the early 1990s.

14. We should remember that our model takes for granted that LDCs in Latin America have not had access to unrestricted voluntary lending from private commercial sources. Thus, for most of the 1980s and 1990s, we have assumed that foreign saving has been exogenous.

15. Of course, this result is tied to the definition of foreign saving, which implies in our case that foreign reserves accumulation is now exogenous and equal to zero $(\Delta R = 0)$.

16. Sarkar (1993) distinguishes the "profit squeeze" factor and the "realization" factor, while post-Keynesians frequently make an analogous distinction between "exhilirationist" and "stagnationist" regimes. An exhilirationist regime is one in which economic growth is driven by rising profitability, so that redistribution favoring capitalists stimulates expansion; this is the tradition that stretches from Ricardo to Arthur Lewis. A stagnationist regime is one in which economic growth is driven by rising wages, so that redistribution favoring workers stimulates expansion; this is the tradition that stretches from Hobson to Kalecki and other post-Keynesians.

17. This is, of course, much more in line with Kalecki's degree of monopoly theory, which includes, among several features, the degree of industrial concentration.

18. See Arestis (1984, 1992, and 1996) for exceptional efforts on this front.

CHAPTER 6

Conclusions

Since the early 1980s, stabilization and structural adjustment policies have dominated the agenda of Latin American countries. During this period domestic policy intervention by multilateral institutions has been decisive. The 1980s were difficult years for LDCs in Latin America, since most suffered low or negative per-capita income growth rates, high inflation, and adverse trends in trade and capital flows. With some exceptions, prospects for the decade beginning in 2000 are not brighter after more than 18 years of harsh stabilization, this despite the fact that most countries have taken big steps toward orthodox economic reforms. There is a chance that continued capital inflows along with the lower inflation profile, can facilitate a return to better growth rates as the decade advances, but the social and distributional requirements will be demanding. The cures prescribed by the multilateral institutions to resolve the basic macroeconomic problems are almost exhausted. However, the IMF/World Bank duet has emerged from the 1980s asserting powerful leverage over economic policy in the region (as the dramatic increase in the number of agreements with these Bretton Woods institutions shows).

The practice of conditionality and performance criteria needs to be evaluated. It is striking to note that the policy package usually prescribed by the IMF has remained static over the years. This is also the case for the theoretical framework, the analytical tools, and the models that underlie conditionality. A much broader focus includes trade and financial liberalization, as well as market reforms looking for price realignments, but all this still requires orthodox demand restraint and exchange rate adjustment.

Despite the importance of the theoretical content of economic policy packages supported by multilateral institutions, studies dealing with these theoretical constructs are few and not very comprehensive. We have made an effort to relate and integrate the various analytical tools. We have shown, by way of achieving a synthesis, that quite traditional policy prescriptions for stabilization and structural adjustment fit readily into the framework of the orthodox open economy monetary models. We have followed closely the chronological order through which these models have been digested into the orthodox policy prescriptions. The exposition not only shows relevant assumptions but also reveals how the various theoretical models are components of much broader perspective within which they appear complementary.

The merit of making explicit the understanding of the models upon which stabilization and adjustment policies are based is that this explicitness aids the task of criticism. We have argued that there are a number of grounds for questioning the appropriateness of the typical stabilization and adjustment package. Weaknesses arise from three sources. First, there are weaknesses that are a result of erroneous premises and assumptions. Second, there are theoretical weaknesses that are intrinsic to the models. Finally, weaknesses have been observed at the empirical level when the theory is subject to the historical and empirical test.

On theoretical grounds, we have raised serious doubts about the effectiveness of devaluation. Devaluation will also be contractionary (at least in the short run) due to supply-and-demand effects. Furthermore, we have surveyed the literature on the impact of devaluation on both the trade balance and output, and found that while the findings are rather optimistic with respect to the trade balance, with respect to output economic contraction seems to be the rule.

The often-ignored inflationary and income distribution effects of devaluation have been pointed out. The structure of the economy is of critical importance here. The capital and intermediate goods content of imports, the structure of output markets, and class conflicts are relevant to the analysis. Devaluation can result in chronic inflation, and real wages will decline as a consequence of the existence of intermediate inputs in the production of tradeables, supply-constrained tradeables, workers' consumption of imported essentials, and non-instantaneous real wage adjustments. We have argued that the fall in real wages and the consequent regressive income distribution may undermine labor intensity (effort), and hence productivity.

The assertion that a current account deficit is the consequence of excess absorption over income is not necessarily true. Here, orthodoxy dogmatically insists on imposing an unverified causal thesis. In reality, an autonomous fall in exports, an autonomous rise in imports, or an autonomous secular or cyclical deterioration in the real terms of trade, for instance, may cause a current account deficit. If the external imbalance originates in a sudden worsening of the terms of trade, a fiscal surplus could be transformed into a fiscal deficit through a decline in tax receipts; the causality is then inverted. It is possible that an increase in aggregate demand caused by a greater fiscal deficit results in an increase in private savings and not an increase in the current account deficit.

In discussing fiscal deficit reduction, we have stressed the need to specify the means by which an overall program of fiscal austerity is achieved. If complementarity between both public and private investment dominates, then a reduction in government plans to invest will affect the prospects for growth. I critically survey several empirical studies that verify this complementarity relationship in LDCs and in several Latin American countries.

The Keynesian-oriented synthesis of the elasticity and absorption approaches suffers from additional weaknesses. The highly aggregative frame of reference (one-sector model), the absence of any detailed description of the internal accumulation balance, and the ignored aspects of income distribution and the supply side makes the elasticity-absorption synthesis virtually irrelevant in LCDs.

The monetary approach is internally consistent, but it explains no real variables. Neither production functions nor sectoral articulation is present. The production capacity of the economy is fixed, output variation is ignored, and monetary targets are based on an assumed stability of the demand for money function. The narrow definition of money that is usually employed and the assumed domestic exogeneity of the money supply are at least controversial. The recommended credit squeeze may affect output, as well as demand and absorption. Moreover, if interest rates increase, the interest cost of working capital (as noted by structuralist authors) will also increase and stagflation is then more than a possibility. The financial programming model indicates that a devaluation may eventually help through expenditure switching, but this policy measure in the best of cases is bound to take some time to have a positive impact on production (as discussed previously).

The analysis and policy implications of structural adjustment or supply-oriented policies have also been subjected to a broad criticism. The integrated model, which seems to be one more attempt to link formally supply-oriented policies and growth, is also shown to be replete with difficulties. The model retains many of the limitations and erroneous assumptions of some of the models criticized previously. The analysis of the impact of an external shock and the formulation of an appropriate policy response to such a shock clearly illustrate the fragility of the IMF/World Bank model in the particular conditions of Latin American countries, where the simplifying assumptions of the model simply do not hold. But in addition, we have demonstrated that the link between supply-oriented policies and economic growth is not straightforward either. Financial liberalization may not increase the willingness to save (which is implicit in the integrated model). Internal deregulation is no guarantee of avoiding inefficiency, and the proposals for trade liberalization as an instrument to eliminate the inefficiencies of a protected domestic market are not self-evident, and are often overstated. We have not only analyzed but also revised the empirical literature where trade liberalization does not lead to outward orientation and to greater overall efficiency and growth. In general, it is clear that the links among structural adjustment, economic efficiency, and growth cannot be established. We have pointed out the failure of structural adjustment itself and the constraints that orthodox short-run stabilization imposes on growth. In sum, the overall picture suggests that the theoretical constructs of IMF/WB thinking are not based on firm foundations. The empirical investigation and the historical lesson reveal that orthodox packages are becoming less and less successful.

We have questioned the McKinnon–Shaw hypothesis and the way orthodoxy understands the functioning of finance in LDCs in four ways. First, we have argued that raising interest rates to positive levels is unlikely to raise savings in LDCs. Foreign exchange constraints and the dependence on imported capital goods also imply that it is not sufficient to raise savings in order to increase investment and growth. Second, investment behavior will not respond to interest rate incentives if retained profits are the main source of investment finance in LDCs (the Lewis hypothesis). Third, higher interest rates could eventually increase financial fragility and reduce productive investment. Finally, we have shown how recent empirical studies in LDCs cast serious doubts upon the validity of the McKinnon and Shaw assumptions.

What we hope to have done in this work is to indicate certain alternative directions in which the theory and policy of stabilization and growth may perhaps be profitably considered and extended. Our study indicates that it is time, therefore, to move beyond the comforting answers offered by models that claim a universal validity, and begin to pay attention to alternative approaches that have undertaken the difficult and arduous task of sorting out the messy and incomplete record offered by economic history. We have argued that interaction between post-Keynesians and structuralists is a step in the right direction and as such is rewarding. We have presented a model that combines elements of both post-Keynesian economics and structuralism. Its attractiveness, we suggest, lies in its capacity for making sense of the reality we experience in Latin American economies. In this respect, it offers a sharp contrast to the orthodox approach, which is ultimately inadequate because its constructs are groundless. We have proposed a model that stands out from conventional macromodels for stabilization and adjustment in many respects. It is post-Keynesian in the sense that it takes as its central focus an approach to economic reality based on a money-production-distribution-class relationship. Oligopolistic product markets, collective bargaining in labor markets, differentiated marginal propensities to save, and a tight link between the monetary and the real sector help us to determine the rate of profits, real wages, overall activity, and the amount of money in the economy. We make some minimal, but essential sectoral distinctions so as to reflect the principal internal characteristics of LDCs. An enclave, a primary (food, basics, or necessities), and an industrial sector are clearly distinguished, where production, pricing, and demand formation are set according to specific structural features. The model, although nourished and stimulated by specific theoretical sources, is considerably richer as it includes not only primary and secondary sector supply and demand constraints, respectively, but also a foreign exchange and a government budget constraint (introducing additional transmission mechanism for policy variables). Moreover, we added a fully specified external sector with capital inflows rationing, where, instead of deriving the conditions for improving the balance of payments at a given level of income, we studied the conditions that enable a country to achieve a higher growth path consistent with payments equilibrium. Additionally, we have introduced a fiscal constraint where the government faces certain limits on financing its deficit and, as a consequence, has to adjust public investment. The entire system of the basic model responds to exogenous shocks through changes in basic good prices, industrial output, international reserves, and public investment.

Extensions have been incorporated formally into the basic model, and solutions have been obtained. The first extension is related to inflation dynamics. Inflation is the outcome of structural disequilibrium and conflictive claims among economic classes and/or sectors. In such a situation the model shows that this sort of economy becomes highly susceptible to inflation. A second extension is related to balance-of-payments constrained growth. We differ from Taylor (1982, 1983, and 1991); Dutt (1990); and Rao (1993) in that our rate of growth (from the saving side) in the manufacturing sector implicitly assumes that the economy simultaneously faces a fiscal and an external constraint.

We have been explicitly concerned with policy issues in this work, and the principles of the model developed here do have significant policy implications that are worth noting. First, one essential point that derives from the model developed is that policy instruments with a highly aggregative impact are insufficient and sometimes inappropriate to meet the stabilization targets of a non-inflationary increase in output and employment without balance-of-payments difficulties. Demand-side policies, for instance, appear entirely insufficient to resolve all macroeconomic imbalances. An increase in government expenditure deteriorates the fiscal balance and does not have any significant effect on manufacturing output and the external balance. Changes in direct taxation have unpredictable consequences. The sale of government bonds (or other financial assets) to the public or/and the banking sector improves the fiscal balance and the level of economic activity, but it may also have the undesired effect of raising the rate of inflation and the trade deficit. We have also analyzed events beyond the control of the government, such as changes in private investment and debt relief, and found that relevant trade-offs between industrial output, the price of basics, and the balance of payments appear.

Second, it has been shown that the adoption of supply-side measures that stimulate capital-augmenting investment in the primary sector will facilitate the expansionary effect of demand and/or income policy by minimizing the damage that such a policy is likely to inflict on the inflationary front. In fact, the price of basic goods declines as public investment in the primary sector increases and the production frontier expands.

Third, if the government is concerned with bringing about an increase in economic activity without deteriorating the level of reserves, it should direct its policy to the promotion of manufacturing exports where macro-increasing returns apply. As an extension of the basic model, we have analyzed and demonstrated the positive effect that an introduction of a subsidy rate has on output growth, without causing any deterioration in the external balance. In a dynamic context, this is an obvious alternative to expansionary objectives of demand-side policies.

Fourth, an additional way of addressing output growth aspects is by introducing behavioral investment functions and changes in the stock of capital in each sector. One preliminary result indicates that an increase in autonomous investment in manufacturing output increases the steady state rate of growth of the economy, but the probability of a greater non-inflationary profit rate is high.

Fifth, a higher equilibrium growth rate is expected when government savings increase, but the system again shows a strong inflationary bias. In fact, growth can be stimulated via larger investments in the public sector, and one way in which the public sector can increase its financing is by selling a greater amount of bonds to the public.

Sixth, regarding income redistribution policies (in this growth context), we have identified the intersectoral savings flows effect and the effect of capacity utilization on investment demand. These effects make the relationship between income distribution and growth ambiguous.

Finally, the relationship between income distribution and growth is examined in a purely dynamic context, in which both the markup and the steady state rate of growth change over time. The markup is endogenized, and the saving-investment balance permits the existence of two regimes (stagnationist and nonstagnationist). Each of these regimes permits two possible equilibria. In the stagnationist case, the economy may be trapped into a situation of low growth and very high income inequality. Income, industrial, or competition policies that try to affect the markup may lead the economy to a better position in terms of the growth-distribution record. But these policies will not work in a nonstagnationist regime, in which case policies that increase public savings are more appropriate.

The results that we have obtained are generally richer and in many instances different from those obtained in the open economy macromodels that support IMF/WB thinking. A comparative analysis between the policy recommendations and goals of the orthodox approach, on the one hand, and those of what might be characterized as post-Keynesian and structuralist, on the other, inevitably involves simplifications. Nevertheless, we offer a brief outline in order to illustrate these basic differences. Based on our findings, the following outline in table 6.1 summarizes and compares the orthodox (IMF/WB) and heterodox approaches in relation to goals and policy recommendations.

The policy recommendations for stabilization derived from the IMF/WB framework are focused on the demand side. Policies are mainly adopted with the intention of solving the aggregate demand-and-supply imbalance by reducing absorption. In addition, the monetary approach has identified excessive expansion of the money supply over money demand as the key to external and internal stabilization. A domestic credit crunch forced by a public sector fiscal adjustment is recommended. To solve indeterminacy, the orthodox approach introduces from the external balance a relationship between reserves variation and the price level (and the exchange rate). Thus, exchange adjustment will complement demand management in its stabilization objective. Though our model recognizes that excess demand may be a peculiar characteristic of primary sector activities, this implies that the elimination of excess demand and of potential inflationary conditions should be pursued on the basis of policies that increase the supply of goods. Therefore, in the orthodox framework, while the supply side places great emphasis on growth, it plays a crucial role for stabilization in the post-Keynesian/structuralist approach. If the government increases its investment

Table 6.1 Policy Implications of the IMF/WB Approach and the Post-Keynesian/Structuralist Model

IMF/World Bank Approach		*Post-Keynesian/Structuralist Model*	
Goals	*Measures*	*Goals*	*Measures*
Stabilization			
External Balance	– Absorption Reduction	External Balance	– Greater Public Sector
Low Inflation	(a) Fiscal Contraction	Low Inflation	Borrowing/Debt Relief
	(b) Domestic Credit	Higher Industrial Output	– Higher Public Sector Investment
	Contraction		(in the Primary Sector)
	– Devaluation		– Subsidies to Manufacturing Output
Long-run			
Output Growth	– Relative Price Realignments	Output Growth	Stagnationist regime
	– Trade Liberalization	Better Distribution	– Incomes Policy
	– Financial Liberalization		– Industrial and Competition Policies
	(higher propensity to save)		Nonstagnationist Regime
			– Higher public savings and investment

spending (in order to solve the primary sector bottleneck) and simultaneously borrows from the public or the banking system on a scale sufficiently to keep the fiscal balance constant, the effect on industrial output will be positive, but the trade balance will deteriorate. It seems evident that stabilization policy should pay greater attention to external constraints. Our model suggests that a good way to do this would be to establish a subsidy rate for manufacturing output. When dealing with the long run, the integrated model resembles the policy package that emanates from the IMF/WB perspective. Three policies (domestic price realignments, trade liberalization, and financial liberalization) must be in action to achieve the central objective, namely, an increase in output growth. The model is superior on this front since it allows us to evaluate the relationship between income distribution and growth. In this sense we have identified two possible regimes. Incomes and competition policies can be indispensable if the economy resembles a stagnationist regime. On the other hand, governments must no doubt improve public savings and the conduction of public investment toward the primary sector if the economy presents a nonstagnationist regime.

References

Aceituno, G. *et al.* (1984) *Economía Mexicana: Modelo Macroeconomico*, Mexico: CIDE.

Agenor, P. and P. Montiel (1996) *Development Macroeconomics*, Princeton: Princeton University Press.

Agosin, M. (1996) "Relación de dos Regiones: La Inversión en la America Latina y en el Asia Oriental," *Trimestre Economico*, Vol. 63, No. 3, 1139–1169.

Agosin, M. and R. Ffrench-Davis (1993) "La Liberalización Comercial en America Latina," *Revista de la Cepal*, No. 50, 41–62.

Alexander, S. (1952) "The Effects of a Devaluation on the Trade Balance," *IMF Staff Papers*, Vol. 2, 263–278.

—— (1959) "The Effects of Devaluation: A Simplified Synthesis of the Elasticities and Absorption Approaches," *American Economic Review*, Vol. 49, No. 2, 22–42.

Altimir, O. (1996) "Inequality, Employment and Poverty in Latin America: Effects of Adjustment and of the Change of Development Style," paper presented at the International Workshop on Income Distribution and Social–Political Stability, Hitotsubashi University, 26–28 January.

Amsden, A. (1989) *Asia's Next Giant*, Oxford: Oxford University Press.

Arellano, J.P. (1986) "La Literatura Economica y los Costos de Equilibrar la Balanza de Pagos en America Latina," R. Cortazar (ed.), *Políticas Macroeconomicas: Una Perspectiva Latinoamericana*, Santiago: CIEPLAN.

Arestis, P. (1986) "Wages and Prices in the UK: The Post-Keynesian View," *Journal of Post Keynesian Economics*, Vol. 8, 339–358.

—— (1988) "The Demand for Money in Small Developing Economies: An Application of the Error Correction Mechanism," in P. Arestis (ed.), *Contemporary Issues in Money and Banking: Essays in Honor of Stephen Frowen*, London: Macmillan Press.

—— (1989) "On the Post Keynesian Challenge to Neoclassical Economics: A Complete Quantitative Macro-Model for the U.K. Economy," *Journal of Post Keynesian Economics*, Vol. 11, No. 4, 601–629.

—— (1990) "Post-Keynesianism: A New Approach to Economics," *Review of Social Economy*, Vol. 48, No. 3, 222–246.

—— (1992) "Economic Policies in a Post-Keynesian World," in W. Milberg (ed.), *The Megacorp and Macrodynamics: Essays in Memory of Alfred Eichner*, Armonk, NY: M.E. Sharpe.

—— (1996) "Post-Keynesian Economics: Towards Coherence," *Cambridge Journal of Economics*, Vol. 20, No. 1, 111–135.

Arestis, P. and C. Driver (1984) "The Policy Implications of Post-Keynesianism," *Journal of Economic Issues*, Vol. 18, No. 4, 1093–1105.

Arestis, P. and A. Eichner (1985) "The Post-Keynesian and Institutionalist Theory of Money and Credit," *Journal of Economic Issues*, Vol. 22, 1003–1022.

Arida, P. and E. Bacha (1987) "Balance of Payments: A Disequilibrium Analysis for Semi-industrialized Economies," *Journal of Development Economics*, Vol. 27, 85–108.

Arndt, H.W. (1982) "Two Kinds of Credit Rationing," *Banca Nazionale del Lavoro Quarterly Review*, No. 143, 417–425.

—— (1985) "The Origins of Structuralism," *World Development*, Vol. 13, 151–159.

Arrau, P., J. De Gregorio, C. Reinhart, and P. Wickham (1991) "The Demand for Money in Developing Countries: Assessing the Impact of Financial Innovation," IMF Working Paper, No. WP/91/45.

Avramovic, D. (1988) *Conditionality: Facts, Theory and Policy*, Helsinski: WIDER.

Bacha, E. (1983) "A Critique of Southern Cone Monetarism," *International Social Science Journal*, Vol. 35, No. 3.

—— (1990a) "IMF Conditionality: Conceptual Problems and Policy Alternatives," in S. Dell (ed.), *The International Monetary System and its Reform, Part V*, New York: North-Holland.

—— (1990b) "A Three-Gap Model of Foreign Transfers and the GDP Growth Rate in Developing Countries," *Journal of Development Economics*, Vol. 32, 279–296.

—— (1992) "External Debt, Net Transfers, and Growth in Developing Countries," *World Development*, Vol. 20, No. 8, 1183–1192.

Baer, W. (1967) "The Inflation Controversy in Latin America: A Survey," *Latin American Research*, Vol. 2, No. 2, 3–25.

Bagchi, A. (1990) "The IMF View of International Economic Policy and the Relevance of Sraffa's Critique of Economic Theory," in K. Bharadwajand and B. Schefold (eds.), *Essays on Piero Sraffa*, London: Unwin Hyman, Ltd.

Balassa, B. (1981) "The New Industrializing Developing Countries after the Oil Crisis," *Weltwirtschafitliches Archiv*, Vol. 117, No. 1, 142–194.

Banco Interamericano de Desarrollo (1991) *Progreso Económico y Social en America Latina*, Washington, D.C.: Informe 1991.

Bandeira, O., G. Caprio, P. Honohan, and F. Schiantarelli (1998) "Does Financial Reform Raise or Reduce Savings?" Boston College, Mimeo.

Barbone, L. (1984) "Essays on Trade and Macro Policies in Developing Countries," unpublished Ph.D. dissertation, MIT.

Bhaduri, A. (1992) "Some Unconventional Implications of Conventional Stabilization Policies," *Indian Economic Review*, Vol. 27 (special issue), 129–134.

Bhaduri, A. and S. Marglin (1990) "Unemployment and the Real Wage: the economic basis for contesting political ideologies," *Cambridge Journal of Economics*, Vol. 14, 375–395.

Bharadwaj, K. (1979) "Towards a Macroeconomic Framework for a Developing Economy: The Indian Case," *The Manchester School*, Vol. 47, No. 3, 270–302.

Bhattacharya, B. (1991) "Macro Imbalances, Stabilisation Programme and Union Budget," *Economic and Political Weekly*, Aug., 2005–2009.

Bhagwat, A. and Y. Onitsuka (1974) "Export/Import Responses to Devaluation Experience in the Non-industrial Countries of the 1960s," *IMF Staff Papers*, July.

Bilson, J. (1984) "The Process of Balance of Payments Adjustment," in J. Muas (ed.), *Adjustment, Conditionality and International Financing*, Washington, D.C.: IMF.

Blackwell, C. (1978) "Monetary Approach to the Balance of Payments Needs Bleeding with Other Lines of Analysis," *IMF Survey*, Vol. 7.

Bleaney, M. (1999) "Trade Reform, Macroeconomic Performance and Export Growth in Ten Latin American Countries," 1979–95, *The Journal of International Trade and Economic Development*, Vol. 8, No. 1, 89–105.

Blecker, R. (1989) "International Competition, Income Distribution, and Economic Growth," *Cambridge Journal of Economics*, Vol. 13, 395–412.

Blejer, M. and M. Khan (1984) "Government Policy and Private Investment in Developing Countries," *IMF Staff Papers*, Vol. 31, 379–403.

Bock, D. and C. Michalopoulos (1986) "The Emerging Role of the Bank in Heavily Indebted Countries," *Finance and Development*, Vol. 33, 22–25.

Borpujari, J. (1985) "Savings Generation and Financial Programming in a Basic Need constrained Developing Country," in A. Gutowski *et al.* (eds.), *Financing Problems of Developing Countries*, London: Macmillan.

Brailovsky, V. (1981) "Exchange Rate Policies, Manufactured Exports and the Rate of Inflation," Mexico: Instituto de Planeación Industrial, Mimeo.

Branson, W. (1986) "Stabilization, Stagflation, and Investment Incentives: The Case of Kenya 1979–1980," in S. Edwards and L. Ahamed (eds.), *Economic Adjustment and Exchange Rates in Developing Countries*, Chicago: The University of Chicago Press.

Braun, O. and L. Joy (1968) "A Model of Economic Stagnation: A Case Study of the Argentine Economy," *Economic Journal*, Vol. 78, No. 312, 34–42.

Brems, H. (1957) "Devaluation, A Marriage of the Elasticity and Absorption Approaches," *Economic Journal*, Vol. 67, 145–159.

Bresser-Pereira, L. (1990) "The Perverse Logic of Stagnation: Debt, Deficit, and Inflation in Brazil," *Journal of Post Keynesian Economics*, Vol. 12, No. 4, 503–518.

Bresser-Pereira, L. and Y. Nakamo (1987) *The Theory of Inertial Inflation: The Foundations of Economic Reform in Brazil and Argentina*, New York: Lynne Riener Publications, Inc.

Bruno, M. (1979) "Stabilization and Stagflation in a Semi-Industrialized Economy," in R. Dornbusch and J. Frenkel (eds.), *International Economic Policy: Theory and Evidence*, Baltimore: John Hopkins University Press.

Buffie, E. (1984) "Financial Repression, the New Structuralists, and Stabilization Policies in Semi-industrialized Economies," *Journal of Development Economics*, Vol. 14, No. 13, 305–322.

Buira, A. (1983) "IMF Financial Programs and Conditionality," *Journal of Development Economics*, Vol. 12, 111–120.

Calabi, A. (1982) "Price Formation in Brazilian Industry," unpublished Ph.D. dissertation, University of California at Berkeley.

Calvo, G., L. Leiderman, and C. Reinhart (1993) "Capital Inflows and the Real Exchange Rate Appreciation in Latin America," *IMF Staff Papers*, Vol. 40, No. 1, 108–140.

Campbell, C.D. (1970) "The Velocity of Money and the Rate of Inflation: Recent Experiences in South Korea and Brazil," in D. Miselman (ed.), *Varieties of Monetary Experience*, Chicago: University of Chicago Press.

Cardoso, E. (1979) "Inflation, Growth and the Real Exchange Rate: Essays on Economic History in Brazil and Latin America," Ph.D. dissertation, MIT.

—— (1981) "Food Supply and Inflation," *Journal of Development Economics*, Vol. 8, No. 3, 269–284.

—— (1993) "Private Investment in Latin America," *Economic Development and Cultural Change*, Vol. 41, No. 4, 834–848.

Cardoso, E. and A. Helwege (1992) "Below the Line: Poverty in Latin America," *World Development*, Vol. 20, No. 1, 19–37.

Carvalho, F. (1984–85) "Alternative Analysis of Short and Long Run in Post-Keynesian Economics," *Journal of Post Keynesian Economics*, Vol. 7, No. 2, 214–234.

Chand, S. (1989) "Toward a Growth-Oriented Model of Financial Programming," *World Development*, Vol. 17, No. 4, 473–490.

Chandrasekhar, C.P. (1995) "The Macroeconomics of Imbalance and Adjustment," in P. Patnaik (ed.), *Macroeconomics*, Delhi: Oxford University Press.

Chen, C. (1975) "IS, LM, BT and a Synthesis of the Elasticity, Absorption, and Monetary Approaches to Devaluation," *Southern Economic Journal*, Vol. 42, No. 1, 132–36.

Chica, R. (1983) "La Dinámica de los Precios en la Industria Manufacturera Colombiana 1958–80," *Revista de Planeación y Desarrollo*, 33–68.

Chichilnisky, G. and L. Taylor (1980) "Agriculture and the Rest of the Economy," *American Journal of Agricultural Economics*, Vol. 62, No. 2, 304–310.

Cho, Y. (1990) "McKinnon-Shaw versus the Neostructuralists on Financial Liberalization: A Conceptual Note," *World Development*, Vol. 18, No. 3, 477–480.

Chossudovsky, M. (1992) "Under the Tutelage of the IMF: The Case of Peru," *Economic and Political Weekly*, Feb., 340–348.

Cline, W.R. (1983) "Economic Stabilization in Developing Countries: Theory and Stylized Facts," in J. Williamson (ed.), *IMF Conditionality*, Cambridge: MIT Press.

Clower, R. (1967) "A Reconsideration of the Microfoundations of Monetary Theory," *Western Economic Journal*, Vol. 6, No. 1, 1–9.

Connors, T. (1979) "The Apparent Effects of Recent IMF Stabilization Programs," International Finance Discussion Paper 135, Board of Governors of the Federal Reserve System.

Considera, C. (1981) "Precos, Mark-up e Distribucao Funcional da Renda na Industria de Transformacao: dinamica de longo e de curto prazo 1959/80," *Pesquisa e Planejamiento Economico*, Vol. 11, No. 3, 10–30.

—— (1983) "Comportamiento Oligopolista e Controle de precos Industriais," *Pesquisa e Planejamiento Economico*, Vol. 13, No. 1, 456–478.

Conway, P. (1994) "IMF Lending Programs: Participation and Impact," *Journal of Development Economics*, Vol. 45, 365–391.

Cooper, R. (1971) "Currency Devaluation in Developing Countries," Essays in International Finance, No. 86, International Finance Section, Princeton University.

Copelman, M. (1996) "Financial Innovation and the Speed of Adjustment of Money Demand: Evidence from Bolivia, Israel, and Venezuela," Board of Governors of the Federal Reserve System, International Finance Discussion Papers, No. 567.

Corbo, V. (1982) "Inflación en una Economía Abierta: El Caso de Chile," *Cuadernos de Economía*, April.

Corbo, V., M. Goldstein, and M. Khan (1987) *Growth Oriented Adjustment Programs*, Washington, D.C.: IMF and World Bank.

Corbo, V. and K. Schmidt-Hebbel (1991) "Public Policies and Saving in Developing Countries," *Journal of Development Economics*, Vol. 36, No. 1, 89–115.

Corbo, V. and P. Rojas (1992) "World Bank-Supported Adjustment Programs: Country Performance and Effectiveness," in V. Corbo, S. Fischer, and S. Webb (eds.), *Adjustment Lending Revisited*, Washington D.C.: The World Bank.

Cripps, F. and W. Godley (1976) "A Formal Analysis of the Cambridge Economics Policy Group Model," *Economica*, Vol. 43, 335–348.

Crockett, A. (1981) "Stabilization Policies in Developing Countries: Some Policy Considerations," *IMF Staff Papers*, Vol. 28, No. 1, 54–79.

—— (1992) "The International Monetary Fund in the 1990s," *Government and Opposition*, Vol. 27, No. 3, 267–282.

Cypher, J. (1990) "Latin American Structuralist Economics: An Evaluation, Critique, and Reformulation," in J. Dietz and D. James (eds.), *Progress toward Development in Latin America: From Prebisch to Technological Autonomy*, Boulder & London: Lynne Rienner Publishers.

Darby, M. (1980) "The Monetary Approach to the Balance of Payments: Two Specious Assumptions," *Economic Inquiry*, Vol. 18, No. 2, 321–326.

David, W. (1985) *The IMF Policy Paradigm*, New York: Praeger Publishers.

Davidson, P. (1978) *Money and The Real World*, London: Macmillan.

Deaver, J. V. (1970) "The Chilean Inflation and the Demand for Money," in D. Miselman (ed.), *Varieties of Monetary Experience*, Chicago: University of Chicago Press.

de Melo, J. and J. Tybout (1986) "The Effects of Financial Liberalization on Savings and Investment in Uruguay," *Economic Development and Cultural Change*, Vol. 34, 561–588.

Demery, L. and T. Addison (1987) "Stabilization Policy and Income Distribution in Developing Countries," *World Development*, Vol. 15, No. 12, 1483–1498.

Demirguc-Kunt, A. and E. Detragiache (1998) "Financial Liberalization and Financial Fragility," paper presented at the April 1998 Annual Bank Conference on Development Economics, World Bank.

de Paiva, M., W. Fritsch, and E. Modiano (1990) "Debt, Growth and Structural Adjustment in Latin America: An Appraisal of the Baker Initiative," in S. Dell (ed.), *The International Monetary System and its Reform*, Part V, New York: North-Holland.

Diamand, M. (1976) "Towards a Change in the Economic Paradigm through the Experience of Developing Countries," *Journal of Development Economics*, Vol. 5, No. 1, 19–53.

Dias Carneiro, D. and R. Werneck (1990) "Deuda Externa, Crecimiento Económico y Ajuste Fiscal," in E. Lora (ed.), *Inflación y Estabilización en America Latina*, Bogota: Tercer Mundo Editores.

Diaz Alejandro, C. (1963) "A Note on the Impact of Devaluation and the Redistributive Effect," *Journal of Political Economy*, Vol. 71, No. 6, 577–580.

—— (1981) "Southern Cone Stabilization Plans," in W. Cline and S. Weintraub (eds.), *Economic Stabilization in Developing Countries*, Washington, D.C.: The Brookings Institution.

—— (1984) "IMF Conditionality: What Kind?" *Pakistan Institute of Development Economics Tidings*, No. 4, 7–9.

Dixon, R. and A. Thirlwall (1975) "A Model of Regional Growth-Rate Differences on Kaldorian Lines," *Oxford Economic Papers*, Vol. 27, No. 2, 201–214.

Dollar, D. and K. Sokoloff (1990) "Patterns of Productivity Growth in South Korean Manufacturing Industries," *Journal of Development Economics*, Vol. 33, No. 2, 245–256.

Donovan, D. (1982) "Macroeconomic Performance and Adjustment under Fund Supported Programs: The Experiences of the Seventies," *IMF Staff Papers*, Vol. 29, No. 2, 171–203.

Dooley, M., E. Fernandez-Arias, and K. Kletzer (1996) "Is the Debt Crisis History?: Recent Private Capital Inflows to Developing Countries," *The World Bank Economic Review*, Vol. 10, No. 1, 27–50.

Dornbusch, R. (1973) "Currency Depreciation, Hoarding and Relative Prices," *Journal of Political Economy*, Vol. 81, No. 4, 893–915.

—— (1980) *Open Economy Macroeconomics*, New York: Basic Books.

—— (1982) "Stabilization Policies in Developing Countries: What have we Learned?" *World Development*, Vol. 10, No. 9, 701–708.

—— (1987) "Exchange Rates and Prices," *American Economic Review*, Vol. 77, No. 1, 93–106.

Dornbusch, R. and A. Reynoso (1989) "Financial Factors in Economic Development," *American Economic Review*, Vol. 79. No. 2, 204–209.

Doroodian, K. (1993) "Macroeconomic Performance and Adjustment under Policies Commonly Supported by the International Monetary Fund," *Economic Development and Cultural Change*, Vol. 41, No. 4, 849–863.

Dow, S. (1985) *Macroeconomic Thought: A Methodological Approach*, Oxford: Basil Blackwell.

Downward, P. and P. Reynolds (1996) "Alternative Perspectives on Post-Keynesian Price Theory," *Review of Political Economy*, Vol. 8, No. 1, 67–78.

Dutt, A.K. (1984) "Stagnation, Income Distribution and Monopoly Power," *Cambridge Journal of Economics*, Vol. 8, 25–40.

—— (1990a) "Sectoral Balance in Development: A Survey," *World Development*, Vol. 18, No. 6, 915–930.

—— (1990b) *Growth, Distribution and Uneven Development*, Cambridge: Cambridge University Press.

—— (1991) "Stagnation, Income Distribution and the Agrarian Constraint: A Note," *Cambridge Journal of Economics*, Vol. 15, 343–351.

Easterly, W. (1985) "A Computable General Equilibrium Model of Mexico with Portfolio Balances with Application to Devaluation," unpublished Ph.D. dissertation, MIT.

Eatwell, J. and A. Singh (1981) "¿Se Encuentra Sobrecalentada la Economía Mexicana?: Un Análisis de los Problemas de la Política Económica a Corto y Mediano Plazo," Mimeo.

ECLAC (1990) *Transformación Productiva con Equidad*, Santiago: CEPAL.

—— (1995) *Preliminary Overview of the Economy of Latin America and the Caribbean*, Santiago, ECLAC Publication 1892-P.

Edwards, S. (1986) "Are Devaluations Contractionary?" *Review of Economics and Statistics*, Vol. 68, 501–508.

—— (1989) "Debt Crisis, Trade Liberalization, Structural Adjustment, and Growth: Some Policy Considerations," *Contemporary Policy Issues*, Vol. 7, 30–41.

—— (1990) "El Fondo Monetario Internacional y los Países en Desarrollo: Una Evaluación Crítica," *Trimestre Económico*, Vol. 52, No. 3, 611–663.

Eichner, A. (1975) *The Megacorp & Oligopoly: Macrofoundations of Macrodynamics*, New York: M.E. Sharpe.

—— (1979) "A Look Ahead," in A. Eichner (ed.), *A Guide to Post-Keynesian Economics*, New York: M.E. Sharpe.

—— (1987) The "Macrodynamics of Advanced Market Economies," New York, M.E. Sharpe.

Elmslie, B. and W. Milberg (1993) "History and Hysteresis: Foundations of Convergence and Divergence," University of New Hamphire, Mimeo.

Eshag, E. (1989) "Some Suggestions for Improving the Operation of the IMF Stabilisation Programmes," *International Labour Review*, Vol. 128, No. 3, 297–320.

Evans, D. (1990) "Outward Orientation: An Assessment," in C. Milner (ed.), *Export Promotion Strategies*, New York: New York University Press.

Eyzaguirre, N. (1989) "Saving and Investment under External and Fiscal Constraints," *CEPAL Review*, No. 38, 31–47.

Fajnzylber, F. (1981) "Some Reflections on South-East Asian Industrialization," *CEPAL Review*, No. 15, 111–132.

Fani, R., J. de Melo, A. Senhadji, and J. Stanton (1991) "Growth-Oriented Adjustment Programs: A Statistical Analysis," *World Development*, Vol. 19, No. 8, 957–967.

Fausten, D. (1989) "A Note on External Adjustment," *Kredit and Capital*, Vol. 22, No. 3, 344–361.

Feinberg, R. (1986) "The Changing Relationship between the World Bank and the International Monetary Fund," in S. Dell (ed.), *The International Monetary System and its Reform, Part V*, New York: North-Holland.

Felix, D. (1964) "Monetarist, Structuralist, and Import-substitution: A Critical Appraisal," in W. Baer. and I. Kerstenetzky (eds.), Homewood, IL: Richard Irwin.

Fernadez-Arias, E. and P. Montiel (1996) "The Surge in Capital Inflows to Developing Countries: An Analytical Overview," *The World Bank Economic Review*, Vol. 10, No. 1, 51–77.

Ffrench-Davis, R. (1988) "An Outline of the Neo-structuralist Approach," *CEPAL Review*, No. 34, 37–44.

FitzGerald, E.V.K. (1980) "A Note on Capital Accumulation in Mexico: The Budget Deficit and Investment Finance," *Development and Change*, Vol. 11, 391–417.

—— (1989) "The Analytics of Stabilisation Policy in the Small Semi-industrialized Economy," in E.V.K. FitzGerald and R. Vos (eds.), *Financing Economic Development: A Structural Approach to Monetary Policy*, Aldeshot: Gower Publishing Company Limited.

—— (1990) "Kalecki on Financing Development: An Approach to the Macroeconomics of the Semi-industrialised Economy," *Cambridge Journal of Economics*, Vol. 14, No. 2, 183–203.

—— (1996) "International Capital Markets in Open-economy Macroeconomics," *Oxford Development Studies*, Vol. 24, No. 1, 79–92.

Flores, L.B. and R. Espinasa (1979) "Dependent Capitalist Accumulation: Some Basic Issues," unpublished M.Ph. dissertation, The Hague: Institute of Social Studies.

Foxley, A. (1983) *Latin American Experiments in Neoconservative Economics*, Berkeley: University of California Press.

—— (1988) "The Foreign Debt Problem from a Latin American Viewpoint," in R. Feinberg, and R. Ffrench-Davis (eds.), *Development and External Debt in Latin America*, Notre Dame, IN: University of Notre Dame Press.

Frankel, J.A. and C. Onkongwu (1996) "Liberalized Portfolio Capital Inflows in Emerging Markets," *International Journal of Finance and Economics*, Vol. 1, No. 1, 1–23.

Frenkel, J. (1976) "The Monetary Approach to the Exchange Rate," *Scandinavian Journal of Economics*, Vol. 2, 200–224.

Frenkel, J. and H. Johnson (1976) *The Monetary Approach to the Balance of Payments*, London: Allen and Unwin.

Frenkel, J., T. Gylfason, and J. Helliwell (1980) "A Synthesis of Monetary and Keynesian Approaches to Short-run Balance of Payments Theory," *Economic Journal*, Vol. 90, No. 359, 582–592.

Frenkel, J. and M. Khan (1992) "Adjustment Policies of the International Monetary Fund and Long-run Economic Development," *The Bangladesh Development Studies*, Vol. 20, No. 2, 1–22.

Frenkel, R. (1979) "Decisiones de Precio en Alta Inflación," *Desarrollo Economico*, Vol. 19, No. 75, 291–331.

—— (1984) "Inflación, Shocks y Mark-up: Argentina 1975–1982," *Ensayos Economicos*, No. 30, 39–81.

—— (1986) "Salarios e Inflación en America Latina: Resultados de Investigaciones Recientes en la Argentina, Brazil, Colombia, Costa Rica y Chile," *Desarrollo Economico*, Vol. 25, No. 100, 587–622.

Fry, M. (1982) "Models of Financially Repressed Developing Economies," *World Development*, Vol. 10, No. 9, 731–750.

Gafar, J. (1982) "Devaluation and its Impact on the Demand for Imports in an Open Economy: The Case of Jamaica," *The Indian Journal of Economics*, Vol. 63, 223–237.

Ghatak, S. (1981) *Monetary Economics in Developing Countries*, New York: St. Martin's Press.

Gibson, B. (1990) "Restructuring the Nicaraguan Economy," *International Journal of Political Economy*, Fall, 81–96.

Giovannini, A. (1983) "The Interest Elasticity of Savings in Developing Countries: The Existing Evidence," *World Development*, Vol. 11, No. 7, 601–607.

—— (1985) "Savings and Real Interest Rates in LDCs," *Journal of Development Economics*, Vol. 18, No. 1–2, 567–589.

Giovannini, A. and B. Turtelboom (1994) "Currency Substitution," in F. Van der Ploeg (ed.), *The Handbook of International Macroeconomics*, Cambridge: Blackwell Publishers.

Goldstein, M. and P. Montiel (1986) "Evaluating Fund Stabilization Programs with Multicountry Data: Some Methodological Pitfalls," *IMF Staff Papers*, Vol. 33, 304–344.

Gomes, L. (1990) *Neoclassical International Economics: A Historical Survey*, New York: St. Martin's Press.

Gonzalez-Arrieta, G. (1988) "Interest Rates, Savings and Growth in LDCs: An Assessment of Recent Empirical Research," *World Development*, Vol. 16, No. 5, 589–605.

Görgens, E. (1998) "IMF and World Bank Development Strategies—From Development Policy Dirigisme to Market Economy Principles—and Back?" *Economics*, Vol. 57, 115–130.

Greenaway, D., W. Morgan, and P. Wright (1997) "Trade Liberalization and Growth in Developing Countries: Some New Evidence," *World Development*, Vol. 25, No. 11, 1885–1892.

Greene, J. and D. Villanueva (1991) "Private Investment in Developing Countries: An Empirical Analysis," *IMF Staff Papers*, Vol. 38, No. 1, 33–58.

Griffith-Jones, S. (1983) "The Growth of Transnational Finance," in D. Tussie (ed.), *Latin America in the World Economy: New Perspectives*, New York: St. Martin's Press.

Guillen-Romo, H. (1988) "De la Crisis Financiera a la Austeridad Hayekiana en México," UAM-Iztapalapa, Mexico, Mimeo.

—— (1990) "Inflación y Concertación: La Vigencia de Aujac y Noyola," in E. Gutierrez (ed.), *Testimonios de la Crisis*, Vol. 3, Mexico City: Siglo XXI Editores.

Gylfason, T. (1987) "Credit Policy and Economic Activity in Developing Countries with IMF Stabilization Programs," *Princeton Studies in International Finance*, No. 60.

Gylfason, T. and M. Schmid (1983) "Does Devaluation Cause Stagflation?" *The Canadian Journal of Economics*, Vol. 16, 508–521.

Hamouda, O. and G. Harcourt (1989) "Post-Keynesianism: From Criticism to Coherence," in J. Pheby (ed.), *New Directions in Post-Keynesian Economics*, Adelshot, UK, Edward Elgar.

Haque, N. and M. Khan (1998) "Do IMF-Supported Programs Work? A Survey of the Cross-Country Empirical Evidence," Working Paper No. WP/98/169, IMF Research Department, Washington, D.C.

Harris, D. (1967) "Income, Prices, and the Balance of Payments in Underdeveloped Economies: A short-run model," *Oxford Economic Papers*, Vol. 22, No. 2, 156–172.

Harris, G. and N. Kusi (1992) "The Impact of the IMF on Government Expenditures: A Study of African LDCs," *Journal of International Economics*, Vol. 4, No. 1, 73–85.

Harrison, A. and G. Hanson (1999) "Who Gains from Trade Reform? Some Remaining Puzzles," *Journal of Development Economics*, Vol. 59, 125–154.

Henry, S.B.G., M. Sawyer, and P. Smith (1976) "Models of Inflation in the United Kingdom: An Evaluation," *National Institute Economic Review*, No. 77, 60–71.

Hicks, N.L. (1991) "Expenditure Reductions in Developing Countries Revisited," *Journal of International Economics*, Vol. 3, No. 1, 29–37.

Hirschman, A. (1949) "Devaluation and the Trade Balance: A Note," *Review of Economics and Statistics*, Vol. 31, 50–53.

—— (1958) *The Strategy of Economic Development*, New Haven: Yale Economic Press.

Hoeven van der, R. (1987) "External Shocks and Stabilisation Policies: Spreading the Load," *International Labour Review*, Vol. 126, No. 2, 134–150.

Hughes, H. (1976) "Capital Utilization in Manufacturing in Developing Countries," World Bank Staff Working Paper, No. 242.

Hussain, M.N. and A. Thirlwall (1984) "The IMF Supply-Side Approach to Devaluation: An Assessment with Reference to the Sudan," *Oxford Bulletin of Economics and Statistics*, Vol. 46, No. 2, 145–167.

Hynes, A. (1967) "The Demand for Money and Monetary Adjustment in Chile," *Review of Economic Studies*, Vol. 34, 285–294.

Interamerican Development Bank (1997) *Progreso Económico y Social en América Latina*, Washington, D.C.: IDB.

IMF (1977) *The Monetary Approach to the Balance of Payments*, Washington, D.C.: IMF.

—— (1994) *Official Financing for Developing Countries*, Washington, D.C.: IMF.

—— (1995) *Private Market Financing for Developing Countries*, Washington, D.C: IMF.

—— (1996) *World Economic Outlook*, Washington D.C.: May, IMF.

—— *Annual Report*, various issues, Washington, D.C.

Jadresic, E. (1985) "Formación de Precios Agregados en Chile: 1974–1983," *Colección Estudios CIEPLAN*, June, 292–325.

Jameson, K. (1986) "Latin American Structuralism: a methodological perspective," *World Development*, Vol. 14, No. 2, 222–232.

Jenkins, R. (1991) "Learning from the Gang: Are There Lessons for Latin America from East Asia?" *Bulletin of Latin American Research*, Vol. 10, No. 1, 37–54.

Johnson, H. (1958) "Towards a General Theory of the Balance of Payments," in H. Johnson, *International Trade and Economic Growth*, Cambridge: Harvard University Press.

—— (1975) "The Monetary Approach to the Balance of Payments: A Diagrammatic Analysis," *The Manchester School*, Vol. 43, 220–274.

—— (1976) "Elasticity, Absorption, Keynesian Multiplier, Keynesian Policy, and Monetary Approaches to Devaluation," *American Economic Review*, Vol. 66, No. 3, 448–452.

—— (1977) "The Monetary Approach to the Balance of Payments: A nontechnical guide," *Journal of International Economics*, Vol. 7, 251–268.

Johnson, O and J. Salop (1980) "Distributional Aspects of Stabilization Programs in Developing Countries," *IMF Staff Papers*, Vol. 27, No. 1, 1–23.

Kaldor, N. (1955–56) "Alternative Theories of Distribution," *Review of Economic Studies*, Vol. 23, 94–100.

—— (1961) "Capital Accumulation and Economic Growth," in V. Lutz (ed.), *The Theory of Capital*, London: Macmillan.

—— (1964) "Economic Problems in Chile," in N. Kaldor (ed.), *Essays in Economic Policy*, Vol. 2, London: Duckworth.

—— (1970) "The New Monetarism," *Lloyds Bank Review*, No. 97, 1–17.

—— (1976) "Inflation and Recession in the World Economy," *Economic Journal*, Vol. 86, 703–714.

—— (1978) "The Role of Industrialization in Latin American Inflations," in N. Kaldor, *Further Essays in Applied Economics*, Vol. 6, London: Duckworth.

—— (1983) "Devaluation and Adjustment in Developing Countries," *Finance and Development*, Vol. 20, No. 2, 35–37.

—— (1986) *The Scourge of Monetarism*, Second Edition, Oxford: Oxford University Press.

Kalecki, M. (1943) *Studies in Economic Dynamics*, London: George Allen & Unwin.

Kalecki, M. (1971) *Selected Essays on the Dynamics of the Capitalist Economy*, Cambridge: Cambridge University Press.

—— (1976) "The Problem of Financing Economic Development," In M. Kalecki (ed.), *Essays on Developing Economies*, Hassocks, Sussex: Harvester Press.

—— (1976) *Essays on Developing Economies*, Hassocks, Sussex: Harvester Press.

Kamarck, A. (1984) "The World Bank and Development: A Personal Perspective," *Finance and Development*, Vol. 31, 26–29.

Kamas, L. (1992) "Devaluation, National Output and the Trade Balance: Some Evidence from Colombia," *Weltwirtschaftliches Archiv*, Vol. 128, 425–445.

Katseli, L. (1983) "Devaluation: A Critical Appraisal of the IMF's Policy Prescriptions," *American Economic Review*, Vol. 73, No. 2, 359–363.

Kay, C. (1989) *Latin American Theories of Development and Underdevelopment*, London: Routledge.

Keynes, J.M. (1935) *A Treatise on Money*, Vol. I, London: Macmillan.

—— (1936) *The General Theory of Employment, Interest and Money*, London: Macmillan.

—— (1937) "The General Theory of Employment," *Economic Journal*, Vol. 51, 209–223.

Khaler, M. (1990) "Orthodoxy and Its Alternatives: Explaining Approaches to Stabilization and Adjustment," in J. Nelson (ed.), *Economic Crisis and Policy Choice: The Politics of Adjustment in the Third World*, Princeton: Princeton University Press.

Khan, M. (1974) "Import and Export Demand in Developing Countries," *IMF Staff Papers*, Vol. 21, 678–693.

—— (1990) "The Macroeconomic Effects of Fund-Supported Programs," *IMF Staff Papers*, Vol. 37, 195–231.

Khan, M. and M. Knight (1981) "Stabilization Programs in Developing Countries: A Formal Framework," *IMF Staff Papers*, Vol. 28, No. 1, 1–53.

—— (1982) "Some Theoretical and Empirical Issues Relating to Economic Stabilization in Developing Countries," *World Development*, Vol. 10, No. 9, 709–730.

—— (1985) "Fund Supported Adjustment Programs and Economic Growth," Occasional Paper, Washington, D.C.: IMF.

Khan, M. and P. Montiel (1989) "Growth-Oriented Adjustment Programs: A Conceptual Framework," *IMF Staff Papers*, Vol. 36, No. 2, 279–306.

Khan, M., P. Montiel, and N. Haque (1990) "Adjustment with Growth: Relating the Analytical Approaches of the IMF and the World Bank," *Journal of Development Economics*, Vol. 32, No. 1, 155–179.

Kharadia, V. (1988) "The Behaviour of Income Velocity of Money in India: Implications for Monetary Theory and Policy," *The Indian Economic Journal*, Vol. 36, No. 1, 39–50.

Killick, T. (1984) *The Quest for Economic Stabilization: The IMF and the Third World*, New York: St. Martin's Press.

Killick, T., M. Malik, and M. Manuel (1995) "What Can We Know about the Effects of IMF Programmes?" *World Economy*, Vol. 15, 575–597.

Kirkpatrick, C. and Z. Onis (1985) "Industrialisation as a Structural Determinant of Inflation Performance in IMF Stabilisation Programmes in Less Developed Countries," *The Journal of Development Studies*, Vol. 21, No. 3, 347–361.

Kirkpatrick, C. and F. Nixson (1987) "Inflation and Stabilisation Policy in LDCs," in N. Gemmell, (ed.), *Surveys in Development Economics*, London: Basil Blackwell.

Knight, J.B. (1976) "Devaluation and Income Distribution in Less-Developed Economies," *Oxford Economic Papers*, Vol. 28, No. 2, 200–227.

Korner, P., G. Mass, T. Siebold, and R. Tetzlaf (1984) *The IMF and the Debt Crisis*, London: Zed Books.

Kregel, J. (1977) "Some Post-Keynesian Distribution Theory," in S. Weintraub (ed.), *Modern Economic Thought*, Philadelphia: University of Pennsylvania Press.

Krueger, A. (1985) "The Experience and Lesssons of Asia's Super Exporters," in V. Corbo, A. Krueger and F. Ossa (eds.), *Export-oriented Development Strategies*, Boulder: Westview.

Krugman, P. and L. Taylor (1978) "Contractionary Effects of Devaluation," *Journal of International Economics*, Vol. 8, No. 3, 445–456.

Lasa, A. (1992) "Tres Años de Política de Estabilización Concertada en Mexico, 1988–1990," *Investigación Económica*, No. 201, 157–195.

Lavoie, M. (1984) "The Endogenous Credit Flow and the Post Keynesian Theory of Money," *Journal of Economic Issues*, Vol. 16, No. 3, 771–797.

—— (1990) "Money in a common research programme for post-Keynesianism and Neo-Ricardianism," paper presented at the University of Tennessee International Workshop in Post-Keynesian Economics, June 29–July 4.

Leon Astete, J. and C. Oliva (1992) "Componente no-estacionario y la Paridad del Poder de Comprea en 12 Países Latinoamericanos," *Cuadernos de Economía*, Vol. 29, No. 88, 481–504.

Lewis, A. (1954) "Economic Development with Unlimited Supply of Labor," *The Manchester School*, Vol. 22, No. 2, 139–191.

Lichtensztejn, S. (1983) "IMF-Developing Countries: Conditionality and Strategy," in J. Williamson (ed.), *IMF Conditionality*, Cambridge: MIT Press.

Liu, P. (1992) "Purchasing Power Parity in Latin America: A Co-integration Analysis," *Weltwirschaftliches Archiv*, Vol. 128, No. 4, 662–679.

Liu, P. and P. Burkett (1995) "Instability in Short-run Adjustment to Purchasing Power Parity: Results for Selected Latin American Countries," *Applied Economics*, Vol. 27, 973–983.

Loxley, J. (1986) *Debt and Disorder: External Financing for Development*, Boulder and London: Westview Press.

Lustig, N. (1991) "From Structuralism to Neostructuralism: The Search for a Heterodox Paradigm," in P. Meller (ed.), *The Latin American Development Debate: Neostructuralism, Neomonetarism, and Adjustment Processes*, Boulder: Westview Press.

Mahdavi, S. and S. Zhou (1994) "Purchasing Power Parity in High Inflation Countries: Further Evidence," *Journal of Macroeconomics*, Vol. 16, 403–422.

Mallan, P. and J. Wells (1984) "Structural Models of Inflation and Balance of Payments Disequilibria in Semi-Industrialised Economies: Some Implications for Stabilisation and Growth Policies," in B. Csikos-Nagy, D. Hague, and G. Hall, *The Economics of Relative Prices*, New York: St. Martin's Press.

Mamingi, N. (1996) "How Prices and Macroeconomic Policies Affect Agricultural Supply and the Environment," The World Bank, Policy Research Department, Washington, D.C.

Mann, A. and M. Pastor (1990) "Orthodox and Heterodox Stabilization Policies in Bolivia and Peru: 1985–1988," *The Journal of Interamerican Studies and World Affairs*, Vol. 31, No. 4, 163–192.

Marglin, S. and A. Bhaduri, (1988) "Profit Squeeze and Keynesian Theory," WIDER Working Paper 39.

Massad, C. (1991) "External Events, Domestic Policies and Structural Adjustment," *CEPAL Review*, No. 43, 11–22.

McKinnon, R. (1973) *Money and Capital in Economic Development*, Washington, D.C.: The Brookings Institution.

—— (1993) *The Order of Financial Liberalization*, Baltimore: Johns Hopkins Press.

McNown, R. and M. Wallace (1989) "National Price Levels, Purchasing Power Parity, and Cointegration: A Test of Four High Inflation Economies," *Journal of International Money and Finance*, Vol. 8, 533–545.

Meade, J. (1951) *The Theory of International Economic Policy*, Vol. 1: *The Balance of Payments*, London: Oxford University Press.

Meller, P. (1987) "Review of the Theoretical Approaches to External Adjustment and Their Relevance for Latin America," *CEPAL Review*, No. 32, 169–208.

Melnick, R. (1991) "Financial Services, Cointegration and the Demand for Money in Israel," Bank of Israel, Mimeo.

Meyer, P. and J. Neary (1975) "A Keynes-Friedman Money Demand Function," *American Economic Review*, Vol. 65, 678–690.

Mill, C. and R. Nallari (1992) "Analytical Approaches to Stabilization and Adjustment Programs," EDI seminar paper, No. 44, Washington, D.C.: The World Bank.

Modiano, E. (1983) "A Dinamica de Salarios e Precos na Economia Brasileira: 1962–82," *Pesquisa e Planejamiento Economico*, Vol. 13, No. 1, 39–68.

—— (1987) "El Plan Cruzado: Bases Teóricas y Limitaciones Prácticas," *Trimestre Económico*, 223–250.

—— (1989) "A Short-run Model of a Semi-Industrialized Economy," in S. Chakravarty (ed.) *The Balance between Industry and Agriculture in Economic Development: Manpower and Transfers*, Vol. 3, New York: St. Martin's Press.

Moore, B. (1979) "The Endogenous Money Stock," *Journal of Post-Keynesian Economics*, Vol. 2, No. 1, 49–70.

—— (1988) *Horizontalists and Verticalists: The Macroeconomics of Credit Money*, Cambridge: Cambridge University Press.

Morriset, J. (1993) "Does Financial Liberalization Really Improve Private Investment in Developing Countries?" *Journal of Development Economics*, Vol. 40, No. 1, 133–150.

Morroni, M. (1992) *Production Process and Technical Change*, Cambridge: Cambridge University Press.

Mosley, P., J. Harrigan, and J. Toye (1990) *Aid and Power: The World Bank and Policy Based Lending*, London: Routledge.

Mundell, R. (1968) *International Economics*, New York: Macmillan.

Musalem, A. (1989) "Private Investment in Mexico: An Empirical Analysis," PRE Working Paper 183, Washington, D.C.: The World Bank.

Mussa, M. (1997) "IMF Surveillance," *American Economic Review, Papers and Proceedings*, Vol. 87, No. 2, 897–913.

Mussa, M. and M. Savastano (1999) "The IMF Approach to Economic Stabilization," Working Paper WP/99/104, IMF Research Department, Washington, D.C.

Myrdal, G. (1957) *Economic Theory and Underdevelopment Regions*, London: Gerald Duckworth.

Nazmi, N., P. Samaniego, and D. Lafuente (1998) "Tipo de Cambio Real e Inversión en Economías Pequeñas y Abiertas: Evidencia para el Ecuador," Mimeo, Banco Central de Ecuador.

Nicolini, J.L. (1991) "Un Modelo de Ajustes Macroeconomicos con Deuda Externa," *Desarrollo Economico*, Vol. 31, No. 122, 127–140.

Niehans, J. (1984) *International Monetary Economics*, Baltimore: The Johns Hopkins University Press.

Noorbakhsh, F. and A. Paloni (1997) "Assessing the Effect of Structural Adjustment Programmes on Export Performance in Developing Countries," Working paper, Centre for Development Studies, University of Glasgow.

Noyola, J. (1956) "El Desarrollo Economico y la Inflación en México y Otros Países Latinoamericanos," *Investigación Económica*, Vol. 16, 603–648.

Obadan, M. and B. Ekuerhare (1989) "The Theoretical Bases of Structural Adjustment in Nigeria: An Appraisal," *International Social Science Journal*, No. 120, 125–145.

Ocampo, J.A. (1991) "Determinantes y Perspectivas del Crecimiento en el Mediano Plazo," in E. Lora (ed.), *Apertura y Crecimiento: El Reto de los Noventa*, Bogota: Tercer Mundo Editores.

Ocampo, J.A., J. L. Londoño, and L. Villar (1985) "Ahorro e Inversión en Colombia: Evolución Histórica y Determinantes," *Coyuntura Económica*, Vol. 15, No. 2, 13–89.

Olivera, J.H. (1964) "On Structural Inflation and Latin American 'Structuralism'," *Oxford Economic Papers*, Vol. 16, No. 3, 321–332.

—— (1970) "On Passive Money," *Journal of Political Economy*, Vol. 78, 805–814.

Pack, H. (1993) "Productivity and Industrial Development in Sub-Saharan Africa," *World Development*, Vol. 21, No. 1, 1–16.

Padoan, P.C. (1986) *The Political Economy of International Financial Instability*, London: Croom Helm.

Palley, T. (1994) "Competing Views of the Money Supply Process: Theory and Evidence," *Metroeconomica*, Vol. 45, No. 1, 67–88.

Palma, J.G. (1989b) "Structuralism," in J. Eatwell, M. Milgate, and P. Newman (eds.) *The New Palgrave: Economic Development*, New York & London: W.W. Norton.

Palma, J.G. and M. Marcel (1989a) "Kaldor on the 'Discrete Charm' of the Chilean Bourgeoisie," *Cambridge Journal of Economics*, Vol. 13, No. 1, 245–272.

Parkin, V. (1991) *Chronic Inflation in an Industrializing Economy: The Brazilian Experience*, Cambridge: Cambridge University Press.

Pasinetti, L. (1962) "Rate of Profit and Income Distribution in Relation to the Rate of Economic Growth," *Review of Economic Studies*, Vol. 29, 267–279.

Pastor, M. (1987) *The International Monetary Fund and Latin America: Economic Stabilization and Class Conflict*, Boulder: Westview Press.

—— (1989) "Current Account Deficits and Debt Accumulation in Latin America," *Journal of Development Economics*, Vol. 31, No. 1, 77–97.

Polak, J.J. (1957) "Monetary Analysis of Income Formation and Payment Problems," *IMF Staff Papers*, Vol. 6, No. 1, 1–50.

—— (1983) "Monetarist Policies on a World Scale," in K. Jansen (ed.), *Monetarism, Economic Crisis and the Third World*, London: Frank Cass.

—— (1991) "The Changing Nature of IMF Conditionality," Essays in International Finance, No. 184, Princeton, NJ: Princeton University.

—— (1997) "The IMF Monetary Model at Forty," Working Paper WP/97/49, IMF Research Department, Washington, D.C.

Polanyi, K. (1992) "IMF Structural Adjustment: Short-term Gain for Long-term Pain?" *Economic and Political Weekly*, Vol. 18, No. 1, 97–101.

Rabin, A. and L. Yeager (1982) "Monetary Approaches to the Balance of Payments and Exchange Rates," Essays in International Finance, International Finance Section, Princeton University.

Ramos, J. (1986) "Políticas de Estabilización," in R. Cortazar, (ed.), *Políticas Macroeconómicas: Una Perspectiva Latinoamericana*, Santiago, CIEPLAN.

—— (1990) "Neo-Keynesian Macroeconomics as Seen from the South," *CEPAL Review*, No. 38, 7–30.

Rangel, I. (1963) *A Inflacao Brasileira*, Rio de Janeiro: Tempo Brasilero.

Rao, M. (1993) "Distribution and Growth with an Infrastructure Constraint," *Cambridge Journal of Economics*, Vol. 17, No. 4, 369–389.

Rattso, J. (1984) "Macroeconomic Adjustment in a Dual Economy under Policy Controlled Domestic Terms of Trade," *Indian Economic Review*, Vol. 23, No. 1, 45–59.

—— (1989) "Macrodynamic Adjustment Mechanism in a Dual Semi-Industrialized Economy," *Journal of Development Economics*, Vol. 30, 47–69.

Reichmann, T. and R. Stillson (1978) "Experience with Programs of Balance of Payments Adjustment: Stand-by Arrangements in the Higher Credit Tranches," *IMF Staff Papers*, Vol. 25, 119–139.

Rittenberg, L. (1991) "Investment Spending and Interest Rate Policy: The Case of Financial Liberalization in Turkey," *Journal of Development Studies*, Vol. 27, No. 2, 151–167.

Rivera-Batiz, F. and L. Rivera-Batiz (1985) *International Finance and Open Economy Macroeconomics*, New York: Macmillan.

Robichek, E. (1971) "Financial Programming Exercises of the International Monetary Fund in Latin America," Washington, D.C., Mimeo.

Roddick, J. (1988) *The Dance of the Millions*, London: Latin American Bureau Ltd.

Rodriguez, F. and D. Rodrik (1999) "Trade Policy and Economic Growth: A Skeptic's Guide to Cross-National Evidence," NBER Working Paper Series, No. 7081, Cambridge.

Rodrik, D. (1995) "Why is there Multilateral Lending," in M. Bruno and B. Pleskovic (eds.), *Annual World Bank Conference on Development Economics*, Washington, D.C.: The World Bank.

Rogoff, K. (1996) "The Purchasing Power Parity Puzzle," *Journal of Economic Literature*, Vol. 34, 647–668.

Ros, J. (1980) "Pricing in the Mexican Manufacturing Sector," *Cambridge Journal of Economics*, Vol. 4, No. 3, 211–231.

Ros, J. and N. Lustig (1993) "Mexico," in L. Taylor (ed.) *The Rocky Road to Reform: Adjustment, Income Distribution and Growth in Developing Countries*, Cambridge: The MIT Press.

Rosales, O. (1988) "An Assessment of the Structuralist Paradigm for Latin America Development and Prospects for its Renovation," *CEPAL Review*, No. 34, 19–36.

Rosenthal, G. (1992) "Balance Preliminar de la Economía de America Latina y el Caribe," *Comercio Exterior*, Vol. 42, No. 2, 131–50.

Rowthorn, R. (1981) "Demand, Real Wages and Economic Growth," *Studi Economici*, Vol. 18, 2–53.

Sachs, J. and A. Warner (1995) "Economic Reform and the Process of Global Integration," *Brookings Papers on Economic Activity*, Vol. 1, 1–117.

Salai-Martin, X. (1997) "I Just Ran Two Million Regressions," *American Economic Review*, Vol. 82, 178–183.

Sagasti, F. and G. Arévalo (1992) "America Latina en el Nuevo Orden Mundial Fracturado: Perspectivas y Estrategias," *Comercio Exterior*, Vol. 42, No. 12, 1102–1110.

Sargan, J. (1964) "Wages and Prices in the United Kingdom: A Study in Econometric Methodology," in P. Hart, G. Mills, and J. Whitaker (eds.), *Econometric Analysis for National Economic Planning*, London: Butterworth.

Sarkar, P. (1991) "IMF/World Bank Stabilisation Programmes: A Critical Assessment," *Economic and Political Weekly*, Vol. 26, No. 40, 2307–2310.

—— (1993) Distribution and Growth: A Critical Note on 'Stagnationism', *Review of Radical Political Economics*, Vol. 25, No. 1, 62–70.

Sau, R. (1988) "Economic Stabilisation Programme," in R. Sau, *Production, Trade and Development: Towards a Keynes-Ricardo Approach*, Calcutta: K. P. Bagchi & Company.

Sau, R. (1992) "Financial Programming for Stabilisation: Some Notes on the IMF Model," *Economic and Political Weekly*, Vol. 27, 531–534.

Sawyer, M. (1982) "Collective Bargaining, Oligopoly and Macroeconomics," *Oxford Economic Papers*, Vol. 34. No. 3, 428–448.

—— (1985) *The Economics of Michal Kalecki*, London: Macmillan.

Scheetz, T. (1986) *Peru and the International Monetary Fund*, Pittsburgh: University of Pittsburgh Press.

Schmidt-Hebbel, K. and S. Webb (1992) "Public Policy and Private Savings," in V. Corbo, S. Fischer, and S. Webb (eds.), *Adjustment Lending Revisited*, Washington D.C.: The World Bank.

Schydlowsky, D. (1979) "Capacity Utilization, Growth, Employment, Balance of Payments and Price Stabilization," in J. Berhman and J. Hanson, *Short-term Macroeconomic Policy in Latin America*, Conference Series No. 14, Cambridge: NBER.

—— (1990) "Macroeconomic Policies: In Search of a Synthesis," *CEPAL Review*, No. 40, 29–35.

Seers, D. (1962) "A Theory of Inflation and Growth in Underdeveloped Economies," *Oxford Economic Papers*, Vol. 14, No. 2, 173–195.

Serven, L. and A. Solimano (1993) "Debt Crisis, Adjustment Policies and Capital Formation in Developing Countries: Where do we Stand?" *World Development*, Vol. 21, No. 1, 127–140.

Shafik, N. (1992) "Modelling Private Investment in Egypt," *Journal of Development Economics*, Vol. 39, 263–277.

Shaikh, A. (1980) "Laws of Algebra and Laws of Production: The Humbug Production Function," in E. Nell (ed.), *Growth, Profits and Property*, Cambridge: Cambridge University Press.

Shaw, E. (1973) *Financial Deepening in Economic Development*, New York: Oxford University Press.

Sheperd, W. (1985) *The Economics of Industrial Organization*, New Jersey: Prentice Hall.

Shieh, Y. (1981) "Monetary Approaches to Devaluation: A Comment," *Southern Economic Journal*, Vol. 47, No. 4, 11147–11151.

Siddharthan, N. (1989) "Impact of Import Liberalisation on Export Intensities: A Study of the Indian Private Corporate Sector," *The Indian Economic Journal*, Vol. 37, No. 2, 103–111.

Singh, A. (1986) "Tanzania and the IMF: The Analytics of Alternative Adjustment Programmes," *Development and Change*, Vol. 17, 425–454.

—— (1995) "Competitive Markets and Economic Development: A commentary on World Bank Analysis," *International Papers in Political Economy*, Vol. 2, No. 1, 1–40.

Sinha, D. and T. Sinha (1998) "An Exploration of the Long-run Relationship between Saving and Investment in Developing Countries: A Tale of Latin American Countries," *Journal of Post Keynesian Economics*, Vol. 20, No. 3, 435–443.

Sisson, C. (1986) "Fund-Supported Programs and Income Distribution in LDCs," *Finance and Development*, Vol. 33, No. 1, 33–36.

Smith, P. (1979) "Keynes' Finance Motive: Some Theory and Evidence," *Journal of Post Keynesian Economics*, Vol. 1, No. 1, 56–78.

Solimano, A. (1986a) "Contractionary Devaluation in the Southern Cone: The Case of Chile," *Journal of Development Economics*, Vol. 23, 135–151.

—— (1986b) "Aspectos Conceptuales sobre Política Cambiaria Relevante para America Latina," in R. Cortazar (ed.), *Políticas Macroeconómicas: Una Perspectiva Latinoamericana*, Santiago: CIEPLAN.

Stein, H. (1992) "Deindustrialization, Adjustment, the World Bank and the IMF in Africa," *World Development*, Vol. 20, No. 1, 83–95.

—— (1994a) "The World Bank and the Application of Asian Industrial Policy to Africa: Theoretical Considerations," *Journal of International Economics*, Vol. 6, No. 3, 134–55.

—— (1994b) "Theory of Institutions and Economic Reform in Africa," *World Development*, Vol. 22, No. 12.

Stein, H. and E.W. Nafzinger (1991) "Structural Adjustment, Human Needs, and the World Bank Agenda," *The Journal of Modern African Studies*, Vol. 29, No.1, 173–189.

Steindl, J. (1952) *Maturity and Stagnation in American Capitalism*, New York: Montly Review Press.

—— (1985) "El Control de la Economia," *Lecturas de Economía*, No. 17, 159–73.

Stern, N. (1973) *The Balance of Payments: Theory and Economic Policy*, Chicago: Aldine.

Steward, F. and E.K. FitzGerald (1998) "The IMF and the Global Economy: Implications for Developing Countries," Working Paper No. 3, Queen Elizabeth House, University of Oxford.

Stiglitz, J. (1998a) "Sound Finance and Sustainable Development in Asia," The World Bank, Mimeo.

—— (1998b) "Towards a New Paradigm for Development: Strategies, Policies, and Processes," 1998 Prebisch Lecture at UNCTAD, Geneva, October.

Stiglitz, J. and A. Weiss (1981) "Credit Rationing in Markets with Imperfect Information," *American Economic Review*, Vol. 71, No. 2, 393–410.

Storm, S. (1997) "Domestic Constraints on Export-led Growth: A Case-study of India," *Journal of Development Economics*, Vol. 52, No. 1, 83–119.

Studart, R. (1993) "Financial Repression and Economic Development: Towards a Post-Keynesian Alternative," *Review of Political Economy*, Vol. 5, No. 3, 277–298.

Sunkel, O. (1960) "Inflation in Chile: An Unorthodox Approach," *International Economic Papers*, No. 10, 107–131.

Sutton, M. (1984) "Structuralism: The Latin American Record and the New Critique," in T. Killick (ed.), *The IMF and Stabilization: Developing Countries Experiences*, New York: St. Martin's Press.

Tarp, F. (1993) *Stabilisation and Structural Adjustment: Macroeconomic Frameworks for Analysing the Crisis in Sub-Saharan Africa*, London & New York: Routledge.

Taylor, L. (1982) "Food Price Inflation, Terms of Trade and Growth," in M. Gertsovitz (ed.) *The Theory and Experience of Economic Development*, London: George Allen and Unwin.

—— (1983) *Structuralist Macroeconomics: Applicable Models for the Third World*, New York: Basic Books.

—— (1985) "A Stagnationist Model of Economic Growth," *Cambridge Journal of Economics*, Vol. 9, 383–403.

—— (1987a) "IMF Conditionality: Incomplete Theory, Policy Malpractice," in R. Myers (ed.), *The Political Morality of the International Monetary Fund*, Vol. 3, New Brunswick, NJ: Transaction Books.

—— (1987b) "Macro Policy in the Tropics: How Sensible People Stand," *World Development*, Vol. 15, No. 12, 1407–1435.

—— (1989) "Macro Constraints on India's Economic Growth," *Indian Economic Review*, Vol. 23, No. 2, 145–165.

—— (1991) *Income Distribution, Inflation and Growth: Lectures on Structuralist Macroeconomic Theory*, Cambridge: The MIT Press.

—— (1993) "The Rocky Road to Reform: Trade, Industrial, Financial, and Agricultural Strategies," *World Development*, Vol. 21, No. 4, 577–590.

Thirlwall, A.P. (1979) "The Balance of Payments Constraint as an Explanation of International Growth Rate Differences," *Banca Nazionale del Lavoro Quarterly Review*, No. 128, 45–53.

—— (1983) "Foreign Trade Elasticities in Centre-Periphery Models of Growth and Development," *Banca Nazionale del Lavoro Quarterly Review*, No. 146, 249–261.

—— (1988) "What is Wrong with the Balance of Payments Adjustment Theory," *The Royal Bank of Scotland*, No. 157, 3–19.

Thirlwall, A.P. and N. Hussain (1982) "The Balance of Payments Constraint, Capital Flows and Growth Rate Differences Between Developing Countries," *Oxford Economic Papers*, Vol. 34, No. 3, 498–509.

Thorp, R. (1990) "Structuralist Attempts at Short-term Management in the 1980s: The Case of Perú under Alan García," in H. O'Neill (ed.), *Third World Debt: How Sustainable are Current Strategies and Solutions?* London: Frank Cass.

Tsiang, S.C. (1961) "The Role of Money in Trade-Balance Stability: A Synthesis of the Elasticity and Absorption Approaches," *American Economic Review*, Vol. 51, No. 5, 912–936.

—— (1977) "The Monetary Theoretic Foundation of the Modern Monetary Approach to the Balance of Payments," *Oxford Economic Papers*, Vol. 29, No. 3, 319–338.

UNCTAD, (1989) *Trade and Development Report*, New York: United Nations.

Van Wijnbergen, S. (1982) "Stagflactionary Effects of Monetary Stabilization Policies: A Quantitative Analysis of South Korea," *Journal of Development Economics*, Vol. 10, 133–169.

—— (1983) "Interest Rate Management in LDCs," *Journal of Monetary Economics*, Vol. 12, No. 3, 433–452.

Villanueva, J. and J.C. Echeverry (1991) "Fijación de Precios en la Industria Manufacturera bajo Condiciones de Hiperinflación," *Desarrollo Económico*, Vol. 31, No. 121, 73–89.

Vos, R. (1982) "External Dependence, Capital Accumulation, and the Role of the State: South Korea 1960–77," *Development and Change*, Vol. 13, 91–121.

—— (1988) "Capital Accumulation and Basic Needs: The Macroeconomic Framework," in R. Teekens, (ed.), *Theory and Policy Design for Basic Needs*, Brookfield: Avebury.

—— (1993) "Aid Flows and the International Transfer Problem in a Structuralist North-South Model," *Economic Journal*, No. 103, 494–508.

Warman, F. and A. Thirlwall (1994) "Interest Rates, Saving, Investment and Growth in Mexico 1960–90: Test of the Financial Liberalization Hypothesis," *Journal of Development Studies*, Vol. 30, No. 3, 629–649.

Wachter, S. (1976) *Latin American Inflation: The Structuralist-Monetarist Debate*, Lexington, MA: Lexington Books.

—— (1988) "State Intervention in Outward Looking Development: Neoclassical Theory and Taiwanese Practice," in G. White (ed.), *Development States in East Asia*, London: Macmillan.

—— (1990) *Governing the Market: Economic Theory and the Role of the Government in East Asian Industrialization*, Princeton: Princeton University Press.

Wang, F. (1990) "Reconsidering the East Asian Model of Development: Evidence from Taiwan," unpublished Ph.D. dissertation, University of California, Los Angeles.

Weintraub, S. (1973) "Marginal Productivity and Macro Distribution Theory," in S. Weintraub, *Keynes and the Monetarists*, New Brunswick: Rutgers University Press.

Werneck, R. (1986) "Poupanca Estatal, Dívida Externa e Crise Financeira do Sector Publico," Texto Discussao, No. 21, Rio de Janeiro, PUC, Departamento de Economia.

Williamson, J. (1983) *The Open Economy and the World Economy*, New York: Basic Books.

—— (1990) "The Design and Implementation of IMF Conditionality," in S. Dell (ed.), *The International Monetary System and its Reform*, Part V, New York: North-Holland.

—— (1990) *Latin American Adjustment: How Much Has Happen?*, Washington, D.C.: International Economics Institute.

World Bank (1980) *Annual Report*, Washington, D.C.: The World Bank.

—— (1981) *Accelerated Development in Sub-Saharan Africa: An Agenda for Action*, Washington, D.C.: The World Bank.

—— (1983) *World Development Report*, Washington, D.C.: The World Bank.

—— (1984) *Structural Adjustment Lending Report*, Washington, D.C.: The World Bank.

—— (1989) *Sub-Saharan Africa—From Crisis to Sustainable Growth: A Longer Term Perspective Study*, Washington, D.C.: The World Bank.

—— (1989) *World Development Report*, Washington, D.C.: The World Bank.

—— (1989) *Report on Development and Financial Structure*, Washington, D.C.: The World Bank.

—— (1991a) *World Tables*, Washington, D.C.: The World Bank.

—— (1991b) *World Development Report: The Challenge of Development*, Washington, D.C.: The World Bank.

—— (1993) *The East Asian Miracle: Economic Growth and Public Policy*, New York: Oxford University Press.

—— (1994) The Caribbean Region: A Review of World Bank Assistance, Report No. 13708, Washington, D.C.: The World Bank.

—— (1994) *World Debt Tables 1994–1995: External Finance for Developing Countries*, Washington, D.C.: The World Bank.

—— (1995) *Structural and Sectoral Adjustment: World Bank Experience, 1980–92*, Washington, D.C.: The World Bank.

Zulu, J. and S. Nsouli (1985) "Adjustment Programs in Africa: The Recent Experience," IMF Occasional Paper 34, Washington, D.C.

Index

absorption approach, 18, 36, 39, 42, 54–8,
   59, 79
  and its deflationary bias, 103–5
  and the budget deficit, 105–8
  policy recommendations, 55–6
  see also devaluation
agricultural sector, *see* primary sector
autonomous investment and growth, 205–7

basic model, 144–54
  and reserve variations, 152, 183
  and the equilibrium level of public
    investment, 183
  and the foreign exchange constraint,
    160–2
  and the four equation system, 223
  external sector adjustment, 151–2
  equilibrium conditions, 134–58, 182–4
  fiscal closure, 150–1, 162–4
  growth extension, 167–73
  monetary block, 152–3, 164–5
  policy implications, 184–97, 215–7
  see also primary sector
  see also industrial sector
basics, *see* primary sector
budget deficit
  as a source of instability, 39
  and distortions, 40
  reduction, 107–8, 197–200

capital-augmenting investment, 216
capital flows, 32, 119–20, 218
  causes of, 10, 178–9
  see also Latin American countries
capital income taxes, 187–9
conditionality, 2, 14–23, 29–31, 33
  cross, 29, 33
  phases in Latin America, 19–23
credit expansion

  in the Polak model, 45–6
  in the Chicago version, 46, 48–9
  in financial programming, 49, 53–4
credit rationing, 121–2
currency substitution, 88–9

debt burden, 4
debt crisis, 1–5
  in Latin America, 2–4
debt relief, 191–3, 215, 217
demand for money
  influence of domestic credit, 89–90
  in the Polak model, 44
  in the Chicago version, 46–7
  in the financial programming model,
    44–50
  specification, 87–9
  stability, 86–7
devaluation, 38–9, 79
  and effects on the external accounts,
    97–9, 128–9
  and inflation, 96–7, 129
  and output contraction, 101–4
  and real wages, 97
  and supply and demand elasticities, 94–6
  and tradable and non-tradeables, 128–9
  and income distribution, 97–8
  and the fallacy of composition, 97
  and the Marshall-Lerner Condition, 54,
    62, 94–6
  impact on primary exports, 95
  in the absorption approach, 57–8
  see also elasticity approach

elasticity approach, 36, 59, 79
elasticity-absorption synthesis, 60
elasticity-absorption-monetary synthesis,
  109–10
enclave, 154, 179